MOTHER'S
101
WORKSHOP
PROJECTS

HOW-TO AND HANDICRAFT IDEAS FOR THE HOME FROM THE EDITORS OF THE MOTHER EARTH NEWS®

THE MOTHER EARTH NEWS, Inc.
Hendersonville, North Carolina
Distributed by Brick House Publishing Co., Inc.

Published 1984

Printed in the United States of America

THE MOTHER EARTH NEWS, Inc.
105 Stoney Mountain Road,
Hendersonville, North Carolina 28791

Library of Congress Catalog Card Number 84-060260
ISBN 0-938-43206-0

THE MOTHER EARTH NEWS

magazine is published at 105 Stoney Mountain Road, Hendersonville, North Carolina 28791. It is the bi-monthly publication edited by, and for, today's turned-on people of all ages . . . the creative ones, the doers, the folks who make it all happen. All material in MOTHER'S 101 WORKSHOP PROJECTS has previously appeared in, or has been adapted from, THE MOTHER EARTH NEWS magazine or a related publication. Not all facts and figures are necessarily current.

This book was produced by the staff of THE MOTHER EARTH NEWS, with special appreciation to the following: EDITORIAL—Arthur T. Snell and Barbara S. Henderson (directors), Lorna K. Loveless, Clark Center, Donald R. Osby, Richard Freudenberger, David Schoonmaker, Kathleen Seabe, Bruce Woods, Robert G. Miner, Katherine Keen; DESIGN AND LAYOUT—Wendy Simons (director), Jennifer Fisher, Joni Gilmour, Anna Gravley, Susanne Mickler-Callahan, Marsha Drake, Charles R. Milstead, Kathy Ochsner, Susan M. Wood; PHOTOGRAPHY—Steve Keull (director), Jack Green, Ken Cross, Ken Forsgren; TYPESETTING—Carolyn Dellinger Sizemore (director), Sherry Seagle, Carolyn Frederick, Spanky Alexander; PRODUCTION—Garry R. Ramo (manager), Mark Hillyer, Gerald B. McMillan.

MOTHER'S 101 WORKSHOP PROJECTS

TOOLS FOR HOME AND GARDEN

YARD, GARDEN, & OUTDOOR LIVING

HOME AND HOME FURNISHINGS

HOMESTEAD WORKSHOP PROJECTS

HOME AND HOME FURNISHINGS

PLAIN PINE TABLE

This is the kind of project that almost suggests itself if you have a surplus of 3- and 4-foot lengths of lumber left over from carpentry work and other do-it-yourself projects. In fact, the design shown here was born of just a few minutes' contemplation of some old spare boards.

To build a structurally sound table, it's a good idea to use only seasoned wood. Green or found boards should be dried indoors for at least six months, and you should feed any cupped or twisted planks to the shop stove. Pallet boards and packing-crate planks are good for workshop projects, but only about one-tenth of the wood will be usable.

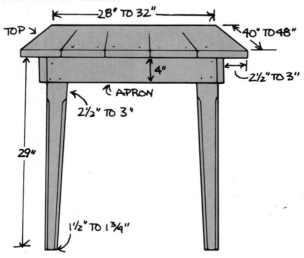

The only carpentry you'll need to know to build a plain pine table involves making right-angle saw cuts, doing a little surface planing, and fashioning simple joints. The only fasteners required are glue and nails. If a power saw is available, the table's legs can be given pleasing tapers, all of which should be on the inside faces of the uprights to help counter the tendency of softwood table legs to go pigeon-toed. The supports' corners can be chamfered with a pocketknife and plane.

Thanks to the availability of reliable waterproof glues, the wobbly legs and warped tops that once characterized softwood tables can be prevented. Water-mix resorcinol glue may be your best all-around buy, but if you have an inexpensive source of epoxy, go ahead and use it: It's a better gap-filler than resorcinol glue.

You'll find it saves time and wood to predrill holes so 8- or 10-penny finishing nails won't split the lumber. Be sure to clamp the pieces of the apron to the legs securely while the glue between them sets.

A finished table should have its top boards edge-fitted and glued. If—on the other hand—you intend your plain pine table for rough use, just make the unit strong and neat, and never mind the cracks.

If the boards you have on hand are too short or too thin to use for a kitchen table, you might consider making a typewriter table. Two-by-fours are not useful in kitchen-table construction but can be ripped into perfectly proportioned typing-table legs that taper from 1-5/8" on the top to 1-1/4" at the bottom. Typewriter tables should be 26" to 30" long by 18" to 20" wide. They ought to be 27" high for manual typewriters and an inch or two shorter for electric models. You might also think about building a television stand, which should be about 18" high with an 18" X 24" top.

The basic table design can be adapted by adding drawers, and any homebuilt unit can be made more attractive by filling nail holes and giving the work a hand-rubbed finish or a coat of paint. However, it's far easier to build plain carpentered tables—constructed of pine, off-color oak, or unidentified packing lumber—and finish them with just some sealer and a little linseed oil.

CEDAR-LINED CHEST

Over the years, cedar's pleasant aroma and insect-repellent qualities have made it a popular material for the construction of fine chests, wardrobes, and closets.

So sought after is this fragrant wood, that it is increasingly difficult to find. Those lucky enough to locate it in board form can expect to pay dearly for it.

But there's a way to combine luxury with practicality at a price that's right! It's a chest made of regular plywood with a heart that's pure cedar.

LIST OF MATERIALS

ITEM	LENGTH/SIZE	PURPOSE
5/8" plywood	21" X 21"	box bottom
1 X 4 pine	10'	side panel stiles
	12'	pedestal, gussets, corner braces
	14'	side panel rails
1 X 6 pine	8'	lid
doorstop pine	7'	panel inserts and molding
	(3) 8'	panel inserts
1/4" lattice strips	8'	joint splines
3/8" cedar	16 sq. ft.	lining
3/8" dowel	4"	screw-hole plugs
flathead wood screws	(56) No. 8 X 1-1/4"	sides and bottom
	(12) No. 8 X 3/4"	molding
brass-plated piano hinge w/screws	1-1/16" X 20"	lid
brass-plated curved friction lid support w/screws	5-1/2" overall	lid

BEG, BORROW, OR . . . BUY: Collect your tools and materials. You'll need all the lumber and hardware called for in the accompanying list, plus some yellow carpenter's glue, a table saw to make accurate cuts, a power drill with several different sized bits and a countersink (a No. 8 Stanley Screw-Mate bit, which makes pilot, shank, and countersink hole in one pass, would be a real boon), sandpaper in a variety of grits, some shellac (and pumice), clear varnish or tung oil, a tape measure, a screwdriver, and—because you'll need to do some fancy finish work—a router.

To make your lumber shopping less of a chore (if, that is, you don't have enough usable scraps around to piece your project together), note that the list indicates specific board lengths that will allow you to arrange your cuts to produce a minimum of waste. Although it would be best to use tongue-and-groove strip cedar for the lining, the cost of such lumber may motivate you to substitute less expensive cedar particleboard.

TAKE A FEW TIPS: This cabinet isn't difficult to assemble, but there are a few tricks you ought to be aware of that will make its construction easier. For one thing, the pedestal should be assembled first, and that entire support can be cut from your 12-foot length of 1 X 4. Note, however, that it's only 2-3/4" tall, so you'll have to rip the entire 3-1/2"-wide board down to size before going on to make the miter cuts for the joints and gussets. Save the leftover strip, because you'll need it later.

Each of the four identical sides starts with a 3/4"-thick 21" X 21" perimeter frame that consists of two 14"-long vertical stiles and full-width top and bottom rails. These four components are held together at the joints with 1/4" X 1-1/2" X 3" splines that are glued into kerfs sliced across the mating surfaces of the seams.

A 3/8"-wide by 5/8"-deep rabbet, cut into the inner face of the bottom rail, will accommodate the 5/8" X 20-1/4" X 20-1/4" plywood base once everything's assembled, and a similar groove (this one 1/2" deep and 1/2" wide), routed into the inside edges of the framework, provides a seat for the 1/2" X 3-1/2" X 16" pine strips that make up the side panel inserts. Furthermore, the side edges of each completed square have 45° miters on the inside to form clean finish joints.

Here's a helpful hint: Cut the stiles

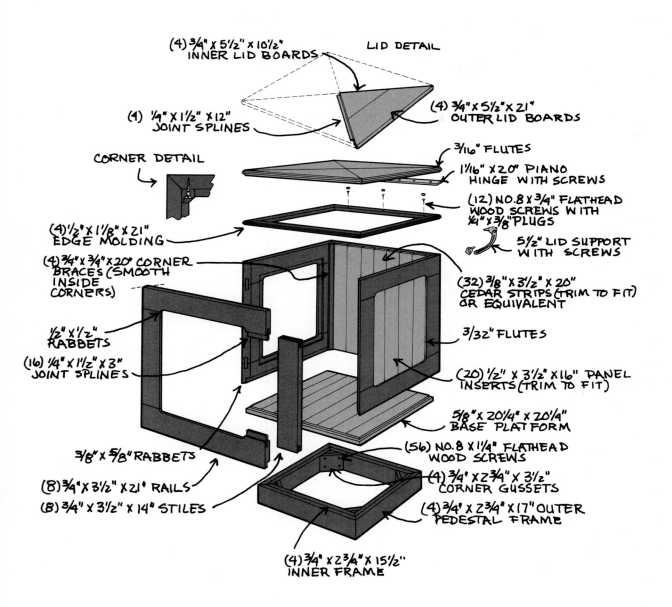

LID DETAIL

(4) 3/4" X 5½" X 10½" INNER LID BOARDS

(4) ¼" X 1½" X 12" JOINT SPLINES

(4) 3/4" X 5½" X 21" OUTER LID BOARDS

3/16" FLUTES

1¹/₁₆" X 20" PIANO HINGE WITH SCREWS

(12) NO.8 X 3/4" FLATHEAD WOOD SCREWS WITH ¼" X 3/8" PLUGS

5½" LID SUPPORT WITH SCREWS

CORNER DETAIL

(4) ½" X 1⅛" X 21" EDGE MOLDING

(4) 3/4" X 3/4" X 20" CORNER BRACES (SMOOTH INSIDE CORNERS)

½" X ½" RABBETS

(16) ¼" X 1½" X 3" JOINT SPLINES

(32) 3/8" X 3½" X 20" CEDAR STRIPS (TRIM TO FIT) OR EQUIVALENT

3/32" FLUTES

(20) ½" X 3½" X 16" PANEL INSERTS (TRIM TO FIT)

5/8" X 20¼" X 20¼" BASE PLATFORM

(56) NO.8 X 1¼" FLATHEAD WOOD SCREWS

(4) 3/4" X 2¾" X 3½" CORNER GUSSETS

3/8" X 5/8" RABBETS

(8) 3/4" X 3½" X 21" RAILS

(8) 3/4" X 3½" X 14" STILES

(4) 3/4" X 2¾" X 17" OUTER PEDESTAL FRAME

(4) 3/4" X 2¾" X 15½" INNER FRAME

from the 10-foot 1 X 4, and the rails from the 14-footer. These boards are most easily routed on a shaper table, although a straightedge clamped to the work at a 3″ width will do in a pinch. You can also add contoured corners and decorate the frame adjacent to the panel inserts with shallow flutes along the edges.

Cut four 3/4″ X 3/4″ X 20″ corner braces from the strip left over after ripping the 12-foot 1 X 4. The sides and braces are locked together with glue and No. 8 X 1-1/4″ flathead wood screws which are installed six to a corner, perpendicular to one another, and through the braces. Once the sides are joined, the plywood bot-

tom of the box can be glued into its rabbet, and the pedestal can be glued underneath and screwed in place from the inside.

To make the lid, you'll need to cut your 1 X 6 into eight pieces, four of which should be 21″ and the other four 10-1/2″ on their longest edges. Because the ends of these sections meet each other at 45° angles cut across their widths, and because you'll naturally want to make the most efficient use of your wood, you'll have to plan your cuts carefully so the angled faces butt against each other. This eliminates the wasteful "wedges" that would otherwise be left between the slices.

These sections, like the side frames, are fastened together with 1/4″ X 1-1/2″ splines set and glued into the mating surfaces of each miter face. The straight edges of the boards are cemented at their joints, too. When the lid's assembled, 3/16″ flutes can be added with the router to its outer edges.

You're not quite ready to install the lid, though. First, the cedar lining, whether it consists of wood strips or of composition board, must be glued in place within the box. Then the edge molding should be ripped from the leftover piece of 1/2″ doorstop pine into two 1/2″ X 1-1/8″ X 42″ pieces—one edge of each of them fluted, with the router, to match the lid—and those two lengths sliced in half to create four 21″-long sections, each with mitered ends. A dozen No. 8 X 3/4″ flathead wood screws hold the trim in place, and the heads should be countersunk so that short plugs made from 3/8″ dowel can be glued over them and sanded flush.

Finally, the hinge is recessed into the lid and into one of the molding sections (here's another job most easily done with a router), and the hinge and cover are fastened into place with the screws provided. A lid support, placed between one side of the box and the hinged top, will keep the lid of the chest open for access when needed.

With everything together, a coat of shellac can be applied and then smoothed with pumice to provide a glossy sheen, or if you'd prefer a more subdued appearance, an oil finish can be rubbed into the wood. No matter how you dress it, though, your home-made chest is sure to be a source of satisfaction, either to you, the builder, or to the lucky person who receives it as a gift.

STORAGE BED

Here's a project that'll help you make good use of that often wasted space beneath your family's beds. Of course there are ready-made "dresser beds" available, but they can be expensive. What's more, plans for making storage beds can be confusing and the projects they propose, very time-consuming.

This practical storage bed, which can help keep any child's room neater, calls for an investment in two 4′ X 8′ sheets of plywood, a bottle of white glue, and some finishing nails.

By following the cutting and assembly instructions, you'll be able to transform any under-bed space into a valuable storage area.

CUTTING: First, trim a 4″ waste strip from one end of each sheet of plywood, then cut off a second strip 17″ wide, also from each sheet. From the 17″ strips, cut pieces 37-1/2″ long to serve as the cabinet's ends. Save the other sections, as they will be used as braces.

From one of the remaining panels, rip a 3″ waste strip off one long edge and then slice a 7″-wide section lengthwise from the stock. From the other large section, cut a 17″ X 75″ piece to serve as the back of the chest, leaving a 31″-wide piece that with the 7″-wide strip cut from the other plywood panel will form the bed's top.

ASSEMBLY: Begin putting the bed together by gluing and nailing the

two end pieces to the back and fasten this assembly to the 38″ X 75″ bottom section. Turn the partially completed bed over and install the narrow top strip and the first brace. Glue and nail the large top section in place, and then position the second brace, securing it to the top. The foot of this brace can be secured by turning the bed over and nailing through from the bottom.

Just follow the easy step-by-step procedure shown in the accompanying photos. You'll also probably want to sand the exposed edges to avoid splinters and to keep any bed coverings from being snagged.

The completed bed can be stained and varnished, painted, or left "raw", but with a mattress or foam pad, it will provide a comfortable sleeper, as well as about 30 cubic feet of out-of-the-way storage space.

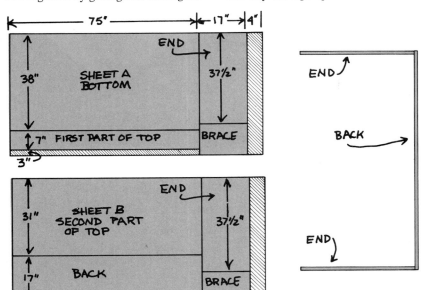

Follow the steps shown in the photos, from left to right, gluing and nailing each piece in place.

1. The end pieces are butted against the back.

2. Next, the bottom panel is attached.

3. Turn the bed right side up and fasten the narrow top strip.

4. The first brace is glued . . .

5. Then it's nailed in place.

6. The large top section is put into position.

7. Support is given by a second brace.

8. Turn the bed upside down to nail the brace.

9. It's no problem to store bulky quilts and blankets.

STORAGE BED

BLANKET RACK

Storage space for blankets during the "in between" months when it can be cool one night and warm the next can be hard to come by, especially when bedroom closets are overflowing with the children's toys, last season's clothing, or assorted containers that are "sure to come in handy someday".

This attractive blanket rack can provide an easy solution that won't crush the down in your comforter or crease the fabric of your favorite bed coverings. Also, the holder's upper wooden rods can be used for drying clothes and hanging towels, and shoes can be racked on the bottom crossbars.

This useful piece of furniture can be yours to enjoy for only a few dollars' worth of wood and a couple of hours of your time. And by building this rack yourself, you'll have a personalized and decorative accessory not to be found in the local department store.

While spruce is an excellent wood for such a rack, equally satisfactory results can be obtained using white pine or fir. In addition to the lumber, you'll need ten No. 12 X 1-1/2" flathead screws, ten 1/2" wooden cap buttons, some glue, and varnish. As for tools, you'll want a ripsaw, a crosscut saw, a saber saw, a hand drill with a No. 12 adjustable countersink bit, a screwdriver, a paintbrush, and some sandpaper.

Start by cutting a pair of 32" lengths of 1 X 12 for the rack's ends, then rip five 1-1/4" X 1-1/4" boards from a 20" length of 2 X 8. (You could also use your ripsaw to divide three 20" 2 X 4's, leaving you with one extra rod.) After cutting the 1 X 12's to length, you can determine the shape you'd like and cut both pieces with a saber saw, or if you prefer, simply assemble the rack with unadorned rectangular sides.

The best way to come up with a pleasing end pattern that's symmetrical is to make a template by folding an 11" X 32" sheet of wrapping paper in half lengthwise. Draw one half of your proposed end board, cut the design from the still-folded paper, open it up, and if you like the result (assuming the removal of the wood will leave

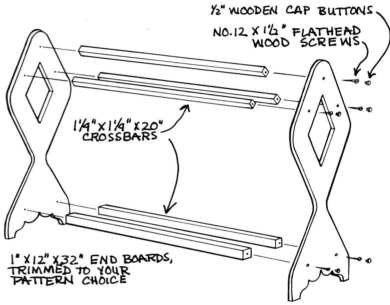

½" WOODEN CAP BUTTONS

NO.12 X 1½" FLATHEAD WOOD SCREWS

1¼" X 1¼" X 20" CROSSBARS

1" X 12" X 32" END BOARDS, TRIMMED TO YOUR PATTERN CHOICE

room for attaching the five crossbars), trace the lines on one of the 1 X 12's. Then, with the boards clamped flat together, cut the two of them at once.

Place the centers of the two lower rods 4" above the floor line and 6" apart. The ends of the three upper pieces form the points of equilateral triangles with 5" sides and having their highest points 2" below the end pieces' top edges.

Mark the two 1 X 12's and, using a No. 12 adjustable countersink tool, bore the holes for the crossbars. This drill/countersink tool not only creates the correct size of hole, but also pro-

vides a 3/16" countersink to permit installation of the 1/2" cap buttons.

Then glue and secure—using No. 12 X 1-1/2" flathead screws—the ends of the rods to the inner faces of the two 1 X 12's. Note that the 1-1/4" faces of the lower crossmembers are parallel to the floor, while the three upper pieces are cocked 45° in an "edge high" position.

Next, glue in the cap buttons and sand all edges and surfaces. Apply a couple of coats of satin urethane varnish (lightly sanded between applications), and the blanket rack will be complete.

"STEP SAVER"

Not only does this little stool save Mom and Pop some steps, but it also gives little ones the all-important opportunity to accomplish things for themselves . . . such as safely getting that umpteenth drink of water, brushing teeth, and washing up.

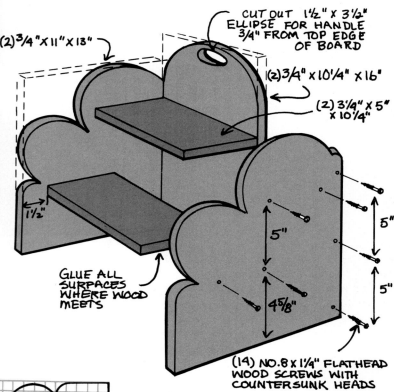

CUT OUT 1½" X 3½" ELLIPSE FOR HANDLE 3/4" FROM TOP EDGE OF BOARD

(2) 3/4" X 11" X 13"

(2) 3/4" X 10¼" X 16"

(2) 3/4" X 5" X 10¼"

1½"

GLUE ALL SURFACES WHERE WOOD MEETS

5"

5"

4⅝"

5"

5"

(14) NO. 8 X 1¼" FLATHEAD WOOD SCREWS WITH COUNTERSUNK HEADS

1 SQUARE = 1 INCH

Making a step saver requires only a few common workshop tools and a 52" length of 1 X 12 board. Best of all, the handy stool can be constructed in an hour, possibly two.

Kick this project off by tracking down a power drill (with an assortment of bits and a countersink), a hand-held electric saber saw, a screwdriver, some white wood glue, and a sheet or two of fine sandpaper. You'll also need 14 No. 8 X 1-1/4" flathead wood screws, a can of wood putty, a piece of string, some polyurethane varnish or shellac, and a paintbrush.

Once you've gathered all the materials and equipment, cut the plank of wood into five pieces with the overall dimensions shown (remember that a standard 1 X 12 is actually 3/4" thick and slightly over 11" wide). Don't worry about rounding the edges right

now; they'll be taken care of in the next few steps.

Set the pieces aside and enlarge the grid so that the squares are 1" X 1" in size. Transfer the shape to the larger grid and trace it onto the two 11" X 13" side pieces.

Next, take the saber saw (or a jigsaw) and cut the scalloped shapes on these two sections. Taking the 3/4" X 10-1/4" X 16" back piece, measure 11" from one end (the edge that you

measure from will become the bottom), and using a pencil, draw a line across the board at this distance. Determine the center of the line and with this mark as the pivot point, draw an arc across the top of the board from one side to the other, using a pencil and length of string as a compass.

You also might want to make a handle for your stool by marking off a 1-1/2" X 3-1/2" ellipse directly in the center of the back piece and about

3/4" down from the top edge. With this done, you can cut the stool's back to the rounded shape shown in the diagram and carve out the hole for the handle (you'll have to drill a starting hole within the handle first, then cut out the little piece of wood with the saber saw).

Now place the back of the stool upright on a flat surface and position the two side sections next to it so that the edges of the 11" X 13" boards are flush with the back of the 10-1/2" X 16" piece. Drill three 7/64" pilot holes about 5" apart through each side board and into the edge of the back piece, and using a 5/32" bit, enlarge the holes in the side boards to accommodate the screw shoulders. To complete this step, countersink these enlarged holes on the outer surface so the screws will be recessed when they're installed.

At this point, temporarily fasten the back and side pieces together, and taking two 3/4" X 5" X 10-1/4" boards, place them in position with the top of the lower step 5" above the bottom of the stool and its forward edge about 1-1/2" behind the stool's front. The upper step should be placed flush against the back of the stool with its business surface 5" above the top of the lower step.

When the step boards have been positioned correctly, drill 7/64" "pilot" holes through the stool sides and into the steps. Two holes located about 4" apart in the end of each step board should sufficient. Then enlarge the holes in the stool sides with a 5/32" bit and countersink the outer surfaces of the holes.

Remove the screws that hold the stool's back and sides together, and smooth all of the surfaces of the wood with fine sandpaper. Run a bead of glue along all the screw-fastened surfaces where wood meets wood and assemble the stool with your No. 8 X 1-1/4" wood screws.

Finally, fill all the screwhead holes with wood putty, sand the filler smooth, and cover the entire step saver with the polyurethane or shellac. Let the finish dry, and your tyke's new "toy" is ready for use.

STUMP STOOL

If you've ever seen a footrest made from a section of tree trunk, then you know what a stump stool is. These eye-catching accessories are functional, handsome additions to any living room. It's almost as easy to make several as just one, so plan on delighting a few of your friends with an unusual gift.

A bucksaw and a rasp are the only tools needed, and a walk in the forest is the price paid for materials. Look for dead trees that have been weathered clean of their bark. The bare trunks are usually a delightful shade of gray or brown, and the wood is strong and lightweight because it's so dry. A tree with a diameter of 9" to 18" is the most suitable size.

Try to find a trunk that's blown over partway, because it will be easier to fell with a bucksaw than one

If you want a completely natural, unfinished piece of furniture, just stop at this point. Otherwise, plane and/or sand the stool's top surface and finish the piece with a stain and a coat of varnish. Work quickly when using stains, since the porous wood will soak up the liquid within seconds. Use a brush-and-wipe, brush-and-wipe system to stain the stool. Then apply varnish, but be prepared here, too, for the wood to absorb much more than you might expect.

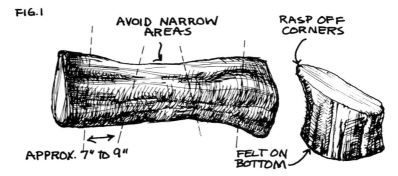

FIG.1

AVOID NARROW AREAS

RASP OFF CORNERS

APPROX. 7" TO 9"

FELT ON BOTTOM

that stands straight up. However, if it's been on the ground for long, it will probably have begun to rot.

It may be more convenient to cut the stools right in the woods and carry home as many as you want in a duffel bag. Once you've felled a tree, make two crosswise cuts for each stool: one at right angles to the tree's centerline, and one at an angle of 30° to the first cut. The short side of the bole should measure approximately 7" to 9", so use the thicker parts of the trunk, as illustrated.

Once you're home, use a file-type wood rasp to round off each stool's sharp edges. The rounded side of the rasp is great for getting into concave crannies, and the flat edge for smoothing out the convex surfaces of the wood.

If the new footrest will be used on a hardwood floor, attach a felt pad to the bottom of the stool to protect the floor's finish. To do this, trace around the stump on a large piece of felt, cut the pad out, and glue it to the wood with carpenter's glue.

For an interesting variation, cut a stool from a tree with a fork in it. Just make the 30° angled cut immediately below the point where the trunk divides and make the perpendicular cut across the two upper branches. This way, the stool will broaden from floor to footrest, and the top surface will have an unusual abstract shape.

The next time you decide to pick up a book or magazine and settle back in a favorite chair, you'll have a one-of-a-kind stump stool on which to rest your feet.

INDIRECT LIGHTING

Lighting fixtures that diffuse glare and soften shadows by deflecting light so it reflects off a wall and the ceiling can make any room seem more attractive and restful. And it's not difficult or expensive for anyone with minimal carpentry skills to brighten dark corners, illuminate hallways, or produce the soothing glow of indirect lighting all over a house.

The fixtures can be adapted to the style of your home and may be as decorative as your talent and budget allow. The valance can be a rustic-looking rough-sawed plank, as shown here, or a sanded board that's painted or stained. A decorator chain might be substituted for the knotted rope, and attractive plant hooks could be used instead of plain utility hooks to support the valance.

LIST OF MATERIALS

QUANTITY	ITEM
1	1 X 6 or 1 X 8 board of appropriate length
3 (or more)	surface-mounted incandescent lamp holders
25' (or so)	No. 18 lamp cord
	insulated staples
	screws (enough to mount lamp holders)
40"	1/4" rope
2	utility hooks with toggle bolts
1	in-line switch
1	plug
3 (or more)	60-watt bulbs

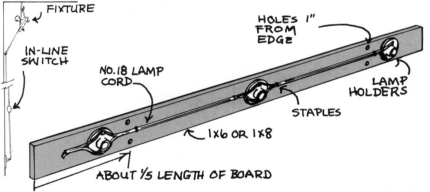

Begin building each fixture by cutting a 1 X 6 or 1 X 8 board to a length slightly shorter than the portion of wall you plan to illuminate. Install a series of surface-mounted lamp holders (available at hardware stores) along the back of the plank at approximately 3-foot intervals.

It's important to use holders with connectors located inside the porcelain housing, to prevent shock in the event the hot and neutral wires have been inadvertently swapped somewhere in the circuit. If exposed terminals are used, always unplug the cord when changing bulbs or making adjustments.

With holders installed, run No. 18 lamp cord from socket to socket, as shown in the drawing, baring the wire to attach it to the terminals. Secure the cord to the wood with insulated staples. Uninsulated staples can damage the wire and become hot.

Once the lamp holders are in place and wired, leave enough cord to comfortably reach the nearest outlet. Then attach a plug to the end of the cord and install an in-line switch at a convenient height.

To support the completed assembly, drill two pairs of holes in the valance, spacing them about one-fifth of the board's length from each of its ends. Using the two sets of holes as guides, fasten the hooks into the ceiling, using toggle bolts, approximately 6" out from the wall.

Knot one end of each of two 20" sections of 1/4" rope, thread the lengths through the pairs of holes in the board with the knots on the visible side, and tie off the working ends. The resulting loops, hung from the utility hooks, should position the plank about 6" down from the ceiling. You may have to retie the loops a couple of times before the plank hangs level.

Once the fixture is suspended to your satisfaction, the lamp will be ready to plug in. Incandescent light bulbs give off a lot of heat, so keep any combustible objects, such as curtains, a safe distance away.

HANGING CRADLE

During the first few weeks after the arrival of a new baby, it's convenient to keep the newcomer as close to hand as possible so the parents can respond promptly to the infant's needs. A cradle is much better for this than a large, cumbersome crib, and this hanging macramé minibed, which is inexpensive to build, can be moved easily from one room of the house to another and even suspended near or over the parents' bed at night.

MAJOR PARTS: The cradle itself consists of three components: a rectangular wooden frame, a flat rectangular bottom, and mesh sides woven from cord or twine. The swinging bed is outfitted with a mattress and bumper pads and is suspended from cords attached at each corner of the frame.

The frame of the cradle shown in the photo is 20″ wide and 28″ long (all the dimensions can be adjusted to make a larger crib) and is constructed of lengths of hardwood 1-3/8″ square. The boards used at the head and the foot are 17-1/4″ long. They are butted between the two 28″ side rails and fastened in place with glue and one No. 12 X 5″ flathead wood screw at each corner.

A more complex but stronger joint can be made by boring the end- and sidepieces as shown in the diagram and cinching the corners together with a 1/4″ X 2-1/2″ bolt. To do this, for each corner drill a 5/8″ hole 1/2″ deep in the outside face of the side rail, with the center of the hole 5/8″ in from the end. Drill another hole of the same diameter 1″ deep into the inside face of the adjoining end board,

with the center of this hole 1-1/4″ from the end of that piece of wood. Align the two pieces as they will be when the frame is completed, clamp them in this position, and drill a 5/16″ hole, starting in the center of the 5/8″ recess in the side rail and continuing until the bit breaks through to the 5/8″ X 1″ hole in the end board. Unclamp the two pieces, apply glue to the sections that abut one another, and assemble the two boards, locking them in place with the 1/4″ X 2-1/2″ bolt fitted with washers and a nut as shown.

Whichever corner-joining method is used, pairs of 1/4″ holes spaced 3/4″ apart and with 2″ between each set are bored through the frame, with nine pairs of holes in each of the sidepieces and five pairs in each of the end boards. To eliminate splinters, the frame should be sanded after the holes are drilled.

The bottom board of the bed can be made of 1/4″ plywood or 3/16″ hardboard cut to a 16″ X 24″ rectangle, which is slightly smaller than the frame so that the mesh sides will slope inward toward the bottom. Drill the

same number and size of holes that are in the frame around the perimeter of this board, but slightly reduce the space between the sets

TYING THE KNOTS: For the lacing used to make the sides of the cradle, No. 36 braided hammock twine is ideal, but cotton twine (prewashed to remove the starch) or nylon sash cord (without any preservatives or tar compounds added) can also be used. Making the sides requires 56 nine-foot sections (504 feet) of macramé material, and about 45 feet more is needed if the finished cradle is to be hung with the same cord.

In order to fashion the mesh sides, you'll need to temporarily suspend the frame so it hangs level at a comfortable working height. Tie a long piece of twine to each corner, fastening the other ends of the cord to hooks screwed into a ceiling beam or other support.

Once the frame is in place, set the crib bottom on a cardboard box so it will rest about 10″ below the frame. Cut the 9-foot lengths of cord and if using nylon twine, carefully sear—or melt—the ends in a candle flame. For each pair of holes around the frame, take two strands of twine at a time and drop the four ends, two to each hole, through the openings. Adjust the ends of these strands until they all hang the same distance below the rail, and using a macramé knot known as a "square knot sennit", start connecting the strands together to form the sides.

Just how fancy you get in your knot tying depends more on patience than skill, and you may want to use more complex or decorative knots than the square knot sennit. This knot and others can be found in almost any macramé book. The main thing is to keep the openings in the mesh small enough so that a child's head can't possibly poke through one, yet large enough so an infant's hands and feet won't get caught. Proceed with your chosen pattern of knots until the bottom board is reached, then thread the twine in pairs through the holes around the edges and secure the lines under the cradle bottom by tying loose ends together.

5/8″

1/2″

1/4″ X 2 1/2″ BOLT AND WASHER

1/4″ NUT AND WASHER

1 1/4″

5/8″ SOCKET

MATTRESS AND BUMPER PAD: The mattress consists of a 2''-thick foam rubber pad cut to fit inside the bed and covered first with plastic sheeting and then with a piece of absorbent cotton.

The bumper pad gives the infant a soft border around the edges of the bed and is made with an extra section that fits under the mattress and helps hold the padded sides in place. Making the pad requires a yard of 45''-wide material to make the sides, a section of cloth 17'' X 24'' for the bottom, 2 yards of ribbon or bias tape for the ties, and enough batting to pad the sides adequately (batting is made in various thicknesses, and you may be able to get assistance in estimating the amount you need at a fabric store).

To make the side pads, cut out four pieces of cloth, two 17'' X 17'' for the endpieces and two 17'' X 24'' for the sides. Fold the square pieces in half so that opposite edges meet, and fold the rectangular pieces so that the 24''-long edges are together. Make all these folds so the unfinished side of the material is out. Next, cut the ribbon or bias tape into eight equal lengths. Lay one end of each section at one of the folded corners of the pieces of cloth so the end of the ties lap at least 1/2'' over the cloth. Stitch closed the ends of the panels, running the seams 1/2'' in from the edges and down until they are 1/2'' from the opposite edge. Be certain the ends of the ties are caught in the seams. Turn the fabric pockets right side out and press them. Cut the batting into about 6''-wide strips, and trim these into lengths that are 16'' and 23'' long. Taking as many of the batting strips as you need of each length to stuff the pockets adequately, insert them in the cloth pouches. Then cut a 1/2'' square out of each corner of the 17'' X 24'' bottom. Slip the edges between the notches into the openings in the pad pieces they match, and stitch a seam catching all three pieces of cloth for each pad. Then, along a line 2'' out from each of those seams, sew another seam, trapping the padding in the outer 6'' of the bags. Place the bumper pad in the bottom of the cradle and tie the ribbon to the mesh sides of the bed at the corners to hold the pads in place. Then put the mattress in on top of the pad's bottom liner.

FINAL TOUCHES: To attach the suspension ropes to the cradle, tie a strong piece of cord—doubled or tripled if necessary—to each corner of the frame, and join the other ends of these four strands with a knot at a point about 3 feet above the top of the cradle itself. At this junction, a single piece of rope—or several pieces of thinner cord—can be used to suspend the cradle from a hook or eyebolt in the ceiling, a beam, or some other solid overhead support.

If the ceiling is plasterboard, make sure the hook is screwed into something solid—like a joist—so there's no chance it will pull out.

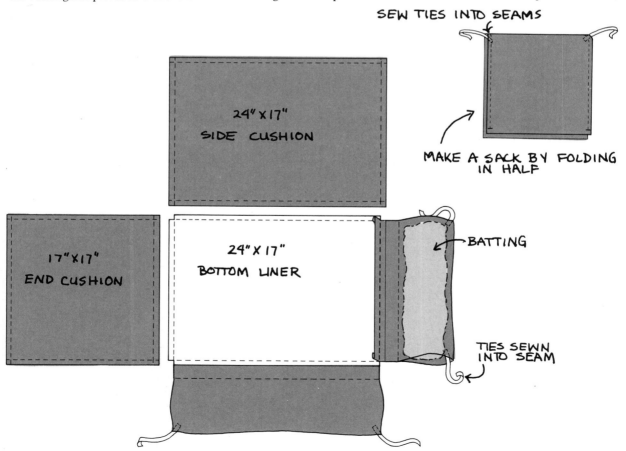

SEW TIES INTO SEAMS

24" X 17" SIDE CUSHION

MAKE A SACK BY FOLDING IN HALF

17" X 17" END CUSHION

24" X 17" BOTTOM LINER

BATTING

TIES SEWN INTO SEAM

REUPHOLSTERING

Because reupholstering an old piece of furniture often costs more than the price of original article, many people are reluctant to have their old sofa or chair recovered. They would like to do the job themselves, but are afraid to tackle an operation that seems complex and mysterious. Stuffed furniture was originally made so that the fabric could be replaced when worn-out. Anyone with basic sewing skills and simple tools (hammer, screwdriver, pliers, staple gun) can reupholster. There's no need to take an expensive course. The furniture itself, as you dismantle it, will show you how it was made.

SIMPLY TAKE IT APART: If, for example, you have a chair you want to overhaul, start by examining it closely. Note the skirt, welting, trim, buttons, and all the other details.

Look over the chair to find the piece of fabric that obviously should come off first: usually the dustcover on the bottom, the skirt or ruffle, or the back. Carefully remove it by prying it loose. Don't *rip* the material free as you'll be using it later as a pattern. Pin a paper on the segment of cloth to identify it as "number one" and to remind you of its location on the chair. Note which section ought to come off next and treat it in the same way.

Keep making notes, mental or written, on how and where the fabric is attached to the frame. Don't disturb the batting or stuffing, and it's best not to remove the cushion casing since the insides usually fall apart. Put a new cover right over the old one.

THAT WASN'T SO HARD: For your first attempt, it's best to choose a piece of furniture whose frame and springs are in good shape. In subsequent jobs, if they're not, this would be the time to refinish any wooden parts, retie the springs, fit new burlap to cover them, and check to see if any additional padding is needed.

In selecting new fabric, it's best to stay away from tapestries, no matter how beautiful and long-lasting they are, because the thick, stiff material is difficult to work with. Medium-weight, softer fabrics are far less troublesome to handle than heavy ones and wear better than one might expect. Before buying any fabric, notice whether any parts of the old covering just removed were cut on the bias to stretch around curves. If so, stay away from stripes or plaids.

Some people make a big point of measuring yardage so closely that not an extra inch of fabric will be left. It's better to take loose measurements, ordering more cloth than the tape shows you'll need. Excess material never goes to waste; in fact, it's one of the bonuses of doing your own upholstering. Leftover material can be used for valances, footstools, covered wastebaskets, and throw pillows. If you buy enough to make matching draperies, it will give the whole room a custom-designed appearance.

NOW PUT IT TOGETHER: Take all the pieces of old covering and flatten them out, clipping open any darts or seams. Arrange the shapes on the new fabric so as to waste as little as possible, and remember to leave an extra inch around each segment. If your earlier research turned up any parts that must be cut on the bias, be sure to lay them out that way. Place the cushion on the yard goods and trace around it twice for the top and bottom. Measure its sides for length and width and mark out a strip to fit. Again, allow for an inch-wide seam allowance on all the cushion pieces. Cut out all the parts and keep each old piece together with its replacement for identification purposes. Use the scraps to make welting, trim, buttons, and such.

When applying the new material, reverse the order in which you stripped off the sections of old covering. The last worn piece removed from the chair will be the first new one to go back on, and so forth. Before fastening any fabric, make sure the padding is smooth and lump-free.

Use a heavy-duty staple gun to attach one side of the first piece of material in the same manner in which the old covering was fastened. Then gently but firmly pull and stretch the cloth from the opposite direction and staple down the far border. Secure the third side, pulling gently from the free edge and fastening it down, too. The manner in which the material is stapled and stretched across the frame is the secret of professional-looking upholstery. The covering should be taut, without sags and wrinkles, but not so tight that there's no give and the fabric tears. If you're not satisfied with the way things are going, remove the section and start over. Mistakes are easily corrected as they happen but impossible to fix later.

Sometimes a section of the original fabric is attached with a metal tacking strip. When this is removed, it's usually bent and impossible to reuse. Tack strips can be purchased, but it isn't necessary to do so. Instead, cut a piece of cardboard the length and width of the metal strip and staple it in place. If the last side of the last piece was originally fastened with such a strip, just secure it with blind stitching.

When covering the cushion, baste the casing first to be sure the fit is good. Then machine-sew the seams, leaving an opening in the back large enough to insert the contents, and blindstitch the slit.

After the chair has been recovered, a critical search may turn up some tiny imperfections. Blind stitches taken here and there will usually eliminate these. To keep mistakes to a minimum, though, beware of shortcuts like stapling the new material right over the old. The result will be anything but professional-looking.

Once you've had the satisfaction of completing your first reupholstered piece, it will be much easier the next time. And who knows? Your skill may prove to be the basis not only for a moneysaving hobby but for a part-time business as well!

AN UPDATED TRADITION:

For centuries, the main characteristic of Japanese interior design has been simplicity. A typical home is sparsely furnished, giving each room an uncluttered atmosphere. For example, a simple, practical bed is made by laying *tatami* (woven mats of rice straw) on the floor and then placing a soft mattress of cotton batting called a *shikifuton*, or underquilt, on top of that resilient base. The cover for each bed is called a *kakefuton*, or overquilt. The whole assembly can be rolled up easily and stored in a large cabinet during the day.

That ancient design has led to an updated version of the shikifuton, consisting of three foam blocks that are covered with fabric and fastened together by cloth "hinges". Because of its unusual construction, this futon can be folded up to serve as an ottoman or a chair, or it can be spread out flat for use as a comfortable pallet.

The construction of this multipurpose sleeper requires three foam rubber blocks, each 27″ X 30″ and 4″ or 5″ thick.

For the futon's covering, you'll need 7 yards of 36″ or 5-1/2 yards of 45″ fabric. Choose a colorful, firmly

FOLDABLE FUTON

You can sleep on it, lounge on it, read on it, exercise on it: The uses for the versatile mattress pictured here are many! And this compact piece of furniture, modeled after the traditional Oriental sleeping mat, is so lightweight that you can carry it almost anywhere. Just follow the instructions, and in a matter of hours you'll have your very own *futon* to use in the bedroom, in the living room, on the patio, or even on camping trips.

woven, heavy cloth such as cotton duck, corduroy, or denim.

FIRST STEPS: Spread out the fabric in a single thickness, and before cutting the material, carefully determine the layout of all the pieces, especially if your material has a directional pattern or nap.

To make an adult-sized shikifuton, cut out two long rectangular panels, 31″ X 55″; two short panels, 28″ X 31″; six 6″ X 28″ side strips; six 6″ X 31″ end strips; and a couple of 1-1/2″ X 31″ hinge strips. These dimensions allow for seams of half an inch all around. The futon shown in the accompanying photos was made with 5″-thick foam. If yours is thicker or thinner, adjust the width of the side and end strips accordingly.

Each long panel of fabric will cover one side of the center cushion and one side of an adjoining end cushion in an overlapping arrangement, as shown in the diagram, while the two shorter panels will each complete the other surface of one end cushion. To make a sturdy, well-constructed futon, it's a good idea to reinforce all your sewing by backstitching at both ends of every seam.

BEGIN AT THE END: The first step is to make the two open "boxes" that will become the covers for the end cushions. Each of these sections requires one short panel, two side strips, and two end strips. Sew a side strip to each 28″ edge of the panel by placing the right sides of the two lengths of cloth together and stitch-

ing to within 1/2″ of the ends of the material. Press both seams toward the panel. Next, with right sides together, sew an end strip to each 31″ side of the panel, once more leaving a 1/2″ opening at each seam's end.

Close the box's corners by joining adjacent side and end strips (always with right sides together), and stop each of those seams 1/2″ from its open end. Then trim away the excess material at the four corners with a pair of pinking shears. After repeating this whole procedure for the other box, set aside the two partially completed end-cushion "jackets".

Prepare the two longer fabric panels by folding one 31″ X 55″ rectangle in half across its width, press the fold line with a warm iron, and lay the piece out flat. Press a hinge strip in half lengthwise, open it, and lay it flat over the crease on the long panel, with the *wrong* sides of the fabric together. Hand-baste that narrow strip onto the larger piece along the matched fold lines. Then stitch it twice, parallel to the centerline and 1/8″ to each side, and pull out all the basting thread. This small strip should be securely attached because

it reinforces the futon's cloth hinges. At the centerline (midway between the two stitched lines), clip a 1/2″ cut on each end through both pieces of fabric. Repeat the entire procedure to attach the other hinge strip to the second long panel.

Take one of the two remaining end strips and, with right sides together, stitch that piece directly to one half of one hinge strip. Sew this seam as close as you can to the line of stitching on one side of the center fold, remembering to leave 1/2″ open at each end.

After fastening the last end strip to the other long panel in the same way, you should have only two side strips left, which will both be attached to the *same* long panel as shown in the drawing. With the right sides together, sew each one to a side of the panel by starting 1/2″ from the free end and stitching right up to the hinge in the center. Press the seams closed, and box the two corners by joining the side strips to the end strip that's stitched to the hinge piece, again leaving the 1/2″ leeway at the free end of the material. Trim the excess fabric from those corners, and you'll have a partially finished long panel, with

two side strips sewn to the end strip at its foldable center.

Now, take this same panel and attach one of the partially completed end covers to it. With right sides facing, stitch one of the longer (end) strips of the end-cushion cover to the unused edge of the hinge strip, again leaving 1/2″ open at each free end. Try to run this seam close to the remaining line of stitching that fastens the hinge strip to the panel.

Use the same procedure to join the other end cover to its panel. Continue attaching each end-cushion cover to its long panel by stitching, with right sides together, along the free end and *one* of the two sides. Leave the other side unsewn for now. Later you'll insert the foam rubber block through this opening. To sew up the one side, start 1/2″ from the free end of the piece and stitch right up to the reinforcement seam on the hinge strip. This is often a rather bulky area, so you might want to pin the rest of the fabric out of the way while working.

FINISHING TOUCHES: To put the futon together, take the long panel that still has a free end strip fastened to its center hinge section and, with right sides facing, stitch that strip to the free end of the center cushion on the other long panel. (Remember to leave 1/2″ openings, as usual, at the ends of the seam.) Box in these two corners and finish attaching the cushion to the other panel by sewing, with right sides together, along one side and across the remaining end.

Carefully trim the seams in bulky areas and corners, turn the whole thing right side out, and you'll be ready to work the foam blocks into their sleeves. Since the spongy material tends to drag against most fabrics, you can make the process easier by wrapping each cushion in a length of lightweight nylon, plastic dry-cleaning bags, or some other slippery material. The foam should then slide more easily into the cloth covers, and you can pull out the wrapping after the block is properly positioned. Finally, hand-stitch the three side seams closed, and your handsome foldable futon is complete.

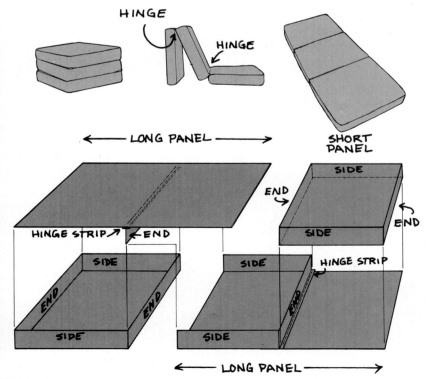

HINGE

HINGE

← LONG PANEL →

SHORT PANEL

SIDE

END

END

SIDE

HINGE STRIP → ← END

SIDE

END

END

SIDE

HINGE STRIP

END

SIDE

SIDE

← LONG PANEL →

OLDABLE FUTON

BUTLER'S TABLE

The butler's tray table was designed hundreds of years ago, no doubt to make it easy for "the help" to deliver milord and milady's tea. It was, after all, a simple matter to load the removable tray with goodies in the kitchen, and then place it atop its waiting legs before a hungry group of gentry.

Even today, in our self-serve society, reproductions of antique butler's tables are often found in American households. And when you think about it, these handy convertible pieces have dozens of uses, from serving breakfast in bed to transporting bowls of midnight popcorn. What's more, you'll find that this mobile "occasional table" is an uncomplicated yet satisfying and attractive shop project.

KEEP THE COST DOWN: Moneywise woodworkers buy large boards and divide them, instead of paying extra for cut-to-size lumber. For example, anyone willing to rip two 8-foot 1 X 8's as shown in the cutting diagram can avoid the addition-al expense of having to buy two (closer-to-size) 1 X 4's plus one 1 X 8.

TAKE IT FROM THE BOTTOM: The tray table's legs and crosspieces are held together by 5/16" X 1-1/2" fluted dowels. Since these wooden pegs enter the corner posts from two different directions, the 3/4" deep holes must be staggered, or the pairs of plugs will run into each other. The dowels should be glued into the holes, and the contact surface between the boards must also be bonded. Once all the pieces are glued and slipped together, apply pressure to the assembly with either four bar clamps or a strap clamp. If you have trouble keeping the legs square, just tack thin strips of wood—such as split lath or 1/4" dowel—between the feet to hold them in position until the adhesive has set.

AND CONTINUE ON TOP: The 1/4" X 1-1/4" fluted dowels that hold the various parts of the table's top together are fitted into holes that must be very carefully aligned, or the ends and faces of the boards won't square up. So before doing any drilling, lay out the various sections and

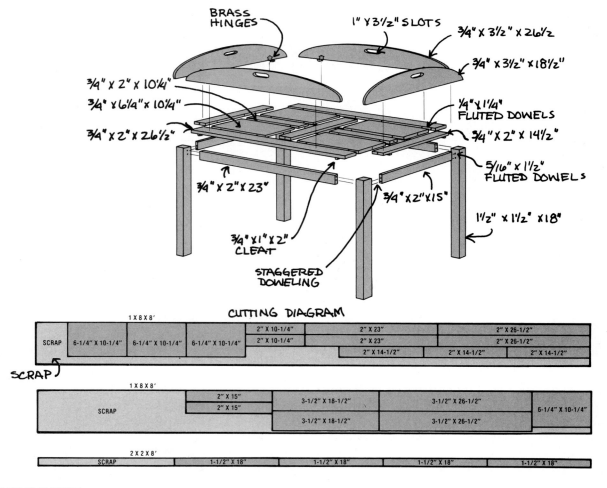

BRASS HINGES

1" X 3½" SLOTS

¾" X 3½" X 26½

¾" X 3½" X 18½"

¾" X 2" X 10¼"

¾" X 6¼" X 10¼"

¾" X 2" X 26½"

¼" X 1¼" FLUTED DOWELS

¾" X 2" X 14½"

5/16" X 1½" FLUTED DOWELS

¾" X 2" X 23"

¾" X 2" X 15"

1½" X 1½" X 18"

¾" X 1" X 2" CLEAT

STAGGERED DOWELING

CUTTING DIAGRAM

1 X 8 X 8'						
SCRAP	6-1/4" X 10-1/4"	6-1/4" X 10-1/4"	6-1/4" X 10-1/4"	2" X 10-1/4"	2" X 23"	2" X 26-1/2"
				2" X 10-1/4"	2" X 23"	2" X 26-1/2"
					2" X 14-1/2"	2" X 14-1/2"	2" X 14-1/2"

SCRAP

1 X 8 X 8'			
SCRAP	2" X 15"	3-1/2" X 18-1/2"	3-1/2" X 26-1/2"
	2" X 15"			6-1/4" X 10-1/4"
		3-1/2" X 18-1/2"	3-1/2" X 26-1/2"

2 X 2 X 8'				
SCRAP	1-1/2" X 18"	1-1/2" X 18"	1-1/2" X 18"	1-1/2" X 18"

mark them, allowing for two dowels in each long dimension and one in each of the shorter sides.

Start assembling the rectangular section of the top by joining two 6-1/4″ X 10-1/4″ boards with a 2″ X 10-1/4″ section between them. Now, secure a 2″ X 14-1/2″ segment to each side of the three-piece unit. Then construct another three-board assembly, attach it to the already assembled five-piece portion, and affix the last 2″ X 14-1/2″ plank to the platform's "unoccupied" edge. Complete this part of the tray by adding the 2″ X 26-1/2″ side boards, and clamp the assembly securely while the glue dries.

Once the adhesive has set sufficiently, remove the clamps and lay the joined boards upside down on your workbench. Position the base unit on top, legs up, leaving about 1/4″ on all sides, and scribe a line on the underside of the tray around the inside of the base's boards. Then, using leftover pieces of wood, make 3/4″ X 1″ X 2″ cleats and fasten them along the inside of the pencil lines with wood screws. Two cleats to each corner will prevent the top from sliding on the base, while still allowing for its easy removal when it is used as a tray.

HANDLES: One simple way to form an accurate curve for the foldup handles, which also serve as edges for the tray, is to make templates from cardboard. Cut out one 3-1/2″ X 18-1/2″ piece and another that's 3-1/2″ X 26-1/2″ and fold each one in half end to end. Once you draw and cut out a suitable curve on both templates, the unfolded cardboard pieces will provide symmetrical arcs.

To make the handgrips, locate the center of each board's long dimension, move in 1-1/4″ from the curved edge, and bore a 1″ hole. Drill another 1″ opening on each side of the centered one, then smooth the edges of the finger slot with a rasp.

FINISHING: Attach the handles to the tabletop with four pairs of brass hinges (the locking type is best), sand the wood surfaces to a smooth, even finish, apply a coat of polyurethane varnish, and when the finish is dry, rub it out with 0000 steel wool.

HOT TUB

Enthusiastic users of hot tubs claim that soaking in steaming water relieves stress, is good for the circulation, induces untroubled sleep, and—perhaps most important—is a particularly enjoyable form of social relaxation. Owning one of these luxurious baths has generally been an expensive proposition, but here is a low-cost alternative: The tank is made of concrete block, the water heater is a woodstove made from an old oil drum, and the pump is salvaged from a garden fountain.

THE BASE: The interior of the tub pictured is about 40″ square, so the instructions given should be adjusted accordingly for a larger one. The first step is to build a concrete base that will be sturdy enough to support both the block tub and the water it will hold. On a level, private, wind-shielded site, dig a 6-foot-square by 6″-deep hole, and line this excavation with a wooden form made from 2″ X 6″ lumber. Then dig out four additional channels 6″ deeper than the rest of the excavation, following the lines that will later mark the four sides of the tub. The trenches will allow for a double-thick concrete base for extra support under the tub's walls.

To strengthen the foundation, install a grid of 16″ squares made from eight lengths of 3/8″ steel reinforcing bar wired together at the intersections, and mark on the forms where the rebar meets the wood, so you can locate those points after the concrete is poured. The grid should lie midway from the top and bottom of the pad after pouring. Put the inlet and outlet pipes in place. To raise the pipes' tips above the level of the poured concrete, fit the ends that will lie within the tub with flanges set on 3″ nipples and fit the far ends with flanges set on 6″ nipples. Then cover the pipe ends with tape to keep the openings clean.

Now, it's time to pour the concrete. A tub this size will take about 3/4 of a cubic yard. You can mix it yourself or buy it ready-mixed. With your hands, reposition the pipe openings and rebar grid, if you didn't wire them in place, and level the concrete's surface with a long 2 X 4. Then sink six U-shaped 12″ X 16″ X 12″ pieces of reinforcing steel, base down, 6″ into the wet cement. These rebar "horseshoes" should be equidistant and lined up at the outside intersection points of the grid (use the frame markings for guidance) so their free ends will poke up into the concrete blocks. For the next two days, spray the new base frequently to let it cure properly.

STACK 'EM UP: Start laying the four levels of blocks for the sides of the tub by lining up string boundaries for the first layer. Set three blocks "longways" and one "endways" on every wall so that the rebar horseshoe uprights go through every other block hole on each side.

Cure the first course by spraying it periodically for two days before adding the other three levels. Then thrust lengths of rebar into the block holes to add to the support already given by the "horseshoe" legs from below. Fill all the openings with con-

The hot tub heater was made by placing a coil of water conduit inside a stovepipe. The tub itself was created by digging and plumbing a foundation pit, filling the hole with cement and rebar, and building concrete block walls.

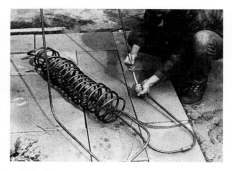

crete and cap the wall with a layer of 8″ X 16″ stepping stones. Add concrete blocks topped with stepping stones to be used as seats, and let it all cure for two weeks.

At this point, it's a good idea to check for leaks. Fill the tub, and if water starts spewing all over the place, add successive layers of a waterproof patching compound, a building block coating, and an airtight water seal until the tub becomes leakproof.

HEAT FEAT: To heat water for the tub, convert an old 55-gallon oil drum into a woodstove. Fabricate a stove door (complete with draft opening) out of 3/16″ steel plate. Using a saber saw, carve the loading hole in the barrel itself, and then secure the door in place with galvanized T hinges.

A heating element, through which cold water will pass to be heated, fits within the smokestack. With a spring-type tubing bender, coil 50

feet of 1/2″ copper tubing into a 6-1/2″-diameter spiral. Since both the intake and the outlet ends of the tubing will emerge from the top of the stack, either double-spiral the coil or bring one straight piece from the bottom up through the coil. Leave a 5-foot section of straight tube from the top of the spiral to each end.

Cut a series of 2″ tabs around the bottom edge of a section of 7″-diameter stovepipe and bend the tabs outward at a 90° angle. Lay the barrel on its side and cut a 7″-diameter hole in its top near the back. Attach the tabbed collar to the drum with sheet metal screws. Assemble the rest of the pipe and snip slots in the top edge to accommodate the two lines of the copper coil. Install a damper above the water-heating spiral and, last, make four spraddled legs to support the heater by using flanges, backing plates, and 2-foot sections of 1/2″ galvanized pipe.

After placing the finished stove a

safe distance from the house, fasten the free ends of the copper coil tubing to some CPVC conduit (regular PVC can't take the heat) with compression fittings, galvanized unions, and two short pieces of galvanized pipe, and run the outlet line through a hose fitting and into the tub. Equip the intake line with a valve, hook it to the pump, and then plumb it to the vat. (If the pump is tied into the line with female fittings and short pieces of hose, it can be disconnected if necessary.)

When it's time to fill the tub with hot water, put a layer of sand in the drum, load the woodstove with scrap lumber, flush water through the system with a garden hose until all the air is out of the pipes, plug the drainpipe, and light the fire. Once the stove gets going, adjust the flow of water from the hose through the heating coil to around 40 gallons per hour so that the temperature of the liquid as it leaves the heater is about 130°F.

When the tub is full (by that time the water will have cooled to 110°), disconnect the hose and start the pump. Be sure to keep the fire small, or the water in the coils will "boil out", causing an air lock that will stop a small pump such as the garden fountain circulator used here. A larger pump, however, should preclude this difficulty. In any case, be certain the pump is well grounded.

When the tub is not in use, cover it with a 4-foot-square piece of plywood to hold the heat in and keep leaves and small animals out. Equip the lid with handles and, for better heat retention, add extruded polystyrene insulation to the underside.

The steaming hot tub that has such a soothing effect on body and spirit is also an excellent breeding ground for infectious germs. Either install a water filter or drain the tub after every three or four sessions. A hose cock on the drain line will be necessary for emptying the tub. Germs can be kept at bay by adding a cup of chlorine bleach per use, and the chemical's unpleasant odor can be masked with lemon, mint sprigs, or scented oils.

EQUIPMENT AND SUPPLIES: For starters, remove the old finish down to the bare wood to insure that the surface is smooth and clean enough to receive a new finish, and then securely refasten all the parts that are loose.

There are many opinions as to the best chemical stripper. Depending on the paint or finish to be removed, some will work better than others; therefore, the wise restorer will have several brands of stripper on his shelves (even a spray can of common oven cleaner for use on old, gray paint.)

Shop around for stripper. Real bargains can be had at flea markets and surplus outlets. Most work calls for the use of a semipaste stripper, although in tight places you might need a liquid product. The semipaste type isn't runny and has the advantage of sticking to an upright surface long enough for the chemicals to do their job.

Here's a list of the equipment you'll need:

[1] Goggles and long-sleeved work clothes.

[2] Cloth gloves. Paint stripper will turn rubber or plastic gloves gummy, ruining them and the work. Leather is also useless.

[3] Hand cream. For skin protection, apply it before you put your gloves on and after you wash up.

[4] One large, flat, dull metal scraper (like a pancake turner or spatula) and many smaller wooden ones. Collect any pointed, flat, or edged implements you can find, such as nutpicks, icepicks, or burnishing tools, for getting into the small channels of carved wooden surfaces.

[5] A bucket or cardboard box to catch all the mess, even if you don't care about the floor of your work space.

[6] A small wooden brush with fine, stiff, nonplastic bristles for use with wet stripper.

[7] A toothbrush (to clean dry surfaces only).

[8] No. 2 and No. 0000 steel wool.

[9] Rags for cleaning up, string for improvising clamps when gluing

REFINISHING

Inexpensive, orphaned furniture begging to be restored to long-lost beauty can be found at almost every yard sale, flea market, and public auction. These real bargains can be coaxed back into a second career of service and, for a small investment, can be made the focus of a nice part-time, or even full-time, business.

Try to select pieces which have all their parts unless you have the equipment, such as a lathe, table saw, jointer, and shaper, to make new parts.

joints, and a lintless cloth for applying varnish.

[10] Glue. White glue or carpenter's glue is easy to use. Forget hide glue, though, and be wary of high-solvent adhesives which can stain or mar a finish.

Don't buy expensive tools unless you have demonstrated to yourself that you'll use them often and skillfully enough to make them cost-effective. The all-important tool—the one you'll need the most—is patience. All the way through every refinishing project, work as thoroughly and as gently with the wood as possible.

PREPARATION: Carefully disassemble as much of the piece of furniture as you can. In areas where its joints and screws are solid, just leave it alone. Work only on unfastening those parts that are already loose. Old glue, paint, or varnish can then be cleaned off, and the parts reattached when the refinishing is complete.

STRIPPING: First of all, wash an inconspicuous part of a piece with soapy water to see what comes off. Sometimes what appears to be black paint turns out to be only water stain. Never wet bare wood, though, or you'll raise the grain.

If the treatment with water is unsuccessful, flow on semipaste stripper, heavily but gently, with a rag swab. Wait an hour. When the chemical has raised the paint, push off the coating from large areas first, detailed areas last. Don't *scrape*: The object is to remove the paint without hurting the wood, so use as little pressure as possible, rather than trying to force off the softened gunk. The stripper is the real tool and

should do most of the work.

Stripper left on too long becomes gummy, and most of it should be removed between stints of paint scraping. When almost all the old finish is safely in the goo bucket, ease off the remainder with No. 2 steel wool and rub the piece dry with a rag.

Details can be cleaned with liquid stripper, which "cuts" differently from the semipaste type. To avoid streaks, keep the liquid stripper off large, flat surfaces, letting it run only into detailed areas.

Remove softened paint with wooden scrapers and a wooden-handled brush, let the surface dry, and brush any remaining gunk out of the crevices with the toothbrush. (Don't use this tool with liquid stripper, though, or the plastic will melt.)

Allow the article you're working on to dry for a day or more. Then rub it— in the direction of the grain only—with No. 2 steel wool. Note that this isn't sanding. You need only to cut the glaze left by the stripper. Finally, dust the piece well with a rag, giving special attention to details.

FINISHING: If the piece you're restoring isn't streaky at this point, that's good. If it is, either lighten the dark areas with liquid stripper on a rag or treat the light spots with a few drops of stain applied in the same way. Evenness, not perfection, is the objective.

Old wood is beautiful in itself and may not require staining. If you feel otherwise, use restraint so that the final effect will be natural. Apply coloring lightly, wait a few minutes, and rub it down with a rag. Don't ever try to get a deep stain in one coat, or the result will look like a bad paint job. Let the finished job dry a day before you varnish it. (Don't apply varnish during damp weather, as moisture affects the drying process, and the finish may remain permanently sticky.)

Pros go over furniture with a vacuum cleaner and "tack rag" immediately before varnishing, but you can get the same effect by rubbing and dusting a surface carefully with a cloth. Then swab on the finish with a lintless rag. Move slowly, working the coating in well, and be sure that no excess is left on corners and edges. Let the piece dry thoroughly, dust it again, and apply another layer (less varnish will be needed this time). Repeat the whole process as often as you want, but keep those coats light!

When you've applied enough thicknesses of varnish to suit you (remember, you want the surface to resemble wood, not glass), rub the dried top layer lightly with No. 0000 steel wool to cut the gloss. The result will be a beautiful low-sheen protective coating, very hard and waterproof, which looks and feels like an expensive oil finish.

Reassemble the piece if necessary, using only enough glue to do the job (excess white glue can be wiped off with a damp rag). Then, if you want a high sheen like that of some old furniture in museums, apply a light coat of paste wax and rub it down.

SALES: Don't be in a hurry to sell an article, or you may get less than it's worth. Unless the item is small, advertise it by itself or with similar pieces. Show it in your living room or any attractive setting, but not in the workshop, unless a clean display area is available. If the piece is really prime, consider having it appraised and then selling it by contacting antique dealers or collectors.

Actually, it's hard to lose money on a nicely finished wooden piece no matter how you handle the transaction. You may be able to do quite well for yourself by rescuing junk store Cinderellas and revealing their true beauty.

PAINTING PRIMER

Protecting and decorating a handcrafted workshop project is an important step in the completion of the item. A coat or two of paint can insure that the final product will stand up to the elements and attractively brighten the space where it is used.

SELECTING A COATING: The kind of paint to use depends on several factors: whether the surface is wood or metal, whether a glossy, semiglossy, or flat finish is desired, whether the item is meant for interior or exterior use, the intended purpose of the object, and the taste of those who will use the finished piece. Enamels and oil-based paints produce opaque finishes ranging from glossy to flat. These coatings flow and level out when applied properly, leaving tough films that do not show brush marks. Enamels and oil paints can be thinned with turpentine or a chemical solvent, which can also be used for cleaning brushes and other equipment. Most enamels can be used on both metal and wood, and when dry, the painted surface is smooth, clean, and soil-resistant and is easily maintained. Enamel is an excellent coating for toys, outdoor and workshop equipment, and other projects on which a bright, durable finish is desired.

Acrylic and latex emulsion paints have the advantage of being easy to work with, water soluble, and quick to dry. However, despite their convenience, these coatings do not yield a truly glossy finish and are not as tough and durable as are oil paints and enamels. The main application for rubber-based paints is in home decorating on walls and trim.

Many older paints contain lead, and they should not be used even though a can with just the right amount in just the right color might be sitting in a dusty corner of the shop. These finishes can cause lead poisoning if even a small amount of the material is ingested. When using any finish, provide adequate ventilation and heed any product warnings.

PREPARING THE SURFACE: The surface must be clean, free from dust or grease, and without dents or other blemishes. Dents in wood can be raised by applying a drop of water or by placing a moist pad over the depression and heating the area with a soldering iron. Nail or screw holes can be filled with wood putty or a mixture of glue and fine sawdust. All areas to be painted should be sanded and any sharp edges rounded very slightly. Open-grained woods and woods with sap streaks or knots need to be sealed with a coat of shellac or other primer.

Metal surfaces should be smoothed by grinding down welds, filing burrs and sharp edges, and rubbing flat areas with emery cloth. A rust preventive primer should be brushed or sprayed on before finishing coats are applied.

APPLYING THE FINISH: Paint used to coat a wood surface is generally applied with a brush, while finishes for metal pieces are often applied from a spray can. Select a quality brush, and dip the bristles about a third of their length into the container. Brush the paint onto the surface with smooth, even strokes, making all the final strokes in the same direction. Some paints need to be flowed on, so follow the instructions on the can and avoid overbrushing. Also, to avoid runs and drips, try not to apply the paint too thickly. Spray paint should be applied sparingly with the can held about a foot away from the surface and moved constantly to prevent runs.

Several thin coats, sanded or rubbed with fine steel wool between coats, will usually yield a better finish than one or two thick coats. Allow ample drying time between applications, and when the project is done, clean the brushes and other materials as directed for the type of paint.

YARD, GARDEN, & OUTDOOR LIVING

LOCATION: For many years, greenhouse manufacturers have been insisting that such structures must be located to face the south. This is a good suggestion, but hardly mandatory. Many excellent greenhouses are attached to the east, west, and even north sides of homes and are filled with healthy plants. Indeed, if you plan to grow orchids, you'll find a northern exposure ideal.

Lean-to construction is probably the most convenient. It allows the greenhouse to abut the living area of your home, adds both beauty and a new feeling of openness, and by eliminating the need for one wall on the new structure, reduces the total cost. If you house is L-shaped and facing the right direction, you'll be able to complete the glassed-in room by constructing only two walls and a roof.

SIZE: An extremely large room for your plants really isn't necessary. With a careful arrangement of tables and benches, more than 100 plants can be accommodated in a greenhouse measuring just 8 X 10 feet.

In general, a conservatory measuring 10 X 12 feet or 10 X 16 feet is all that's needed to add a real touch of elegance to a house. The height of the glassed-in addition can also contribute to the total effect. There's nothing like a tall ceiling to give a greenhouse that old-fashioned conservatory look, and a high roof line is essential if you ever decide to mix in a few big tropical beauties with your smaller potted plants.

TOP LIGHT: When considering your structure's top light, don't plan to make the roof completely of transparent glass or plastic. If you do, the conservatory will be far too hot in the summer and too cold during the winter. There's no need to admit that much sunlight anyway. Almost any plant will do fine with 30% top light, which can be provided by skylights.

MATERIALS: For a durable floor that resists both stains and water, use concrete or brick. They both also retain heat to help keep a greenhouse warm.

While bricks may be expensive, unless you salvage them from a demolished building, most homeowners find it easier to set bricks in sand than to pour and trowel concrete. Brick also makes a very attractive floor, which is an important factor to many people.

Cinders or gravel can be spread several inches deep directly on the ground as makeshift greenhouse flooring. Neither is as satisfying, in terms of looks, usefulness, or durability, as concrete or brick. If used at all, they should be thought of as nothing more than temporary materials, which will eventually be replaced.

The walls, roof, and glazing can be of all new materials if desired, but recycled components can be just as attractive and much less expensive. Salvage yards, bargain centers, and demolition companies can often supply used lumber, doors, and glass at considerably less than the price of new goods. If recycled materials are used, try to obtain all of them before starting to build. It's much easier and far less expensive to construct as much of the greenhouse as possible from existing materials with set dimensions and then build around them, than it is to try to work the other way around.

FOOTINGS AND FOUNDATION: Because the footings and foundation will support the rest of the structure, many people prefer to have them poured and/or laid by professionals. On the other hand, if you decide to tackle these jobs yourself, here is a general outline of the process:

[1] Don't make a move before consulting local building codes and thor-

---

ADD-ON GREENHOUSE

The advantages and benefits of attaching a greenhouse to an existing home are well known, but having this job done professionally, even with a prefabricated model, is an expensive proposition. Even so, there's no reason to do without your own conservatory.

Homemade greenhouses can often be much better than the commercial kind, because when you plan and build your own, you can make certain it's the size and shape and style that's best for your particular needs.

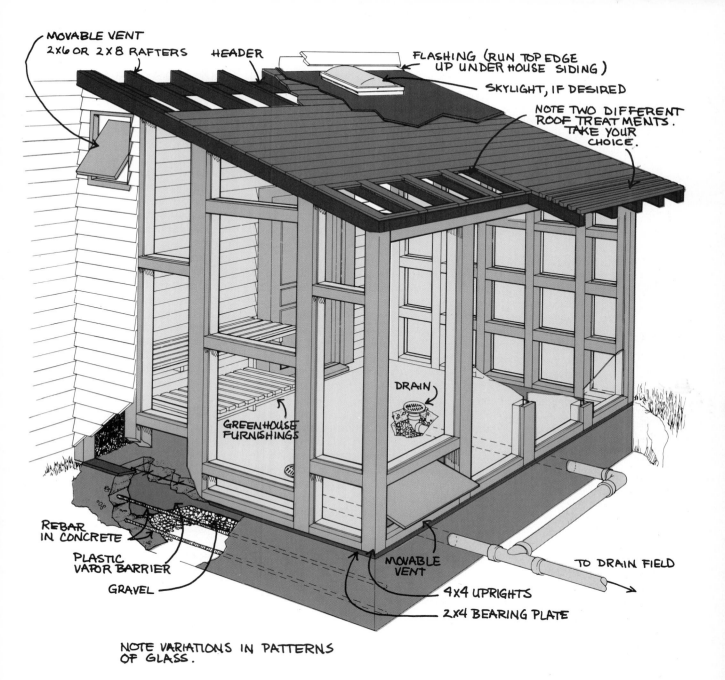

MOVABLE VENT
2×6 OR 2×8 RAFTERS

HEADER

FLASHING (RUN TOP EDGE UP UNDER HOUSE SIDING)

SKYLIGHT, IF DESIRED

NOTE TWO DIFFERENT ROOF TREATMENTS. TAKE YOUR CHOICE.

DRAIN

GREENHOUSE FURNISHINGS

REBAR IN CONCRETE

PLASTIC VAPOR BARRIER

GRAVEL

MOVABLE VENT

4×4 UPRIGHTS

2×4 BEARING PLATE

TO DRAIN FIELD

NOTE VARIATIONS IN PATTERNS OF GLASS.

ADD-ON GREENHOUSE

oughly understanding them. Few things are more discouraging than having to tear out something you've just built because it wasn't constructed exactly to code. These codes are designed for the homeowner's protection, and though they may sometimes seem arbitrary, there are definite reasons for them. If you know nothing about the frost line in your area, for instance, you may question why the local code specifies that all footings must be set 6″ deeper into the ground than you placed yours ... until the night a hard freeze cracks your new foundation so badly that it must be replaced.

[2] Lay out the footings by driving stakes into the ground and running string or cord from one marker to another to indicate where the walls will go. When you're satisfied that you've laid out your walls as accurately and as squarely as possible, dig a trench along the perimeter of the staked area as wide and as deep as the local construction code reqires.

[3] The concrete footings, which should be a minimum of 16″ wide and 6″ deep, will support the foundation. Local codes may allow both to be poured as a unit. If not, or if a block or brick foundation is planned, the footing is poured and allowed to cure before any more work is done. It should be reinforced with rebar, leaving vertical lengths of the steel rod extending above the surface to tie into the foundation.

[4] The minimum width for the foundation is 8″, and it should extend far enough above the ground to keep the base of the wall from being damaged by water. The forms for pouring both footings and foundation can be fashioned from 3/4″ exterior grade plywood or they can be rented from a tool-rental firm, contractor, or cement supplier.

[5] The top of the foundation must be level to accommodate the bearing, or sill, plates. These will be attached by 1/2″ anchor bolts set into the foundation when it's built. You also will have left 2″ drainage holes spaced about 4 feet apart in the foundation walls. The building code may require the installation of tile or gravel drainage channels leading away from these holes.

[6] Once the foundation is in and has cured sufficiently, remove the forms and backfill the foundation with gravel or dirt, again in accordance with local codes.

FLOORING: If the floor is to be made of concrete it must be formed up and leveled in much the same way that the foundation was. Dig out the whole area where the concrete is to be poured so that there will be room for 4″ of gravel and no less than 4″ of concrete.

Be sure that the ground all the way across the area which will be covered by the floor is as level as you can make it, then dump or shovel in the gravel and smooth it out. The crushed stone is topped with tar paper or a sheet of heavy builder's plastic, which will act as a vapor barrier. Reinforcing bars or steel mesh are set in, and the concrete is poured, tamped, and screed.

As the floor begins to cure, it must be troweled smooth. If the weather is hot, the curing concrete should be covered with plastic or burlap and sprinkled with water from time to time to make it cure more slowly and make the finished floor stronger.

You can purchase ready-mixed concrete for the footers, foundation, and floor, or you can rent a powered mixer and make your own. Mix one part cement, two parts sand, and two parts gravel with enough clean water to make the concrete easy to work but not overly "sloppy". Work up each batch by putting the water into the mixer first, followed by the gravel and sand, and finally the cement. Mix the concrete very well, pour it, and tamp it thoroughly to remove any bubbles. Scree the surface, but wait until it begins to set before final finishing.

FRAMING: Redwood, cedar, cypress, and Douglas fir all resist rot and are top choices for the wooden framing in the greenhouse. If these are unavailable, use well-seasoned lumber that will grip nails tightly and that will not warp or twist. All the wood in the structure should be protected with one of the excellent heavy-duty preservatives or paints on the market today.

Though local codes may require more, generally four or five 4 X 4 posts set up in the greenhouse's outer wall are all the heavy vertical structural members needed. Anchor them firmly to the lean-to's foundation by toenailing or bolting them to a 2 X 4 sill, or bearing, plate fastened to the foundation with the anchor bolts. It's a good idea to apply a layer of mastic between the footing and the sill to prevent capillary action from drawing water through the concrete and rotting out the bearing plate.

The beam running across the tops of the uprights can be a 4 X 4 for 4-foot spans, a 4 X 6 for spans of 6 feet, or a 4 X 8 for 8-foot spans. Rafters, spaced either 18″ or 24″ on center, are usually heavy enough if made of 2 X 6's, though many folks like to use 2 X 8's for these members, especially when building flatter roofs.

The simplest way to connect the upper ends of the lean-to greenhouse's rafters to the house is by resting them on, and spiking them to, the top of a 2 X 6 or 2 X 8 ledger which, in turn, is securely spiked directly to the main structure's wall studs.

Be certain that the rafters are braced at each end and in the center with 2 X 6 or 2 X 8 blocks so they won't twist. Each rafter should be notched to fit the ledger strip on one end and the horizontal beam on the other. Mark one rafter, cut it to fit, and then use the first as a pattern to mark the others. Coat each joint and every other wood-to-wood joint in the greenhouse with sealing preservative before nailing the juncture together.

GLAZING, SIDING, AND ROOFING: The glass or plastic used to cover the walls and part of the roof of the conservatory can be purchased new or secondhand, or it may even be salvaged from wrecked houses, stores, barns, factories, and other old buildings. It really doesn't matter if that glass or plastic is in the form of bare panes, old windows already set in frames, rigid panels of fiberglass, or commercial skylights or domes. Almost anything that will transmit light will work. However, the chosen panes of glass or fiberglass should be attractive once they're in place, and should be installed in a safe and permanent manner.

Glass already mounted in wooden frames can be set into tracks on the side of the greenhouse or attached to the building with nails driven right through the frames. Fiberglass can also be nailed directly into place, applying sealing compound where the panels overlap each other. But special channels will have to be cut for bare panes of glass, and they must be set into place with some kind of glazing compound. Special framing will also be necessary for any commercial "bubbles" or skylights that you install in the roof.

Greenhouse glass is graded SSB (single strength B grade), DSB (double strength B grade), SSA (single strength A grade), and DSA (double strength A grade). In general, single strength glass is 1/16" thick and double strength is 1/8" thick, and of course, A is to be preferred over B. This grading system is further complicated by tempered glass, which is five times as strong as standard glass and which comes in 3/16", 7/32", and 1/4" thicknesses, and by wire glass. This, as the name implies, is glass with a grid of wire embedded in it. Both tempered and wire glass are much safer to use than ordinary glass. Indeed, in some states, only one or the other of these types can be used for overhead glass or for the first 16" above the surface of the earth if the glass in the greenhouse runs all the way to the ground.

Regardless of what thickness or grade of glass is used, each pane must be glazed properly. Fit it precisely into its opening with a little space all around, and seat and seal all four edges with a first-class glazing compound. Putty, which was standard for this job for years, is difficult to work with and soon becomes brittle, falls away, and must be replaced. Newer mastic-type glazing compounds are much better and the plastic glazes better yet. Both are extremely easy to put into place with a glazing gun.

The solid portions of the roof, any closed sections of the building's sides, and movable ventilation panels can be fabricated of boards or plywood, recycled or new. Once again, redwood, cedar, or Douglas fir will last longest, but almost any good construction lumber that's protected by a coat of preservative will do.

Plain roll roofing laid down over a base of flat boards or plywood is as inexpensive as any. Metal flashing should be used to waterproof the joint where the greenhouse roof attaches to the wall of the main building. Corner guards, another kind of flashing made especially for the job, should also be used to protect the end grain of any siding applied to the walls of the conservatory.

HEATING EQUIPMENT AND TIPS: Whether or not the greenhouse needs to be artificially heated depends on a great many factors: where you live, what you plan to grow in the building, the size of the structure, what kind of floor it has (a massive cement or brick floor will absorb the sun's rays during the day and then radiate the warmth back at night), what kind of wall the lean-to is built against (a masonry wall will tend to regulate a room's temperature just like a cement floor), how much glass is in the roof and walls of the greenhouse, and so forth.

To keep the conservatory warmer than it would otherwise be from only the heat of the sun, plant a double row of evergreens, a thick hedge, or some shrubs as a weatherbreak between the glassed room and winter storms. Install wooden shutters, roll-up blinds, or heavy drapes inside the glassed portions of the lean-to and use them at night. Weatherstrip all cracks in the greenhouse and install sufficient insulation. Keep in mind that double glazed windows are certainly more expensive than ordinary glazing but, in the long run, more than pay for themselves.

You can, at times, supplement the heat in the conservatory by opening a large door or doors between the lean-to and the house to which it is attached. This works both ways, of course: On cold sunny days, excess heat from the conservatory will flow into the house and help to heat it, while on cold nights some of the warmth from the building's heating system can be allowed to flow the other way. This idea can be refined somewhat by extending one of your regular furnace ducts right into the greenhouse.

If this add-on conservatory is to be used as a hothouse, though, it must be equipped with a heating system of its own. Check local gas, oil, and electric rates and price a wood-burning furnace. Make any choice based on original cost of the setup, availability of fuel, ongoing operating expenses, ease of operation, and whatever other factors are pertinent. Be sure to consult local codes and a knowledgeable dealer in greenhouse equipment for the facts and figures applicable to your situation.

THREE WAYS TO INSTALL GLASS

NOTE GROOVE USED IN ALL VARIATIONS

ADD-ON GREENHOUSE

POLYGONAL TABLE

An unusual design gives this attractive table a versatility unmatched by any conventional picnic table. Rather than the hexagonal unit shown here, a custom-built table could have as few as two or three seats, or as many as you wish. Each diner has plenty of elbowroom and unobstructed legroom and is undisturbed by the coming and going of other people at the table. And this type of table remains stable no matter what combination of seats is occupied.

The polygonal picnicker is sturdy enough to use in any rustic setting, but its clean good looks would make it a welcome addition to a porch, patio, or even breakfast nook, where its many-sided shape takes up less space than the more traditional round or rectangular models.

LIST OF MATERIALS

MATERIAL	SIZE	PURPOSE
No. 1 Common pine, kiln dried	(6) 2 X 4 X 10'	tabletop
No. 2 Common lumber	(6) 2 X 4 X 27-1/2"	tabletop braces
No. 1 Common pine, kiln dried	(2) 2 X 8 X 16'	seats
11-gauge box tubing	(2) 1-1/2" X 20'	legs
14-gauge sheet metal	(6) 10" X 12"	seat bottoms
11-gauge sheet metal	3' X 3', cut to size	seat gussets
carriage bolts w/nuts	(48) 1/4" X 2"	seat fasteners
carriage bolts w/nuts	(6) 5/16" X 3-1/2"	tabletop fasteners
flathead wood screws	(72) No. 12 X 2-1/2"	tabletop braces
glue		adhesive
wood putty		finishing
paint		finishing
marine spar varnish		finishing

TOOL REQUIREMENTS

radial-arm or table saw
power hacksaw
arc welder
hand grinder
power drill
1/4", 9/32", 11/32" metal bits
7/64", 7/16", 9/16" wood bits
3/4" hole saw
belt sander
40-, 60-, 80-grit sandpaper
sliding T-bevel

protractor
(4) bar clamps
(4) C-clamps
saber saw
flathead screwdriver
wrenches
1" wood chisel and mallet
pliers and wire
measuring tape
pencil

TEST YOUR METTLE: Although this shop project could be divided into separate metal- and woodworking stages, the best use of time combines the different tasks into a well-organized series of steps. Cut and weld steel while the glue is drying, and then get back to woodworking as the metal cools. Using the power tools included in the accompanying list, it should take about 40 hours to complete the table. Note that while the instructions contained here are for a six-seat unit, the design may be modified to include the number of sides you want. Here's how to build a duplicate of this truly innovative table:

Step 1. Form the six inner wood triangles by making 30° cuts across a pine 2 X 4 with a radial-arm or table saw. This may require some practice since even very small cutting errors will show up dramatically when fitting the six pieces together.

When the fit is satisfactory, glue the triangles together to form a hexagon, wrap a strand of wire around the assembly, and twist the ends of the wire with a pair of pliers to clamp the six blocks together firmly. Set this aside to dry overnight.

Step 2. While the inner hexagon is curing, cut the 1-1/2" box tubing into six 81-1/2" lengths, designating the location of the six bends on each section to match the drawing. Then set your sliding T-bevel to a 67-1/2° angle (using a protractor to position its blade) and mark across the 1-1/2" tubing at each bend to form two intersecting diagonal cuts with a total included angle of 45°.

These marks describe notches that must be removed from the steel to allow it to bend. Don't cut all the way through the metal, though. Just use a power hacksaw to cut down to the flat, opposite side so that the other 1-1/2" face can become a hinge for the bend. Now, bend the tubes to the shape shown.

Step 3. Set up a roughly right-angled jig on the top of your welding table, using heavy bars held down by C-clamps. Actually, the jig should be positioned at about a 95° angle—to include two bends—because the joints will draw together somewhat as they cool after being welded. Set one of the bent sections in the device and weld along the three open sides of one corner. Wait until this first joint has cooled to check the finished angle and adjust the jig accordingly for future welds. This adjustment must be accurate to insure that the legs are square to the floor and to the tabletop. When you're certain that the jig is producing accurate 90° corners, weld all the remaining joints on the six legs, grinding them afterward to remove burrs.

Step 4. Returning to the wooden tabletop, cut out the second set of 2

X 4's (again, at a 30° angle), using the inner hexagon for the short-side measurement on each board. Throughout this project, cut pieces, whether wood or steel, to fit, rather than rigidly relying on the drawings. Only four new, opposite-facing ring boards can be glued at a time, since they must be cinched across the top with bar clamps. One set of clamps can be positioned beneath the table-top with another going across the upper surface.

At most, only one new ring can be completed per day, because of the hours needed for the glue to cure, so it will take a total of seven days for the tabletop to attain its full width. The rest of the time can be devoted to making the seats and the other metal parts.

Step 5. Using a hacksaw, cut out twelve 4″ right isosceles triangles from the 11-gauge sheet metal. Then weld these seat gussets to the insides of the seat posts in accordance with the drawing of the frame. When the welds are cool, remove any burrs and grind the top of each seat post to a 5°

angle that slopes upward from the center in both directions.

Step 6. Bend each of the six 10″ X 12″ sheet-metal seat brackets up 10° across the center of its 12″ side to form a 170° angle. A seat with this configuration provides thigh support

and is far more comfortable than the conventional flat surface. Following the diagram, drill eight 9/32″ holes 1-1/8″ in from the edges of the bracket. Position each seat bracket with one 10″ edge 1-3/4″ away from the inside lip of the seat post, and

tack the sheet metal to the box tube on the inner contact surface only.

The rear seat gusset is formed by cutting a 3″ X 7″ right triangle from 11-gauge sheet metal, adjusting the base to fit the obtuse angle between the seat post and the seat bracket. This should involve trimming a 5° wedge from the triangle's base, but earlier errors may force you to compensate in order to create the best possible fit.

Once the six rear gussets are prepared, tack one to the base of each seat bracket, using welds no more than 1″ long per section. (Excessive welding will warp the bracket beyond use.) Next, weld the bases of the triangular pieces of steel to their seat posts.

Step 7. Cut the two-piece seats from the 2 X 8 board to the dimensions shown. Bevel the faces where they will touch (to 5° on each board, to fit the angle of the bracket), round the four corners with a jigsaw, and smooth down the edges with a belt sander, file, or coarse sandpaper.

Step 8. After all seven rings of the

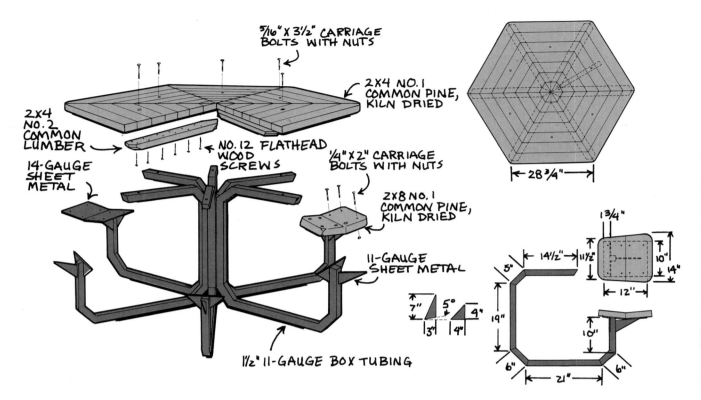

5/16" X 3 1/2" CARRIAGE BOLTS WITH NUTS

2X4 NO. 1 COMMON PINE, KILN DRIED

2X4 NO. 2 COMMON LUMBER

14-GAUGE SHEET METAL

NO. 12 FLATHEAD WOOD SCREWS

1/4" X 2" CARRIAGE BOLTS WITH NUTS

2X8 NO. 1 COMMON PINE, KILN DRIED

11-GAUGE SHEET METAL

1 1/2" 11-GAUGE BOX TUBING

28 3/4"

1 3/4" **14 1/2"** **11 1/2"** **10"** **14"** **12"**

5° **7"** **5°** **4"** **3"** **4"** **19"** **10"** **6"** **21"** **6"**

tabletop have been glued together, saw off six 27-1/2″ lengths of 2 X 4 to use as braces for the hexagon. Cut one end of each board to a 60° point so that all the braces will fit together at the center, and cut a 120° point on the other end to match the shape of the outer lip of the tabletop. Round off the edges on the broader ends to prevent occupants from banging their knees on sharp wood.

Fit the braces together at the center and secure them to the underside of the tabletop with the No. 12 X 1-1/2″ wood screws. To facilitate this operation, you may want to bore lead holes with a 7/64″ bit. Furthermore, all of the screws should be countersunk, using a 7/16″ bit, to a depth of no more than 1/2″, to prevent clothing from getting snagged.

Step 9. In order to fit the table legs snugly to the top, the braces have to be notched near the center. To determine where to put these channels, place the table top-down on the floor or on a bench and, using a leg as a pattern, mark the location directly onto each board. The legs should be centered between the braces. Cut out

the notches with a wood chisel and mallet.

When all the cuts have been made, the legs for the table can be put together, using the still upside-down tabletop as a guide. Once the tubes are all in place and properly aligned, make 4″ welds at the top and bottom where the edges of the six square sections meet.

Turn the legs and top upright to see whether the structure rides evenly on its base and the legs sit level on the floor. If the supports aren't true, they must be forced into place by bending or relieving the joints.

Step 10. Coat the metal parts with primer and then with enamel.

Step 11. Bore 11/32″ holes through the tabletop and the tubular metal supports directly below it at the six points on the fifth wooden hexagon where the steel braces lie. With a 3/4″ hole saw, countersink the top of each opening 1/2″ deep and fasten the table and legs together with 5/16″ X 3-1/2″ carriage bolts and nuts.

Step 12. Locate the seat halves on their brackets, mark the positions for

the necessary mounting holes by using the steel bracket as a template, and drill through the seat boards with a 9/32″ metal bit. Run a 1/4″ carriage bolt through each hole and snug the seats down with nuts from below.

Step 13. To round the corners of the hexagonal tabletop, mark off the edges, using a one-quart paint can lid as a template. Then follow the markings with a saber saw.

Step 14. Flatten irregularities in the surface by rubbing them with 40-grit sandpaper, inspecting the joints as you sand. If thoroughly dry boards were used, the seams should not have pulled apart, but there may be a few small gaps that need to be plugged with wood filler. Fill in the countersunk holes on the top with putty or dowel plugs.

Switch to 60-grit sandpaper to smooth the top, the edges, the corners, and the seats. Finish with 80-grit paper, dust off the surface, and complete the project by protecting the wood against the elements with coats of marine spar varnish or some other durable exterior finish.

ZAPOTEC STOOL

Anyone who's ever been stuck without something sturdy to sit on will appreciate this stool, based on a unique design handed down by the Zapotec Indians of southern Mexico.

To make one, round up a 5-foot length of 1 X 12 (old shelving is fine), 16 four-penny finishing nails, some white or yellow carpenter's glue, a ruler, a protractor, and a saw.

Start by cutting the board into two 14″ and two 16″ lengths, then in one end of each 14″ piece, trim out a shallow V-shaped section having an angle of 135°. A decorative 3-1/4″ X 3-1/4″ X 5″ wedge can be removed from the opposite end of each of these components, but that's optional. From each of the 16″ pieces of lumber, cut two lengthwise parts: the first 6-1/2″ wide, and the second only 2″ wide and trimmed to 14″ in length.

Next, place first one—then the other—of the 6-1/2″ X 16″ seat halves into its angled position on the legs and mark the long inside edge of both planks so you can trim a triangular sliver from each to allow a smooth mitered joint. Then fashion two 3/4″ X 2″ notches in each of the stool's leg planks midway between top and bottom to accommodate the struts.

With all the pieces trimmed to size, assemble your project by simply gluing the parts together and securing them with finishing nails as illustrated in the drawing. After giving it a light sanding, you'll find that this uncomfortable-looking stool is actually a pleasure to sit on, because the hassock was designed with the behind in mind.

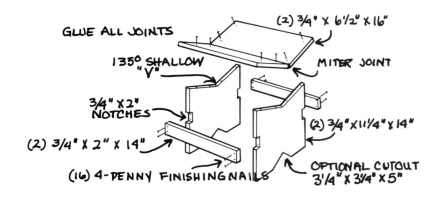

GLUE ALL JOINTS
(2) 3/4" X 6 1/2" X 16"
135° SHALLOW "V"
MITER JOINT
3/4" X 2" NOTCHES
(2) 3/4" X 11 1/4" X 14"
(2) 3/4" X 2" X 14"
(16) 4-PENNY FINISHING NAILS
OPTIONAL CUTOUT 3 1/4" X 3 1/4" X 5"

WOOD PICNIC TABLE

A sturdy benched table is a welcome addition to almost any backyard, and this uncomplicated design can be reproduced by the most amateur carpenter. And not only is it durable, but it's low in cost, too.

The required materials are four pressure-treated 8-foot-long 2 X 4's, three 12-foot 1 X 6's, four 3/8" X 3-1/4" carriage bolts with washers and nuts, and approximately one pound of 8d galvanized nails. Get some varnish, too, if you want the table to last longer. The treated 2 X 4's will cost a little more than untreated ones, but because they form the crucial structural supports, that money will be well spent. The 1 X 6's that form the benches and tabletop should be conventional lumber, since it's likely that food will come into direct contact with these surfaces, and the chemicals used to pressure-treat lumber are toxic.

To begin, saw the 1 X 6 planks into nine 48" lengths. Next, following the cutting diagrams, saw out one

bench support and one leg from each of two 2 X 4's. Cut out a leg, a top support, and a brace from each of the remaining two 2 X 4's.

Start the actual construction by assembling the two end frames. Make each four-piece unit by positioning a tabletop support and a bench support beneath two legs, as shown in the accompanying illustration, and nail the components together. Take care not to nail through the centers of the leg/bench support junctions, since your next step will be to drill holes at these spots, attaching the 3/8" carriage bolts and nuts. For the sake of appearance, place the washers and nuts on the undersides of the joints.

Stand the two frame ends 33" apart and parallel to each other, and connect their top supports by nailing a 1

X 6 across their centers. Nail another plank along the outer edge of each bench support. These decking boards should protrude about 6" beyond their bracers. Now, attach two more planks flush with the *ends* of the top supports and then finish the eating surface by centering a board in each of the two remaining spaces. Nail the last two 1 X 6's next to the existing bench boards, leaving a gap of about 1/4" between adjacent bench planks. Then carefully turn the unit upside down and attach the two 45° braces as shown.

Finish the picnic table with an application or two of a durable, water-resistant coating such as polyurethane (or any of the marine varnishes), and your family and friends will enjoy it for years to come.

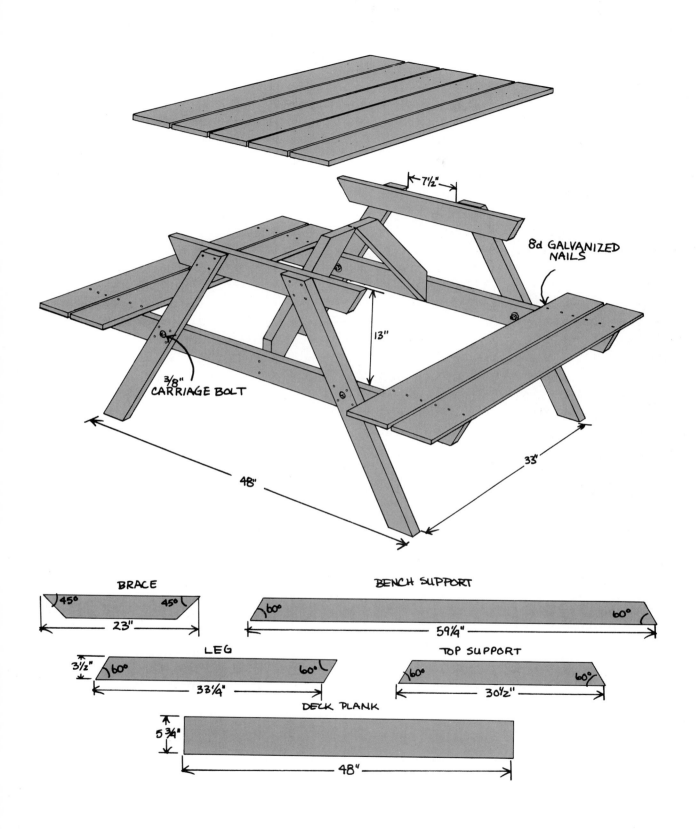

7½"

8d GALVANIZED
NAILS

13"

3/8"
CARRIAGE BOLT

48"

33"

BRACE

45° 45°

23"

BENCH SUPPORT

60° 60°

59¼"

LEG

3½" 60° 60°

33¼"

TOP SUPPORT

60° 60°

30½"

DECK PLANK

5¾"

48"

WOOD PICNIC TABLE

BARBECUE COOKER

Few meals are as downright satisfying as those featuring food cooked over a bed of glowing red coals. While many manufactured smoker/broilers carry a high price tag, that needn't keep you from the enjoyment of outdoor barbecuing. The body of this homemade cooker is built from a discarded storage tank made to keep refrigerant under pressure, and the cost of the rest of the materials should be minimal.

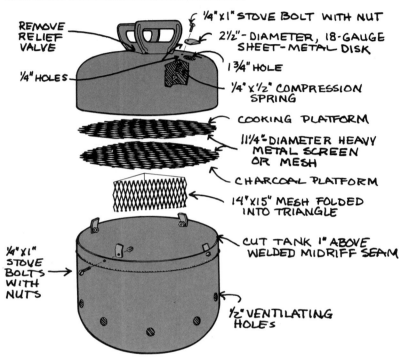

- REMOVE RELIEF VALVE
- ¼" HOLES
- ¼"x1" STOVE BOLT WITH NUT
- 2½"-DIAMETER, 18-GAUGE SHEET-METAL DISK
- 1¾" HOLE
- ¼"x½" COMPRESSION SPRING
- COOKING PLATFORM
- 11¼"-DIAMETER HEAVY METAL SCREEN OR MESH
- CHARCOAL PLATFORM
- 14"x15" MESH FOLDED INTO TRIANGLE
- CUT TANK 1" ABOVE WELDED MIDRIFF SEAM
- ¼"x1" STOVE BOLTS WITH NUTS
- ½" VENTILATING HOLES

GATHER THE MATERIALS: Obtain the storage cylinder from a refrigeration or air-conditioning repair shop. Federal law prohibits refilling these tanks, so the owner should be more than happy to give you a used one. You'll also need a piece of heavy wire mesh or metal lath (the kind used in plaster and stucco work) measuring about 16" X 24", five 1/4" X 1" stove bolts with nuts, a 1/4" X 1/2" compression spring, and a 2-1/2" X 4-1/2" section of 18-gauge sheet metal.

BODY BUILDING: Cut the cylinder in half by first marking a point 1" above the container's welded midriff seam and drilling a 1/4" hole at that spot through the wall of the tank. Then scribe a line at this same level all around the vessel and, using the hole as a starting point, cut the container in half with an electric saber saw.

To make the cooker's draft control, remove the relief valve in the cooker's top portion with a hacksaw and file the remaining nub smooth. Then scribe a 1-3/4"-diameter circle on the top near the handles, cut this piece out with your electric saber saw, and drill a 1/4" hole about 1/4" from the rim of this opening.

To cover the hole, cut a 2-1/2"-diameter sheet-metal disk and bend a small lip on one side of it. Drill another 1/4" hole near the edge of this cap opposite the lip and fasten it to the outside of the cooker's lid with a stove bolt, a spring, and a nut.

Start making the cooking portion of the grill by cutting eight 1/2" ventilation holes around the base of the lower half of the cylinder as shown in the accompanying illustration. Fashion a set of guides for the lid by making four 1" X 1-1/4" sheet-metal tabs and bolting them equidistantly around the upper lip of the bowl. Allow about 3/4" of metal to protrude above the edge, then bend the tabs inward slightly so the lid can be easily slipped on and off.

The cooking grill and the charcoal platform are made by cutting two 11-1/4"-diameter disks from the screen mesh stock (this dimension might vary, depending on the size of your cylinder). The grill rests on the bolts that hold the sheet-metal tabs, and the lower disk is supported by a pedestal made from a 4" X 15" rectangle of screen mesh bent into an equilateral triangle with 5" sides.

NOW HEAR THIS: Before preparing any food in the new grill, it's imperative that you burn out any refrigerant that might remain in the container. Place a pile of charcoal briquets on the lower screen (enough to cover the surface when they're spread out), ignite them, and wait till the coals get white hot with the cooker lid removed. Then replace the top, open the draft control, and let the fire burn itself out. By this time, all the paint on the cooker's surface will have peeled off and the refrigerant residue will be completely gone. When the grill cools down, clean it thoroughly—inside and out—with a stiff wire brush and give its outer surface several coats of heat-resistant paint.

COOKING: Use this smoker/broiler as you would any barbecue cooker. To prepare a slow-cooked meal, fire up the coals, lay your choice of meat on the cooking screen, install the lid with the draft control partially open, and let your dinner broil to perfection. Throw a few hickory chips into the coals to give your meat a hickory-smoked flavor. Or, if you wish, remove the lid altogether and cook over the coals as with a conventional hibachi.

ROPE HAMMOCK

There are few more delightful ways to spend a sunny afternoon than enjoying a cool breeze and listening to the grass grow while you're basking in a hammock. A comfortable net sling in which to laze away those warm spring, summer, and autumn weekend days can be woven in your spare time while the winter cold is in the air, and it will be ready to relax in when the weather begins to warm. This comfortable rope hammock, first described in the July-September 1981 issue of *Handmade* magazine (a quarterly published by Lark Communications, 50 College Street, Asheville, North Carolina 28801), requires only a small investment in materials.

PRELIMINARIES: To make a single-person hammock, you'll need about two pounds (three pounds for a two-person sling) of No. 40 to 46 seine twine, two welded-steel or brass rings 2″ to 3″ in diameter, two hardwood support bars measuring 1-1/2″ X 1-1/2″ X 33″ each (48″ long for the double hammock), a smooth gauge stick that's about 3/4″ X 1-1/2″ X 12″, and a netting shuttle. Hardwood support bars and a scrapwood gauge can be obtained from a lumberyard. Rings, twine, and shuttle are available from craft outlets.

Check the accompanying sketches (Fig. 1) for directions on tying a square knot, a weaver's knot, a half hitch, a lark's head knot, and a plain overhand knot. Then find a comfortable place to sit where there's a handy hook, nail, or knob to hang your work on, and begin.

CASTING ON: Start by cutting a 3-foot length of twine and tying its ends together with a square knot. Hang this starter loop from that handy nail or knob, wind the netting shuttle full of twine (as depicted in Fig. 2 through Fig. 5), and then tie the free end of the shuttle cord to the starter loop, using an overhand knot.

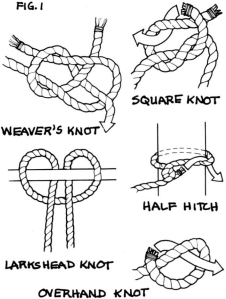

FIG. 1

WEAVER'S KNOT

SQUARE KNOT

HALF HITCH

LARKSHEAD KNOT

OVERHAND KNOT

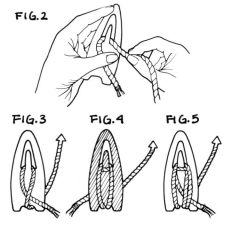

FIG. 2

FIG. 3   **FIG. 4**   **FIG. 5**

Next, take the gauge stick in your left hand (if you're a southpaw, you would reverse any left/right directions given here), and place it *behind* the shuttle cord, right up against the starter loop. Draw the shuttle up in back of the stick, pass it through the starter loop (Fig. 6), then bring it back down in *front* of the stick. Pull the twine taut and pinch it against the stick with your left thumb to hold it in place (Fig. 7). Raise the

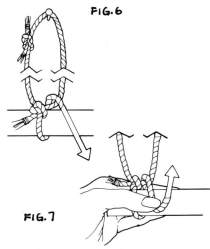

FIG. 6

FIG. 7

shuttle again—still in front of the stick—and make a half hitch around both strands of the starter loop (Fig. 8). Now, pull the twine down in front of the gauge stick, letting go

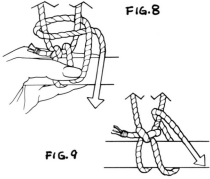

FIG. 8

FIG. 9

with your left thumb and tightening the half hitch as you do so. You've just completed your first cast-on "stitch"!

Repeat the process by bringing the shuttle around and up in back of the stick, passing it through the starter loop, and so on (Fig. 9). Continue until you've made 20 snug and even loops around the gauge stick (30 for the two-person hammock). Incidentally, be sure to make the half hitches in the same direction each time with the "over" strand always taken from the same side so the work will lie smooth (Fig. 10).

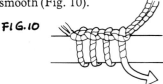

FIG. 10

FIRST ROW: At this point you should flip the gauge stick over so that the shuttle cord hangs on the left side (you'll work from left to right on each row). Then pull out the stick, letting the loops dangle free. Hold the gauge in your left hand, just under the work and bring the shuttle and its cord down in front, up behind and through the first cast-on (not the starter) loop, and down in front of the stick again. Pinch the twine with your thumb, make a half hitch around the two strands of the first cast-on loop, and carry the shuttle down and around the gauge stick again. This time, pass the shuttle through the second cast-on loop and continue as before. Repeat the process through each cast-on loop, making sure to keep the work even. This initial row is the hardest for most people, but with perseverance the task will become easier.

When all the cord on the shuttle is used, reload and tie the free end of the new twine to that of the previous cord using a square or weaver's knot.

SECOND ROW . . . THIRD ROW . . . AND SO ON: Flip the work over when you reach the end of the first row—as you'll do after finishing *each* row—and proceed as before. Keep repeating the process until you've netted the length you want (54 rows should equal about 7 feet of netting).

Anytime after completing the second row, you can cut the starter loop and pull it free from the cast-on loops. After doing so, support your work using a sturdy dowel (see Fig. 11) or whatever you have on hand to hold the piece evenly.

FIG. 11

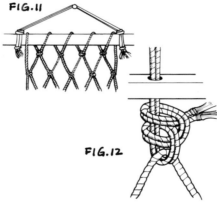

FIG. 12

MOUNTING: Drill 20 holes (30 for a two-person hammock) through each of your two hardwood bars, 1-1/2" on center, the outermost being 2-1/4" from the ends. The end holes should be 1/4" to 5/16" and all the others 3/16" to 1/4" in diameter.

With that done, cut four cords each of the following lengths: 46", 47", 48", 49", 50", 51", 52", 54", 56", 58". You'll have a total of 40 pieces, 20 for each end of the hammock. (If you're making the double model, cut the same 40 lengths *plus* four each of 60", 62", 64", 66", and 68" long, making 60 pieces in all.) These will form the fan-shaped arrays of strings running between the end rings used to hang the hammock and the sup-porting hardwood bars. The longest pieces will be secured to the outside holes in each bar, and the strings will get shorter as they near the center.

Loop one of the four longest cords around a metal ring with a lark's head knot, thread *both* the ends through the outermost hole in one of the bars, and secure the cord to the top left-hand loop of the hammock mesh using a double half hitch. Taking the cords in shorter and shorter lengths as you work toward the center of the hammock, fasten each one from the ring, through the next support-bar hole, to a loop in the net (Fig. 12). When you've attached all 20 strings, repeat the procedure on the other end of the hammock.

FINISHING THE JOB: To end this "knotty" chore, make a pair of three-cord braids. These will be used to add a bit of firmness to the hammock's edges. To allow for the necessary give, you'll want to make each braid three inches shorter than the stretched-out length of the netting. Be generous when cutting the twine because the cords will end up at least 10% shorter after braiding.

Tie the three ends together with an overhand knot, braid the cords (left over middle, right over new middle, and so on), and thread the untied ends through the outside hole in one hardwood bar. Then, make a loose knot in the end of the braid and weave it in and out through the outer meshes of the net (Fig. 13). Undo the loose knot, thread the braid through the outside hole of the bar at the *other* end of the hammock, and make a tight overhand knot to hold it in

FIG. 13

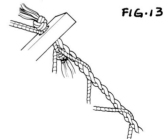

place. Repeat this process on the other side. Now, hang your hammock between two convenient trees . . . and have a swinging summer!

HUMMINGBIRD FEEDERS

It isn't necessary to purchase expensive hummingbird feeders to bring these beautiful birds close enough to be watched and photographed easily. In just a few minutes, and for a few pennies, you can make feeders that will attract even the most finicky hummer.

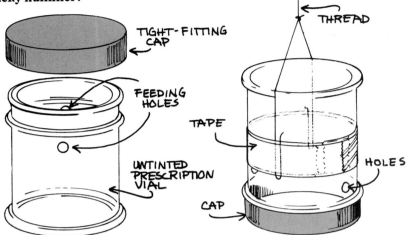

The necessary supplies are clear, untinted prescription vials (the 20-dram size works best) with tight-fitting caps, some transparent tape, a few feet of heavy thread or thin wire, and an ice pick.

For each feeder, heat the ice pick nearly red-hot and punch a pair of holes on opposite sides of the plastic vial near its open end (see diagram). Make sure the holes are very close to—but not covered up by—the rim of the cap when the cap is in place, and that they are small enough to keep insects out and liquid in.

Then take several feet of thread or fine wire and secure the ends to the vial's side with tape. For extra holding power, fold the ends of the thread back over the tape and wrap a second piece of tape around the tube.

That's basically all there is to it. Duplicate your efforts, and you're on your way to assembling a mobile similar to the one shown. This arrangement makes for the most interesting bird-watching, attracting lots of hummers at once.

To fill one of the feeders, remove the cap and hold the vial upright, fill the vial with nectar, cap the container tightly, and quickly invert the tube so the feeder's "dribble holes" are at the bottom. A small amount of liquid may leak out of the holes initially, but the leakage will stop as a vacuum is created inside the feeder.

NECTAR REQUIREMENTS: Hummingbirds—which individually weigh barely more than a dime—expend a phenomenal amount of energy, and it takes incredible amounts of syrup to sustain them: A single hummer will drink about twice its weight in nectar (roughly 40% of its weight in pure sugar) every day.

Of course, syrup from the feeder (or nectar from flowers) is not the only kind of nourishment hummingbirds receive. These little birds also relish a variety of insects, including aphids and mosquitoes. Still, it's amazing that five or six tiny hummers can empty a 20-dram feeder in about an hour.

To make syrup you can either buy a commercial nectar mix (the granulated kind, not a tablet type) or make up your own sugar solution. Note that honey is *not* recommended

as a syrup base. Tests have shown that a diet of straight honey can weaken or sometimes even be fatal to hummingbirds.

The granular mix is convenient but expensive. An 8-ounce package will usually make 48 ounces of feeding solution, and this amount may not last a week if there are five or six hummers in the area.

Considering how frequently refills are needed, the homemade alternative is much more economical. Just stir four or five heaping teaspoons of granulated sugar into a cup of water along with enough red food coloring (vegetable dye) to give the resulting mixture a definite scarlet hue. The color is very important, because hummingbirds have no sense of smell and are attracted to nectar-bearing flowers—and to feeders—by color alone.

HANGING YOUR FEEDER: It's generally a good idea to place the feeder where it won't be exposed to direct sunlight, since sugar solutions can ferment, and sunlight tends to accelerate this process. Nestle it in a spot where it won't be shaken (and perhaps emptied) by wind or by tree limb motion.

Some bird-watchers maintain that the way to bring hummers to the patio is to hang a feeder near flowers that have already attracted the birds. Then over a period of several days or weeks, move the feeder progressively closer to the patio. Chances are, however, they'll find your attractive server no matter where it hangs.

CLOSE ENCOUNTERS: Interestingly, hummingbirds are bold little creatures. It's not at all unusual for them to hover within a few feet of the person refilling the feeder. Some may even be brave (or inquisitive) enough to eat from your hand or perch on your head!

This, of course, is good news for the amateur photographer, who can easily shoot close-ups without a long telephoto lens. Simply wait quietly with camera cocked until the hummers pose. Then click the shutter. You've captured nature at its loveliest.

MATERIALS AND TOOLS:

To build this innovative birdhouse you'll need the following materials: one 8-foot 1 X 8, a 3-foot length of 1/8" X 1/2" or 1/8" X 3/4" aluminum bar, a 3" X 6" sheet of 6-gauge brass, one 12" length of 3/32" brass rod, two 1/2" X 8-32 machine screws with nuts, six 1" X 8-32 machine screws with nuts, one 2" butt hinge, with screws, four 8-32 tee nuts, some 6d finishing nails, and an assortment of metal washers.

In addition, you'll need the following tools: tinsnips, a hacksaw, a drill with several sizes of bits, a saw, a hammer, a screwdriver, pliers, and either a soldering iron and some solder or a couple of feet of small-gauge steel wire.

CONSTRUCTION: Before you can really get started, you'll need to cut the 1 X 8 board into the following pieces: back, 6" X 7-1/4"; front sill, 1-1/2" X 6"; front, 3-1/4" X 4-1/2"; two sides, 5-1/2" X 7-1/4"; bottom, 4-1/2" X 5-1/2"; roof, 7-1/4"

SMALL-BIRD FEEDER

Everyone who loves birdwatching has probably put up a feeder or two around the house. In just a short time, the yard becomes a haven for cardinals, nuthatches, chickadees, and even woodpeckers! Soon, however, other visitors discover this bounty. Grackles, blue jays, and other large birds, as well as squirrels, devour food intended for the others.

The project described below will help eliminate these unwelcome gluttons via its weight-sensitive perch. Birds or animals weighing over 2-1/2 ounces will send its gate crashing shut. Those below that weight will be able to eat freely.

X 13-1/8"; roof, 7-1/4" X 14"; two gables, 6" X 6" X 6-1/8" triangles; perch 3/8" X 6-1/2"; feed-flow ramp, 4-1/2" X 5-1/2"; feed control, 4-1/2" X 4-3/4".

Nail the backs to the sides and attach the front sill to the sides at the lower front. Fasten the front and bottom pieces as shown in Fig. 1.

The roof pieces should be beveled to 60° and nailed together as shown in Fig. 2. Fasten the rear gable in

place so its outside face aligns with the back edge of the roof. When this is done, place the front gable upright on, and flush with, the front of the feeder body. Lower the roof into place, making sure the rear gable, already attached, is aligned with the back. With everything lined up, press down on the roof to hold things in place and nail the roof to the front gable. It may be necessary to drill pilot holes first to minimize move-

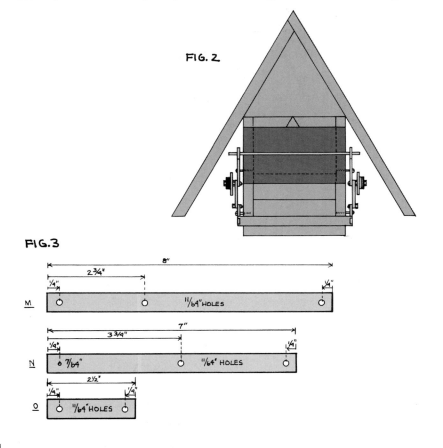

FIG. 2

FIG.3

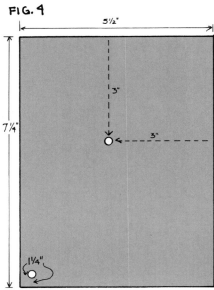

FIG. 4

The hopper gate closes fast when a bird heavier than a cardinal attempts to dine. A side view shows a counterbalanced perch, which is the secret to the feeder's selectivity. Spikes driven up through the roof can discourage marauding squirrels.

ment of the pieces while hammering.

To complete the feeder box, bevel the ends of the feed flow ramp to 45°, insert the piece into the box so that it slants down from back to front, its beveled faces flush with the back and bottom, and nail it in place. Then fasten the feed control to the back of the front, flush with top.

The gate is constructed by scribing a line along the longitudinal center of the brass sheet, centering the brass rod along this line, and soldering or welding it in place. If the rod and brass sheet are to be wired in place,

drill a pair of holes, one on either side of the rod, at both ends and in the middle of the gate. Loops of wire passed through these holes and twisted tightly at the back should hold the components together.

Make the gate operating bars by cutting two 8″ lengths, two 7″ lengths, and two 2-1/2″ lengths of aluminum bar. With an 11/64″ bit, drill a hole 1/4″ from each end in all the pieces. Drill an additional hole in the middle of the 7″ lengths. In the 8″ pieces, drill a third hole 2-3/4″ from one end (see Fig. 3).

Assemble the two sets of operating levers. With a 1/2″ screw and nut, fasten the 2-1/2″ bar to the long end of the 8″ bar. Attach the other end of the 2-1/2″ bar to one end of the 7″ bar with a 1″ screw. The small bar should be outermost when the assembly is installed.

Drill two 7/32″ holes in each side of the feeder box, one 1-1/4″ up from the bottom and 1-1/2″ from the front, and the other 3″ from the top and 3″ from the back (see Fig. 4).

Position a tee nut in each of the holes in the right side of the feeder body, and making certain not to tighten them so far the bars cannot pivot freely, attach one set of levers, using 1″-long screws. Insert one end of the gate rod through the hole in the end of the 8″ bar. Place the other end of the gate rod through the front hole in the other 8″ bar, put the tee nuts in the left-side holes, and attach the left lever assembly. Cut notches in each end of the perch about 1/8″ deep and wide enough to accept the aluminum bar. Fasten the perch between the two levers, using No. 8 X 1/2″ wood screws.

Complete construction of the feed-er by attaching a small block of wood to the outside top of the front to serve as a gate stop. Then center the butt hinge and fasten it to the back wall and rear gable.

All that's left is to counterbalance the gate. Attach metal washers to the 1″ machine screw that connects the 2-1/2″ bar to the 7″ bar. By hanging one 3/8″, one 3/4″, and three 7/8″ washers on both sides, a "perch activation pressure" of about 2-1/2 ounces is achieved. In other words, any bird up to the size of a cardinal will be able to feed, but any larger creature will shut the door in its own face. You can adjust the pressure required to close the gate by adding or removing washers.

Some people may find that squirrels find the new feeder a convenient place for a handout. To prevent them from hanging from the peak of the roof by their hind legs while scooping up the food with their front paws, install a deterrent. This is simply a row of nails driven upward through the roof's overhang and spaced about 1/4″ apart. This will look far more dangerous to the furry animals than it is, and they'll seek a handout somewhere else.

FIG.1

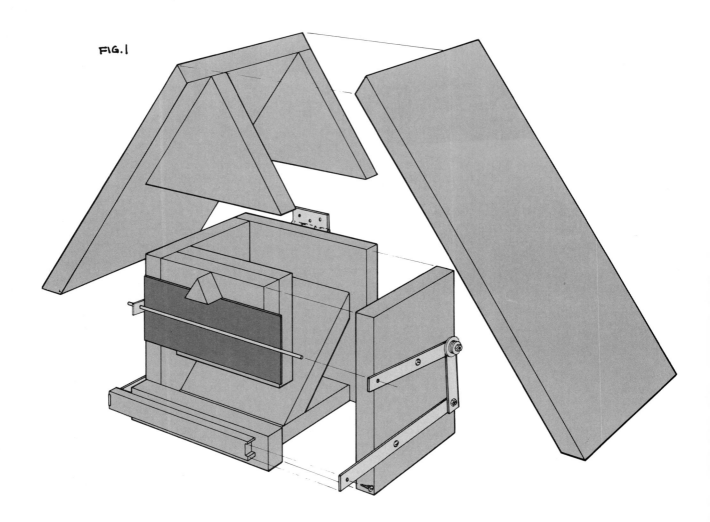

BIRDBATH & FEEDER

A few minutes spent converting dried gourds into birdbaths and feeders can beautify your yard, provide delightful moments of entertainment for all the family, and cut down on the number of insect pests that attack you and your garden during spring and summer months.

The birdbath is made by cutting across a circular gourd to form a dish. Drill four holes at equidistant points around the edge and suspend the bowl from a handy tree limb as shown, with two coat hanger "V"s hooked through the holes. Provide a bath for the birds *only* during warm weather, as a freeze can turn it into a miniature skating rink!

To make a feeder similar to the one shown, use a fine-toothed saw to cut a "bird-sized" opening in an appropriately shaped dried gourd. Then remove the seeds and drill two holes—on opposite sides of the top—to accommodate the hooked ends of a V-shaped piece of coat hanger.

One caution, though: Throughout the winter, when food is scarce, feeder-fed birds may starve if their supply is cut off and inclement weather keeps them from finding other sources. So, if you start hosting your backyard feathered friends during cold weather, be sure that the feeder is always stocked. After all, a little regular attention is a small price to pay for the help and pleasure that the cheerful bathers and diners will give to you in return!

BLUEBIRD BUNGALOW

Once common throughout the rural areas of North America, the bluebird has become a rarity in this country, a problem that can be at least partially solved by providing these valuable and beautiful members of the thrush family with homemade bungalows to help alleviate their housing shortage. Nesting site scarcity, competition for housing areas from imported species such as the English sparrow and the starling, and pesticide poisoning have affected the eastern bluebird (*Sialis sialis*) most adversely, but both the western bluebird (*Sialia mexicana occidentalis*) and the mountain bluebird (*Sialia currucoides*) face the same problems.

By constructing houses for these insect-eating songsters, locating the homebuilt nests in the open areas favored by bluebirds, and evicting any unwanted avian competitors from the nesting boxes, the homeowner can insure that the desired tenants have at least a place to live. Bluebird houses are easily built, being mainly vertical rectangular boxes with an entry hole bored in the face a short ways below the roof, which is pitched slightly to shed water. The dwellings can be attached to fenceposts, power poles, trees, or other supports in open areas such as large yards or fields that bluebirds find appealing.

A shelter built to attract members of the genus *Sialia* must be specifically designed to accommodate the tenants that you're seeking and to discourage occupancy by the birds' rivals.

The front of such a house is the most important component of the entire structure. First, a 3/4"-thick board is cut to 4" X 9-3/4" as shown in the diagram. After the "starling-proof" 1-1/2"-diameter hole is drilled at a slightly upward angle to prevent rain from getting in, the interior of the panel should be grooved horizontally with a chisel or saw. These "steps" will give fledglings a means of leaving the dwelling when they're ready to try their wings. When the front piece is finished, the other main sections should be cut to shape.

Now you're ready to begin the actual assembly of the home. It's easiest first to attach the sides of the box to the back and then to install the bottom, making sure that the sides extend 1/4 inch below the base piece so water won't run down the outer walls and collect in the center of the bottom where it might soak through the floor and dampen the nest. Using wood screws and glue rather than nails to assemble a nest box will give the birdhouse a longer life expectancy.

When the base piece is secured in place, the roof can be attached and the front panel added. In the design shown here, the front can be swung open on the two upper nails (which serve as hinges). So, when positioning the door, leave a gap between its top and the roof to insure that the portal won't bind when you try to pivot it up. The door can be secured in its closed position simply by drilling angled holes through the lower edges of each side into the bottom of the front section. Then slip a large-headed nail into each hole, keeping the door closed and at the same time giving the impression that the box is permanently fastened shut. This helps dissuade human passersby from disturbing the feathered tenants by looking inside the dwelling. As an alternative to building the box so the front swings out, that piece can be fixed permanently in place and a hinge placed at the back of the roof so it can be raised for access to the inside of the nesting box.

Once the home's assembled, drill a 1/4"-diameter hole near each corner and another in the center of the floor to provide drainage in the unlikely event that water gets into the cavity. Next, drill a row of four 1/4" holes along the top of each side just below the overhang of the roof to allow for ventilation. Also, it is a good idea at this point to drill a few 1/8" holes through the back panel above and below the box. Wire can be threaded through these holes and used for mounting the birdhouse on a metal post or on an object into which a nail can't be driven.

While an unpainted structure will look more natural, a coat of latex-base paint *will* probably increase the life span of the dwelling. However, any color applied to the exterior of a bluebird box should be dull tones of light green, gray, or tan. The inside of the home should not be painted. For a look even more natural than an unpainted birdhouse, the box can be covered with bark-sided sawmill slabs.

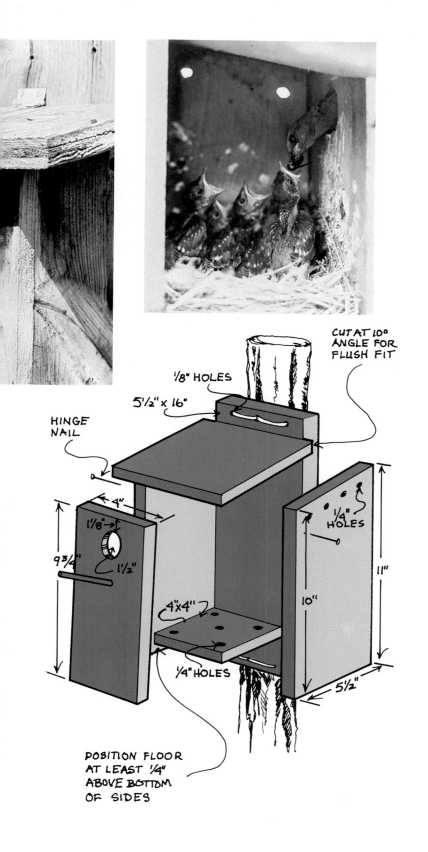

CUT AT 10°
ANGLE FOR
FLUSH FIT

1/8" HOLES

5 1/2" x 16"

HINGE
NAIL

4"

1 1/8"

9 3/4"

1 1/2"

1/8"
HOLES

11"

4"x4"

10"

5 1/2"

1/4" HOLES

POSITION FLOOR
AT LEAST 1/4"
ABOVE BOTTOM
OF SIDES

SITE SELECTION: The design of a bluebird house—no matter how exacting it may seem—is no more critical than is the placement of the homemade nest. Bluebirds prefer homesites that are free of heavy vegetation, where the feathered hunters can hop along the ground in search of insects. The setting should include scattered "observation post" trees. Golf courses and large country cemeteries are excellent bluebird habitats. Orchards, big yards, and sunlit fencerows will also provide all of the necessary amenities.

A fencepost or other sturdy upright pole can serve as a good support for the avian abode. Mount the box from three to five feet above the ground on the side of the post opposite any pasture that might be occupied by livestock, and clear away any surrounding vegetation that might prevent the adult birds from having a clear view of their surroundings when leaving the house. According to some experts, the relatively low positioning of the house will help prevent English sparrows from taking over the dwelling. Should these birds move in anyway, it is best simply to evict them before they lay any eggs.

You'll want to position bluebird homes at least 100 yards apart, and a good rule of thumb is to erect only three houses per acre. Also, try to keep them convenient to your homestead or to a route that you regularly trace in the course of your chores. By being able to visit the birdhouses relatively often, you can enjoy the tenants you've worked to attract as well as deal with unwanted guests.

Bluebirds can produce as many as three broods during a summer, and two could be considered common. You'll increase the chances that your box will house consecutive families if you clean it out, discarding the old nest and unplugging the drainage holes, as soon as the first group of fledglings takes to the trees. If such regular cleaning during the warmer months is impossible, at least clean the quarters each winter so you can enjoy the bluebirds' return the following spring.

BLUEBIRD BUNGALOW

YARD CART

This sturdy, hard-working cart could take the strain out of many gardening and landscaping chores. Tools required for its construction include a saber saw, a circular saw, wrenches, a drill, and a propane torch. By shopping judiciously you can produce an efficient carryall that's comparable to factory-built models costing six times as much.

BUY THE MATERIALS: For this handy cart you'll need two 8-foot lengths of slotted angle iron, a 10-foot length of 3/4″ electrical pipe, some 4″ X 4″ right-angled metal brackets, 1-1/2 sheets of 5/8″ exterior grade plywood, 12 feet of 2 X 2 lumber, yellow carpenter's glue, two wheels with axles, carriage bolts and nuts, and some wood screws.

Be creative in your search for parts. Your local lumberyard may be able to supply you with "cutoffs" at a reduced price. Fleamarkets, auctions, or discount houses could furnish you with the metal parts you'll need. A set of used wheels might be found at a motorcycle dealer or repair shop.

AND GET TO WORK: Start off by trimming one 2′ X 4′ piece of plywood to 24″ X 43″ to form the bottom of the box, and by cutting another piece to make two 12″ X 43″ sidewalls. Slice a 4″ X 8″ wedge off one end of each sidewall. Cut the two 6″ X 30″ "splashboards" and round the top corners. The cart's bottom is re-

Angle iron, which is attached to a 2 X 2, supports each axle. Slotted angle iron provides additional support on the outside of the wheels.

inforced with 2 X 2's laid flat around the underside perimeter of the box, glued into place, and secured with screws for extra support. The angle irons that support the inside of the axles will be bolted to these 2 X 2's.

Outriggers (the V-struts to which the wheels are mounted) are fashioned from two pieces of angle iron cut to 3-foot lengths. Cut a 90° wedge into the slotted edge of each piece of angle iron at a point halfway down the bar. Each piece of iron is then bent to 90° (at the cutout wedge) and a 1/2″ washer is soldered in place at the spot where the axle would pass through the support.

It's possible the wheels you buy will come with axles that are just the right length. If they are too long, you can trim and rethread them, and if they're just a *bit* too long use a pipe-coupling spacer on each side to take up the slack.

Mount each axle so that the leading edge of the tire is 3″ behind the front end of the box. The idea is to position the axles so that the weight will be well distributed when the cart is fully loaded. When mounting the wheels and outriggers, be sure to align the wheels and to block them so they remain straight while you secure them in place. Alternatively, you may want to allow the wheels to slant slightly inward at the bottom, but only if you think your loads will be heavy enough to cause the wheels to deflect to true vertical position.

Use leftover pieces of slotted angle iron to reinforce the corners at the front and rear ends of the box. If you position the front plywood panel at a 45° slant from bottom to top (like a wheelbarrow), it will make it easier to dump the cart's loads. Finally, fashion a support leg made of 3/4″ conduit bent to suit, center it, and mount it about 6″ in from the back edge of the box. Position the leg so you won't kick it when pushing the cart. An electrician could fashion this leg for you, as well as bend the conduit to form the handle.

When the cart's assembled, give it a coat of paint or varnish, and it should last for years.

SOIL SIFTER

An efficient sifter for compost or potting soil can be made by nailing a piece of hardware cloth to the bottom of a 12″ X 18″ frame. The only materials needed are a 4-foot piece of 1 X 4, a 2-foot piece of 1 X 6, a 12″ X 18″ piece of 1/4″ hardware cloth, some 6d nails, and some 3/4″ staples.

LIST OF MATERIALS

WOOD
Sides: 2 pieces 1 X 4 X 18″
Ends: 2 pieces 1 X 6 X 10-1/2″

HARDWARE
1 piece 12″ X 18″ hardware cloth, 1/4″ mesh
3/4″ staples
6d nails

First, cut two 18″ lengths of 1 X 4 and two 10-1/2″ lengths of 1 X 6. Taper the upper corners of the 1 X 6's by marking each end at a point 2″ down from the top and at another point 3-1/4″ in along the top edge. Draw a line connecting the two points and cut along the line.

For the handholds, mark a 1″ X 3-1/2″ rectangle in the upper middle of each end board, as shown, and cut out the rectangles (or long ovals) with a keyhole or coping saw.

Then butt the end boards into the sides and nail the frame together. Give the wood a protective finish, if you like, and staple the hardware cloth to the bottom of the frame.

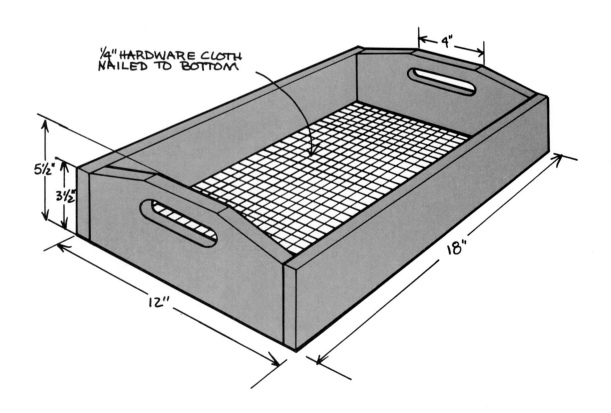

¼″ HARDWARE CLOTH NAILED TO BOTTOM

4″

5½″

3½″

18″

12″

SEED STARTER

Seed germination doesn't have to be a hit-or-miss proposition. In fact, given the right environment and healthy stock, a success rate of close to 100% can be achieved. Much depends on temperature and humidity, and you can insure proper levels of both by building a sprouting cabinet. The glass walls of this cabinet are held in place within grooves cut into upper and lower redwood or cedar frames, and the glass lid is housed in a separate casing. A pair of hinges, a knob, and a side latch allow the cover to be lifted and held up. Warmth is provided by electric heat tape fastened to a piece of foil-backed foam insulation. Plug-in heat tape, generally available at nursery centers, will maintain a thermostatically controlled temperature of 72°F. A sheet-metal tray placed on top of the insulation board provides a platform for the peat medium used. With the addition of seeds and a soaking mist, the box will serve as an ideal miniature nursery.

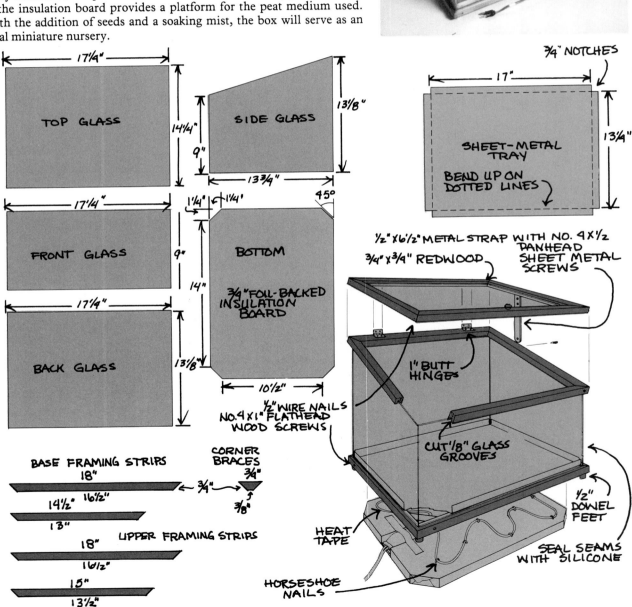

TOP GLASS — 17¼" — 14¼"

SIDE GLASS — 13⅛" — 9" — 13¾"

FRONT GLASS — 17¼" — 9"

BOTTOM ¾" FOIL-BACKED INSULATION BOARD — 1¼" — 1¼" — 45° — 14" — 10½"

BACK GLASS — 17¼" — 13⅛"

SHEET-METAL TRAY BEND UP ON DOTTED LINES — ¾" NOTCHES — 17" — 13¾"

½"x6½" METAL STRAP WITH NO. 4X½ PANHEAD SHEET METAL SCREWS
¾"x¾" REDWOOD
1" BUTT HINGES
CUT ⅛" GLASS GROOVES
½" DOWEL FEET
½" WIRE NAILS
NO. 4X1" FLATHEAD WOOD SCREWS
HEAT TAPE
SEAL SEAMS WITH SILICONE
HORSESHOE NAILS

BASE FRAMING STRIPS
18"
14½" 16½"
13"

CORNER BRACES
¾"
¾"
3/8"

UPPER FRAMING STRIPS
18"
16½"
15"
13½"

BARREL ROOT CELLAR

Many root vegetables, such as white potatoes, sweet potatoes, beets, turnips, parsnips, radishes, and carrots, can be stored in a simple barrel root cellar for winter and spring use. Dig a hole large enough for the container to be placed at a 45° angle and be two-thirds underground. Set the barrel on a few large rocks or bricks for drainage and cover it, leaving the open end exposed, with six inches of dirt, six inches of straw, and a final two inches of dirt. Select firm, sound vegetables; remove any excess dirt but do not wash the produce. Carefully pack the vegetables in straw—layer upon layer—in the barrel and cover the full container with its lid, a foot of straw or leaves, and a board held in place by a large rock. You'll find it easy to open this root cellar and remove the produce inside as needed. If you can't obtain a wooden barrel from hardware stores or lumberyards, a section of culvert drainage tile fitted with plywood ends will work just as well.

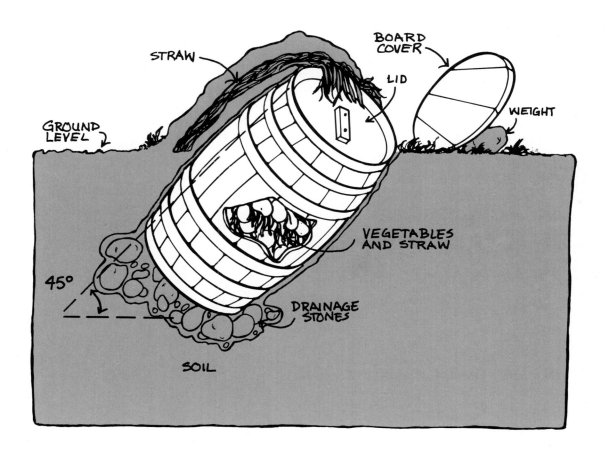

GARDEN SPRAYER

A handy tool for spraying liquid fertilizer, pesticides, and herbicides or for misting plants with water need not be expensive. Make this lightweight, pressurized, portable model, and you'll find it will do the job at a fraction of the cost of a commercial sprayer. Since the storage canisters are made from two-liter plastic soda bottles, you can have a separate tank for each type of liquid.

MATERIALS AND TOOLS: You'll need at least four plastic soda bottles, a football pump, six hose clamps, six No. 5 X 2" machine screws and nuts, the valve stem from an inner tube, two 1/2" pipe to 3/8" hose barbs, a 5/16" X 3" tension spring, a 4-foot length of 3/8" plastic hose, and the 1/2" plumbing parts that are called for in the illustration. You can make a sling out of anything from a webbed belt to a piece of rope, and you'll need a nozzle. The sprayer shown has a brass trigger and wand, which will function well for a long time, but a less costly nozzle can be found on one of any number of bottles of cleaning liquids that have pump/spray tops. Remove the siphon tube, and the adjustable head should work quite well.

The only tools required are a knife, a screwdriver, a drill with a 1/8" bit, and soldering supplies, though soldering can be eliminated if PVC pipe and cement are chosen instead of copper plumbing components. The use of coated thread tape or silicone sealant will help to make the joints airtight.

BUILD THE SPRAYER: The plumbing manifold should be assembled using the illustration as a guide. Once that's done, cut a 5-1/2" length of 3/8" plastic hose and trim the valve stem so the tubing can be clamped over it. By threading the stem into the football pump, pressing the stem's other end inside the hose, and clamping the free end of the tube to the barb at the end of the horizontal manifold tube, you can insure a kink-free connection between the pump and the storage tanks.

Then, to hold everything together as a unit, lash the manifold to the side of the pump with the 2"-diameter hose clamps and, if possible, use these same fasteners to secure the carrying strap. The remaining 42-1/2" of plastic tubing can be clamped to the free hose barb and to the nozzle.

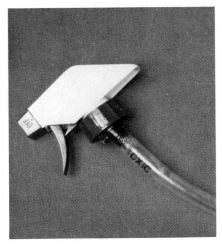

To make the storage tanks, cut the flat plastic collars from the necks of two of the salvaged pop bottles, making sure the surfaces are smooth, then drill three equidistant 1/8" holes around this pair of rings and in those that are still in place on the remaining two bottles. Wrap the "slip" ends of the 1/2" pipe to 1/2" slip PVC adapters with thread tape and insert them into the necks of the containers. The free collars, screwed to their mates on the uncut bottles—with the adapters between—will keep those canisters from blowing off under pressure. (Though you probably won't be able to develop more than about 30 pounds per square inch (PSI) with the hand pump—which is plenty to serve the purpose—bottles that were tested accepted nearly 200 PSI before bursting!)

To use the sprayer, fill one container with the liquid nutrient or pest spray (soapy water, for instance), thread both tanks in place on the manifold, sling the strap over your shoulder so the bottles are "bottoms up" under your arm, and pump away. An average charge will keep the spray going for about five minutes or until the fluid runs out. You can, of course, fill both tanks to increase capacity a bit, but do leave a couple of inches of air space in each so they can be pressurized.

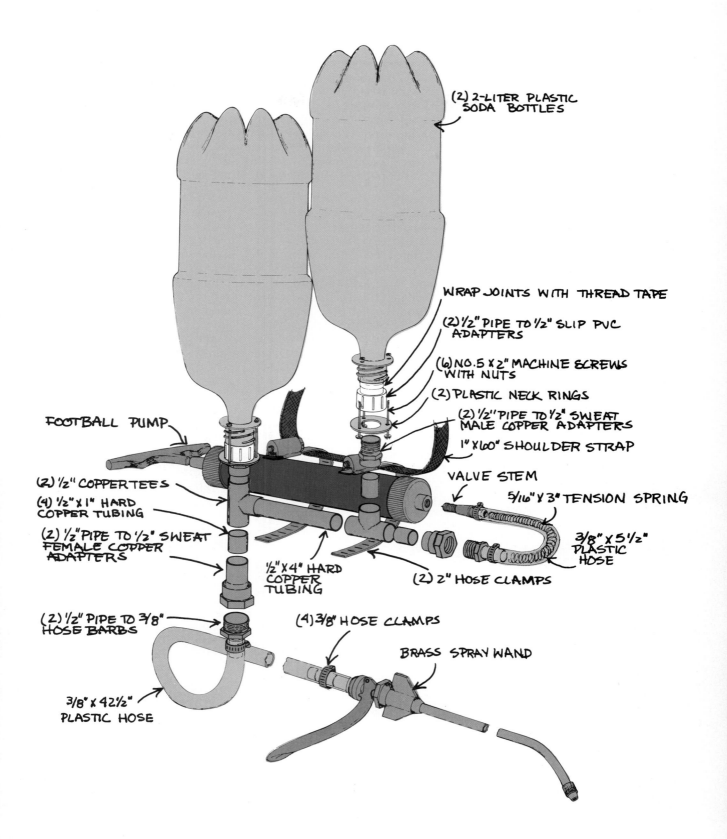

(2) 2-LITER PLASTIC SODA BOTTLES

WRAP JOINTS WITH THREAD TAPE

(2) ½" PIPE TO ½" SLIP PVC ADAPTERS

(6) NO.5 X 2" MACHINE SCREWS WITH NUTS

(2) PLASTIC NECK RINGS

(2) ½" PIPE TO ½" SWEAT MALE COPPER ADAPTERS

1" X 60" SHOULDER STRAP

FOOTBALL PUMP

VALVE STEM

5/16" X 3" TENSION SPRING

(2) ½" COPPER TEES

(4) ½" X 1" HARD COPPER TUBING

(2) ½" PIPE TO ½" SWEAT FEMALE COPPER ADAPTERS

½" X 4" HARD COPPER TUBING

3/8" X 5½" PLASTIC HOSE

(2) 2" HOSE CLAMPS

(2) ½" PIPE TO 3/8" HOSE BARBS

(4) 3/8" HOSE CLAMPS

BRASS SPRAY WAND

3/8" X 42½" PLASTIC HOSE

GARDEN SPRAYER

U-BAR GARDEN TOOL

Anyone who practices biointensive gardening knows that the raised beds of very deeply cultivated soil, before they are ready for planting in the spring, require a great deal of digging even after the ground is initially broken. The time needed for this laborious final preparation of the seedbed can be cut to a small fraction of what it would otherwise take, however. The gardener needs only to build a tool especially designed for the job: a low-technology implement called a U-bar.

To make one for yourself, you'll need to obtain 22 feet of 1-1/4", 11-gauge square steel tubing and 10-1/2 feet of 3/8" rectangular bar stock from a local steel distributor or scrapyard. You'll also need a tape measure, a hacksaw, a protractor, a drill with a 9/16" bit, and access to a welder.

Begin by sawing the bar stock into seven 18"-long sections and cut one tip of each of these pieces at a 45° angle to form the tool's tines. Then using the three-view diagram as a guide, size and trim the square steel tubing that makes up the various parts of the U-bar's frame. (Note that the grips on the handles can be cut and welded or be bent to achieve a comfortable working angle.)

The tines are mounted in the foot bar that forms the base of the tool. Before fastening that component to the handles, drill the seven sockets through the tubing, 4" on center. Insert the prongs (beveled ends facing one direction), and weld them in place from both sides. Now, attach the handles to the foot bar, angling them 30° toward the tines' beveled faces, and complete the implement's construction by welding on the handle braces and the stops as shown. For additional strength at the corners, you might consider adding flat 1/8" steel plate gussets to those joints.

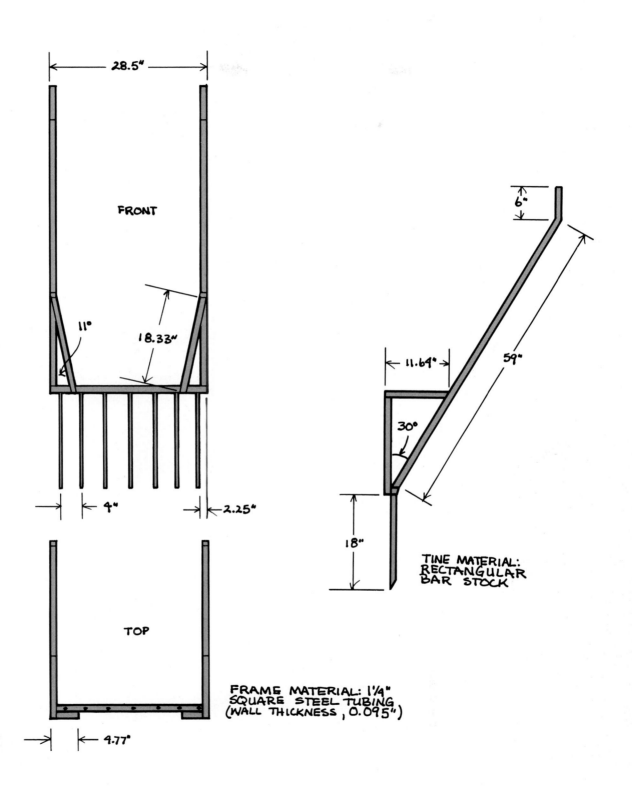

28.5"

FRONT

11°

18.33"

4"

2.25"

6"

11.64"

59"

30°

18"

TINE MATERIAL:
RECTANGULAR
BAR STOCK

TOP

4.77"

FRAME MATERIAL: 1¼"
SQUARE STEEL TUBING
(WALL THICKNESS, 0.095")

TOOL CADDY

More often than not, the tool you need in the garden is the one you left back in the shed or house. But if you happen to have a few wood scraps and an old bucket handle on hand, you can quickly make a carry-all that'll eliminate such problems.

The tray's walls are made from 1 X 6, trimmed to 4-3/4″ wide. Both the bottom and the center divider are made of 1/4″ plywood, and the racks and compartment partition are of 1/2″ pine. To make the caddy, cut and angle the wood according to the dimensions in the diagram and assemble the pieces using nails or screws. Instead of cutting compound angles for the mitered corner joints, just butt the end boards to the sides.

Complete the tote by fastening the wire handle from a worn-out five-gallon plastic bucket to the ends of the box with screw eyes. The caddy's design can be altered to suit the tools you use most.

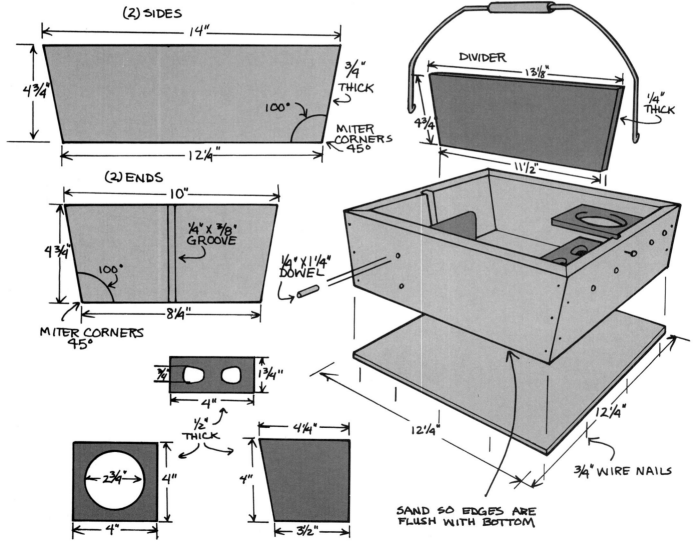

(2) SIDES

14″

4 3/4″

3/4″ THICK

100°

12 1/4″

MITER CORNERS 45°

DIVIDER

13 1/8″

4 3/4″

1/4″ THICK

11 1/2″

(2) ENDS

10″

4 3/4″

1/4″ X 3/8″ GROOVE

100°

8 1/4″

MITER CORNERS 45°

1/4″ X 1 1/4″ DOWEL

3/4″

1 3/4″

4″

1/2″ THICK

2 3/4″

4″

4″

4 1/4″

4″

3 1/2″

12 1/4″

12 1/4″

3/4″ WIRE NAILS

SAND SO EDGES ARE FLUSH WITH BOTTOM

SUNDIAL

An interest in sundials may stem from historical curiosity, a desire to get closer to nature, or a yearning for the uncomplicated in this highly complex world. Building your own helio-clock can be an engrossing project, and it will provide an attractive—and useful—addition to your yard.

GETTING THE LAY OF YOUR LAND: Consult an atlas to determine your exact location in terms of *latitude* and *longitude*. Latitude lines run across the map from east to west (or vice versa) and will be marked "North" if you live above the equator. Longitude marks run north-south and will be designated as "West" if you are located in the Western Hemisphere. (Please note that the remainder of the instructions included here apply only to the Western Hemisphere, north of the equator.)

LAYING OUT THE DIAL FACE: At this point, decide how large a sundial you wish to build. Faces can be designed in any reasonable size (though larger dials allow more accurate readings), but for this project, a 9" cake pan provides a very convenient mold. The diameter of your "clock's" face will become Dimension A in the drawings.

The other dimension needed to lay out a sundial can be calculated by drawing a semicircle using Dimension A as the diameter (Fig. 1). Construct a *tangent* perpendicular to the diameter of the half circle, then scribe a line that diverges from the intersection of the diameter and the tangent at an angle equal to your latitude. The length of the *chord* which is described by that line's intersections with the semicircle will become Dimension B.

Now, begin to draw the dial face on a piece of tracing paper. Prepare a three-sided figure like the one depicted by the *solid* red lines, and according to the dimensions specified (Fig. 2). The *broken* red lines in the same illustration indicate the noon and six o'clock lines which intersect each other at a 90° angle at the focus (or center) of the dial. Extend the two

broken lines perpendicularly from the solid red lines to points that are a distance equal to Dimension A beyond the three-sided figure on the six o'clock line, and a distance equal to Dimension B below it on the noon line, as shown.

Each of the three points thus calculated will serve as a focus from which the hour line determinants (Fig. 2 shows them in blue) will radiate at 15° intervals. But before putting those reference lines on paper, it's necessary to figure out the correction factor for your longitude's difference from your time zone's meridian.

Consult Chart A to learn whether you're situated to the east or to the west of your time zone's meridian. In either case, subtract the smaller number from the larger one. If your location's longitude happens to be *west* of the time zone longitude, correct for the difference by rotating the six o'clock and noon lines *clockwise*—from their three respective focuses—that number of degrees. But if your home is located to the *east* of your time zone's meridian, make the correction by rotating the six o'clock and noon line determinants *counterclockwise*. (A clockwise—west of meridian—correction is shown by the blue lines in Fig. 2.)

CHART A
TIME ZONE MERIDIANS

Eastern Standard Time = 75° West
Central Standard Time = 90° West
Mountain Standard Time = 105° West
Pacific Standard Time = 120° West

With that done, proceed to place the hour line determinants on the paper by marking off a 15° increment for each hour, as shown, and then connecting the focus of the dial to the points where the determinants inter-

sect the solid red lines. These connecting lines, shown in green in Fig. 2, will become the hour lines on the sundial's face. Complete the dial by scribing its perimeter (with a diameter equaling Dimension A) and lettering the Roman numerals.

MAKING THE DIAL: You can cast your sundial's face from concrete. First indent the Roman numerals and the hour lines in the bottom of the 9"-diameter cake pan by means of a 1/4"-blade screwdriver and a rubber mallet. To orient the numerals correctly, lay the paper face down

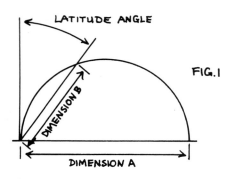

LATITUDE ANGLE

DIMENSION B

DIMENSION A

FIG.1

FIG.2

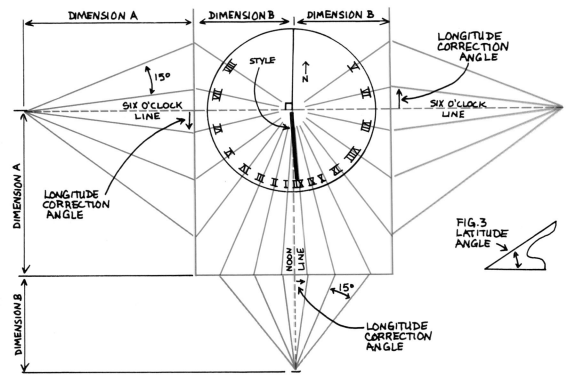

DIMENSION A

DIMENSION B

DIMENSION B

LONGITUDE CORRECTION ANGLE

STYLE

N

15°

SIX O'CLOCK LINE

SIX O'CLOCK LINE

LONGITUDE CORRECTION ANGLE

DIMENSION A

DIMENSION B

NOON LINE

15°

LONGITUDE CORRECTION ANGLE

FIG.3 LATITUDE ANGLE

in the pan so that the markings will appear backwards when they are transferred to the metal. The inscriptions will then be reversed on the casting, and the face will be "right side to". (If you use the cake pan, screwdriver, and mallet technique, be sure to back up the pan with end-grain wood and don't pound *too* hard, or you'll pierce the container's metal bottom.)

Since the style must be attached to the dial face, you must make allowances for it in the casting. Simply poke two six-penny nails through the bottom of the pan on the (corrected) noon line, slip the rubber insulation from some No. 12 wire over the nails, and cast the concrete around them. Also—before you pour—prepare the mount for the dial itself by hanging a 20-penny nail from a wire, exactly in the center of the pan and not quite touching its bottom. (The two smaller nails will leave holes in the finished casting, and the bigger one will remain fixed in the concrete for a later use.)

To get the smoothest surface possible, combine two parts cement and one part sand, oil the inside of the pan, and pour the mixture directly in. Then keep the assembly covered with wet rags for two days to insure very slow curing.

THE STYLE: Your latitude will determine the angle of the style, as indicated in Fig. 3. Although the exact shape—beyond the angle—isn't critical, the accompanying plan gives a basic profile to follow. The illustrated style was made from 18-gauge steel, but any material of similar integrity should be acceptable.

To mount the shadow-caster, you'll need to solder two six-penny nails—with their heads cut off—to the base of the style. Since the spikes must slip into the holes in the concrete face, and the apex of the latitude angle must be at the dial's focus, be sure to space the nails in accord with the prepared apertures.

THE POST: The post's forms are made from 1 X 6 and 1 X 4, with screen door molding tacked inside to provide relief. A 40″ length of 5/16″

steel fuel line is set down the middle of the form, and a piece of lath with a hole serves to hold the tube in place while the concrete is poured. The same two-to-one mixture of cement and sand may be used to form a 39″-long post.

PAINT AND ASSEMBLE: As you can see in the photo, both the dial and the post were painted white, and then the raised Roman numerals, the hour lines, and the style were coated with black paint to provide contrast.

To assemble the pieces, just sink the post—so that it's exactly vertical—to a depth of 6″ to 9″ at the chosen spot in your yard or garden, slide the 20-penny nail on the bottom of the dial into the 5/16″ fuel line in the top of the post, and slip the two nails on the base of the style into the holes in the face.

ORIENTING THE DIAL: If the post was placed vertically, your sundial's face *should* be horizontal, but it's a good idea to check it with a carpenter's level anyway. Once you've made any necessary adjustments, you'll need to orient the *original* noon line (*not* the one shown by the style) to due north. You can do this by sighting down the (now imaginary) line toward the North Star at night by using a compass (corrected

for the local variation between magnetic and true north) or by turning the dial so that it reads noon when your watch does, provided the timepiece is set on standard, not daylight saving, time.

CORRECTION FOR MEAN SOLAR TIME: Vagaries in the earth's orbit and in its relationship to the sun cause the length of the day that we observe to vary through the year. Therefore, corrections must be made to the sundial reading to maintain its agreement with the 24-hour *mean solar day*. If your sundial is intended primarily for aesthetic purposes (and you can afford to disregard 15 minutes here or there), ignore the *equation of time* correction. But if you would like your solar clock to read as accurately as possible, you'll need to keep a listing—such as Chart B—or a graphic representation of correction factors somewhere on or near your sundial.

Of course, once you've gone to all the trouble of making an accurate sundial, there'll probably come a day each spring when public decree will cause your timepiece to be off by one hour throughout the warmer months. It's possible to build a dial to register daylight saving time, but it's far easier just to add in the extra hour yourself and leave the face uncluttered.

CHART B
EQUATION TO MEAN SOLAR TIME

DATE	MINUTES	DATE	MINUTES	DATE	MINUTES
1/1	+ 3	5/1	− 3	9/1	0
1/15	+ 8	5/15	− 3	9/15	− 4
2/1	+ 14	6/1	− 2	10/1	− 10
2/15	+ 13	6/15	0	10/15	− 14
3/1	+ 12	7/1	+ 4	11/1	− 16
3/15	+ 8	7/15	+ 5	11/15	− 12
4/1	+ 4	8/1	+ 6	12/1	− 11
4/15	0	8/15	+ 4	12/15	− 5

TOOLS FOR HOME AND GARDEN

Since there are many possible methods for constructing a convenient worktable, you'll probably want to add your own bits of inspiration in order to make the bench best suit the kinds of projects you most often tackle.

THE TOP: To provide a stable working surface, the bench's top is built from a 4 X 8 foot sheet of 3/4" interior A-B plywood, which is cut into two 4-foot squares that are glued together (and also nailed from the underside) with the grain of the top half at a right angle to that of the bottom layer. The resulting 1-1/2"-thick plank is then fitted with molding made from a 49"-long 1 X 8 board, which is ripped to 1-1/2" widths and mitered at 45° to form the corners of the tabletop.

THE BASE: The foot of the X-shaped base is built by first constructing a rectangular box from two 54-1/4"-long pieces of 1 X 8 with a 12" length of 1 X 8 butted across each end of the assembly. Next, two three-sided frames of 1 X 8 are made, each consisting of a pair of 21-1/8" boards with a 12" length across *one* end. The two smaller structures are then butted—open end in—to the 54-1/4"-long box and secured with three wood screws in each joint. Finally, the "X" is topped with appropriately sized sections of 1/2" plywood tacked to the tops of the 1 X 8's.

PEGBOARD SIDES: Eight 21" X 28-1/2" pieces of pegboard are used to close in the sides of the base's four sections and to support the top. Using these dimensions will produce a table 36-1/2" high, but you could add

---

WORKBENCH

When working on a shop project, it's hard to determine every tool and piece of material that will be needed, and it's even more difficult to keep them all at hand. Having to stop each time to hunt for a required item wastes time and interupts concentration. And often the result is a work surface that's too cluttered to be efficient.

Well, the bench pictured here is the perfect answer to this dilemma. By incorporating large storage areas beneath the tabletop—in the form of drawers and shelved cabinets—and by constructing the sides of the assembly from pegboard which can be equipped with hooks for hanging up tools, a worker can keep all of the equipment needed for a project close at hand *without* littering the work area.

to or subtract from the longer dimension of the pegboard to alter the bench's overall height.

Allow the pegboard to overlap the 1 X 8 base by about 1", and screw the perforated sheets to the wood behind them. For added security, corner braces should be attached near the top of the pegboard sections, on the outside of the right-angle joints. A few inches of plumber's tape (metal strap with holes) and a pair of screws for each brace, applied from the inside so they can't be seen, should suffice.

JOINING THE TOP AND BASE: Because the top is somewhat heftier than the base, it will be easier to join the two if you turn the work surface face down on the floor and fasten the base—upside down—to it. To make the connection, two 54" and four 22" lengths of 1 X 2 are first screwed to the underside of the 1-1/2"-thick table in the same X-pattern as the base, but set so that the distance between the *outside* edges of the cross's arm is 12". The pegboard can then slide *over* this frame on the tabletop's underside and be secured to the 1 X 2's with wood screws.

BUILDING THE STORAGE SPACES: Once the table has been flipped back over so that it's right side up, a decision must be made about what kinds of storage units will be needed in the four cavities. One or more of the four openings may be fitted entirely with drawers, either deep or shallow depending upon the gear you intend to stow in them. Shelves inserted into the columns will provide ready access to bulky tools. And, of course, a column may be left completely open for storage of short lengths of lumber, dowels, or other construction material. Swing-open doors may be built, as well, and attached to any column without drawers. A quick inventory of your tools will help you arrange the available space.

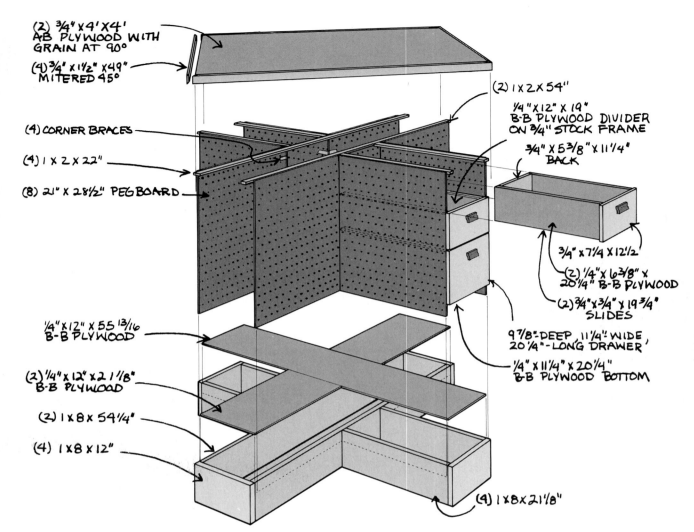

(2) 3/4" X 4' X 4' A-B PLYWOOD WITH GRAIN AT 90°

(4) 3/4" X 1/2" X 49" MITERED 45°

(4) CORNER BRACES

(4) 1 X 2 X 22"

(8) 21" X 28 1/2" PEGBOARD

1/4" X 12" X 55 13/16" B-B PLYWOOD

(2) 1/4" X 12" X 21 1/8" B-B PLYWOOD

(2) 1 X 8 X 54 1/4"

(4) 1 X 8 X 12"

(2) 1 X 2 X 54"

1/4" X 12" X 19" B-B PLYWOOD DIVIDER ON 3/4" STOCK FRAME

3/4" X 5 3/8" X 11 1/4" BACK

3/4" X 7 1/4 X 12 1/2"

(2) 1/4" X 6 3/8" X 20 1/4" B-B PLYWOOD

(2) 3/4" X 3/4" X 19 3/4" SLIDES

9 7/8"-DEEP, 11 1/4" WIDE, 20 1/4"-LONG DRAWER

1/4" X 11 1/4" X 20 1/4" B-B PLYWOOD BOTTOM

(4) 1 X 8 X 21 1/8"

Since the sides of drawers will run flush against the *inside* of the pegboard, those columns with drawers cannot have hooks placed on their pegboard surfaces. Therefore, if you install too many drawers, you may eliminate the bench's tool-hanging capability.

The drawers themselves are built from one-by lumber and 1/4" plywood. To construct each of the smaller ones, you will need two sections of 1/4" X 6-3/8" X 20-1/4" B-B interior plywood (which will form the sides), another piece of B-B plywood that measures 1/4" X 11-1/4" X 20-1/4" (for the bottom), a 3/4" X 5-3/8" X 11-1/4" backboard, a 3/4" X 7-1/4" X 12-1/2" front piece, and two 3/4" X 3/4" X 19-3/4" slides.

Before assembling a drawer, rabbet the inside of the front to a 7/16" depth all around, making the cut 5/8" wide along the top, 9/16" wide on both sides, and 1/4" across the bottom. Then slice a 1/4"-wide, 3/8"-deep dado across the *inside* face of the drawer front 3/4" above the 1/4" rabbeted relief. This slot will accommodate the drawer's bottom. Wood screws are used to hold all the pieces together, and a suitable handle can be fashioned from a scrap of 2 X 4.

The assembly of the large drawers follows the same basic plan as that of the smaller ones. The rabbets on the inside of the drawer front are identical, but the dimensions are slightly different: The sides are made from 1/4" X 9-7/8" X 20-1/4" B-B interior

plywood, and the bottom is a 1/4" X 11-1/4" X 20-1/4" slab of the same material. The drawer's back is a 3/4" X 8-7/8" X 11-1/4" board, and its front is 3/4" X 10-1/2" X 12-1/2".

Dividers should be included as well, to give the drawers secure platforms to slide on. A set can be built from half-lapped rectangles measuring 12" X 19". Made from 3/4" X 3/4" stock, these are covered with 1/4" X 12" X 19" sheets of B-B interior plywood.

FINISH: The top of the workbench may be coated with a heavy layer of polyurethane varnish, both to give it a pleasant natural appearance and to waterproof it. The color of the pegboard side may be left as is or painted along with the drawers with a quality latex enamel.

TOOL RACK

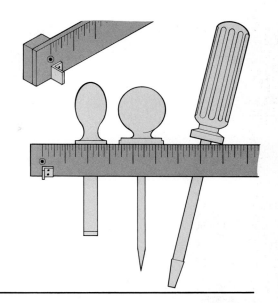

A yardstick is a handy tool to have around any workshop. And if you mount one above your workbench as shown here, you can make it do triple duty.

Screw or nail the wooden measuring stick to the wall with half-inch spacers behind it, and the yardstick will serve as a useful rack for screwdrivers, files, awls, and similar equipment. Then, by placing a small center-punched plug of metal directly on the zero point of the scale, it will be easy to set dividers, compasses, and other scribing instruments properly and quickly. Finally, by attaching a small section of angle bracket below the plug so that its inner face is also right on the scale's zero mark, aligning items on the yardstick for a quick measurement will also be easy.

GARDEN HOSE HANGER

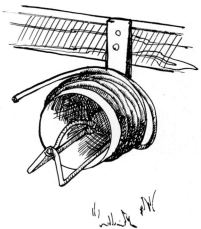

Stop fighting those tangled masses of garden hose and get them neatly off the ground with one or more of these easily made hangers. For each one you'll need a discarded 5-gallon plastic (or metal) container, a 10″ X 20″ piece of 1/2″ plywood, a scrap of 2 X 4, and a small assortment of bolts.

Cut two circles of plywood the same diameter as the inside of the bucket's bottom. Clean the container if necessary, and place one disk on the inside and the other on the outside of the pail's bottom, as shown in the illustration. Then clamp the disks together with four 1-1/2″-long bolts and mount the reinforced bucket to one end of a 24″ length of 2 X 4, using two 1/4″ X 4″ bolts. Using two more 1/4″ X 4″ bolts, attach the free end of the 2 X 4 to the side of a porch or some other convenient spot.

These hangers are so simple to put together that you'll probably want several in order to keep tidily coiled hoses in more than one location.

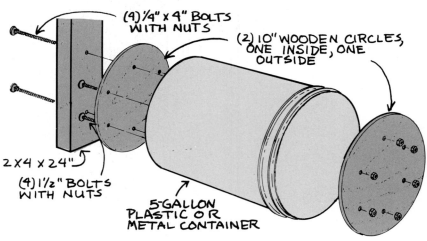

(4) 1/4″ X 4″ BOLTS WITH NUTS

(2) 10″ WOODEN CIRCLES, ONE INSIDE, ONE OUTSIDE

2 X 4 X 24″

(4) 1 1/2″ BOLTS WITH NUTS

5-GALLON PLASTIC OR METAL CONTAINER

RUST PREVENTIVE

For a tough waterproof coating for metal tools, make a mixture of 70% raw linseed oil and 30% turpentine (genuine or mineral). Apply this to chisels, spades, saw blades, and so forth, making sure the steel is dry, so no moisture will be sealed in. The application will dry quickly and can be easily renewed as it wears off. This finish, however, should not be used on wood.

"NEW" TOOLS

It's almost impossible to keep up with the repair and maintenance jobs around a home or farm without a large number of tools: an expensive proposition if you have to buy them new. But, by picking up other people's castoff tools and giving them a bit of tender loving care, it's possible to equip a workshop for pennies a year. In fact, you could even have some tools left over for barter.

TOOL GRAVEYARDS: Starting a collection of discarded treasures takes a good nose for the kind of hiding places where junked tools come to rest. And nothing will get you *into* those places quicker than a willingness to help clean out other folks' attics, basements, barns, and similar graveyards of abused equipment. There you'll find lots of perfectly good tools hidden under coats of rust and neglect. Unwanted tools in excellent condition may be purchased inexpensively at garage sales, auctions, and flea markets.

FROM BEAST TO BEAUTY: To begin the restoration, soak your discoveries overnight in a five-gallon bucket of used motor oil. This will loosen surface rust and corroded joints and also arrest oxidation to prevent further damage.

One of the most valuable items in tool renovation is a vise; it's like a third hand. If you don't have one, use a clamp to fasten the tool to a workbench or table.

When the oil has done its work, it's time to put on safety glasses and get down to business. It's very important to shield your eyes from flying bits of rust and wire. Use the vise and an electric drill with a 3" wire wheel attachment to further clean the tools.

This arrangement is better than a bench grinder with a wire wheel because the workpiece remains stationary, and it's possible to see when the metal is clean. For a thorough and quick job, adjust the direction that the vise faces and clamp the tool in as many different positions as necessary to get comfortably at all the blighted areas. You'll find that the rust will come off easily (but don't try to remove metal with a wire wheel; it just won't do the job).

Once you've cleaned around any nuts, bolts, or other fasteners, disassemble the tool to get at hidden corrosion. Be sure to pay special attention to bearing surfaces and cutting edges, because your tool will be useful as soon as these working surfaces are in good condition.

GET TOUGH: Should a tool refuse to yield to the low-pressure tactics mentioned, there are three "big guns" that can be brought in to attack the job: naval jelly, penetrating oil, and heat.

Where necessary, a thick coat of naval jelly will normally remove even the most stubborn rust. And penetrating oil placed on frozen joints and screws will help to loosen up any tool, especially if you judiciously use a hammer to break the rust bond.

If all else fails, heat the tool with a propane torch over a gas stove or in a forge. Just be careful not to burn your hands, and be aware that too much heat takes the temper out of metal. Once the tool is hot, tap it lightly with a hammer, and attempt to work the offending part free. Unfortunately, there will be times when a tool can't be rescued. Save yourself a lot of time and frustration by learning to recognize one of these "dead pieces" early in the game.

THE FINAL TOUCHES: Once the rust is removed, sharpen the tool's edges, refinish the handles, and add a touch of light machine oil to the bearing surfaces.

A saw-filing jig will be needed to put an edge on a recycled saw. Snips, wire cutters, and similar devices, on the other hand, are easily sharpened with a flat file. A file will remove pit marks from the face of a hammer, too.

Old wooden handles should be sanded to remove paint (the wire wheel would score the wood), and then finished with a half-and-half mixture of boiled linseed oil and turpentine. The notoriously slow drying process of linseed oil can be speeded up somewhat if you add a teaspoon or two of cobalt siccative—available at art supply stores—to one quart of the oil and turpentine mix. After the coating dries, sand the handles with 220 grit sandpaper for a first-rate, beautiful finish that's good for the wood and water-resistant, too.

And, if you find a tool (such as an ax or sledge) that needs a new handle, use ash or a similar hardwood with a clear, straight grain. Then just apply a finish in the manner described above.

TOOL CLEANER

A good way to keep garden tools clean and rust-free is to build an oiling/cleaning pit. Dig a hole about a foot square in a convenient spot, perhaps near the entrance to the toolshed. Line the sides of the hole with wood and fill the pit with sand. The next time you change the oil in your car, tractor, or mower, just pour the old oil into the sand and mix it up. Or if you don't have any used oil, obtain some from a service station. Try to maintain a sandy texture without too much oil; a hand dipped in the sand should pick up just a trace of oil. Tools that are thrust into the mix three or four times should come out clean, oiled, and ready to be put away.

LIST OF MATERIALS

WOOD
Walls: one 6-foot piece of 1 X 12
   or
four 12" pieces of 1 X 12
Lid: one 11-1/4" piece of 1 X 12
   or
one 11-1/4" square sheet of 3/4" exterior plywood
Cleats: one 2-foot piece of 1 X 1
   or
two 10-1/2" pieces of 1 X 1

HARDWARE
8d nails
1-1/4" brads
one door pull
wood preservative

To construct the pit, cut four 12"-long pieces of 1 X 12. Using simple butt joints and 8d nails, fasten the pieces together into a square frame. Dig a hole large enough to accommodate the frame with the upper edges projecting about 2" above the ground. Fill inside the frame with builder's sand, then backfill with soil around the outside of the boards. Pour the old oil onto the sand and work it in with a shovel.

A lid may be fashioned for the tool cleaning pit either by cutting an 11-1/4" section of 1 X 12 or by using an 11-1/4"-square piece of 3/4" exterior plywood. Attach a common door pull handle on top of the lid, and on either side underneath the lid, fasten two 10-1/2" cleats with brads to help keep the cover in place.

So the tool cleaning pit will last, it's a good idea to use rot-resistant wood, or to treat the frame and lid with a preservative.

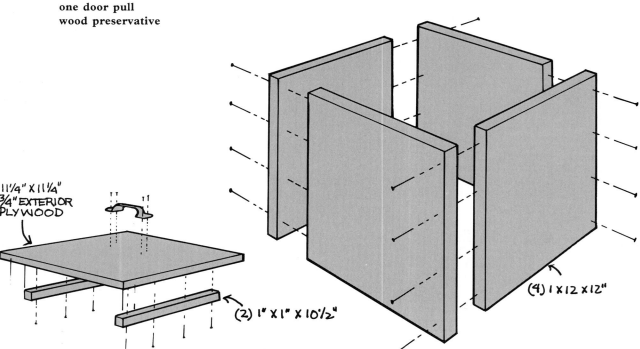

11¼" X 11¼" 3/4" EXTERIOR PLYWOOD

(2) 1" X 1" X 10½"

(4) 1 X 12 X 12"

TOOLS FOR HOME AND GARDEN/TOOL CLEANER

THE WHEEL: The tank-type roller that makes this wheelbarrow so efficient is made from a discarded pressurized-refrigerant cylinder, which can probably be obtained free from a refrigeration or air conditioning shop. Drill a 3/4″ hole in the center of each end of the tank. Position a 3/4″ X 22″ length of rigid conduit through the holes for the axle and weld the shaft in place. Since this is the only part of the construction process that requires more than basic carpentry tools, you may want to have it done by a welding shop.

To enable the metal roller to ride more smoothly over concrete or rocks, try stretching a section or two of truck-sized old inner tube over the cylinder. For ease in slipping the tubing into place, lubricate the surfaces with oil, if necessary. Slices of used tire tread attached to the tank with pop rivets or screws would serve the same purpose.

WHEELBARROW

Few conventional wheelbarrows can cruise over holes and bumpy ground as easily as this homemade garden helper, and no other single-wheel design is as stable. In addition, the load is balanced above the oversized wheel, so less effort is required for lifting. Some of the parts are made from salvaged materials, and once the supplies are on hand, it shouldn't take more than a few hours to complete the project.

THE FRAME AND BED: The wooden frame's triangulated design calls for two 10-foot lengths of 2 X 4. Divide one of these into two 60″ pieces to form the handles. Since the handles angle outward from the axle ends so they can be gripped comfortably, the holes for the bolts that secure the handles to the axle are not perpendicular to the wood surface. To get the correct angle, turn the handles sideways on a flat surface and prop the grip ends with 5″ blocks. At the axle ends of the handles, drill holes 3″ in from the ends and centered on the faces. By boring these holes perpendicular to the surface on which the handles are resting, the proper angle for attaching them to the axle will be obtained.

With a heavy load in the wheelbarrow, there's a danger that the pressure, which will focus at the axle holes, may split the 2 X 4's. To prevent this, brace the wood with two carriage bolts that pass through a pair

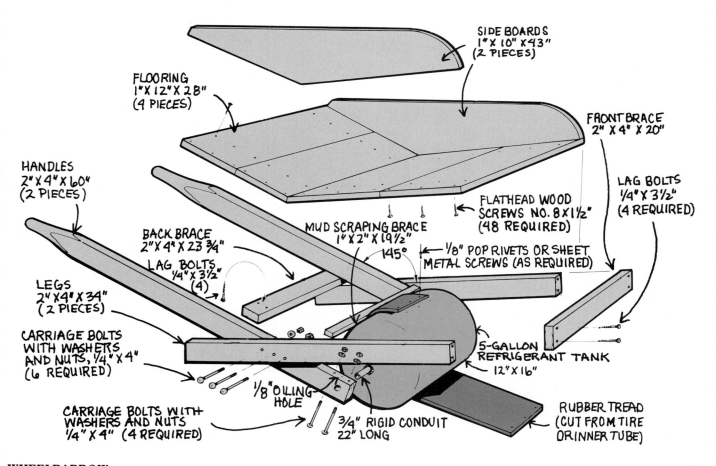

SIDE BOARDS
1″ X 10″ X 43″
(2 PIECES)

FLOORING
1″ X 12″ X 28″
(4 PIECES)

FRONT BRACE
2″ X 4″ X 20″

HANDLES
2″ X 4″ X 60″
(2 PIECES)

LAG BOLTS
1/4″ X 3 1/2″
(4 REQUIRED)

BACK BRACE
2″ X 4″ X 23 3/4″

LAG BOLTS
1/4″ X 3 1/2″
(4)

MUD SCRAPING BRACE
1″ X 2″ X 19 1/2″

145°

FLATHEAD WOOD
SCREWS NO. 8 X 1 1/2″
(48 REQUIRED)

1/8″ POP RIVETS OR SHEET
METAL SCREWS (AS REQUIRED)

LEGS
2″ X 4″ X 34″
(2 PIECES)

CARRIAGE BOLTS
WITH WASHERS
AND NUTS, 1/4″ X 4″
(6 REQUIRED)

5-GALLON
REFRIGERANT TANK
12″ X 16″

1/8″ OILING HOLE

CARRIAGE BOLTS WITH
WASHERS AND NUTS
1/4″ X 4″ (4 REQUIRED)

3/4″ RIGID CONDUIT
22″ LONG

RUBBER TREAD
(CUT FROM TIRE
OR INNER TUBE)

of 1/4″ holes on each side of the axle, using large washers and nuts to provide maximum support for this critical connection. In addition, drill a 1/8″ oil inlet into each axle hole from the top so you can give the conduit periodic lubrication.

Prepare for attaching the handle to the leg by boring a 1/4″ hole approximately 9″ from the axle. The holes in each handle must be the same distance from the axle, or the frame will scissor unevenly. After this is done, slide each handle onto its appropriate axle, and nail a 1″ X 2″ X 19-1/2″ brace across the top of the handles about 1″ behind the wheel. This crosspiece stabilizes the assembly and also acts as a mud scraper.

TOOLS FOR HOME AND GARDEN

To make the wheelbarrow's legs, saw off two 34″ sections from the other 2 X 4. Drill a 1/4″ hole 23″ from the end of each piece and bolt each leg to the outside of a handle with a 1/4″ carriage bolt. The legs can now pivot on these bolts as the handles are moved, thereby allowing the angle between these pieces to be adjusted.

For the front and rear braces, cut the remaining section of 2 X 4 to obtain one length that's 20″ and another that's 23-3/4″. Slide the larger board between the legs and handles from behind until these units form a 145° angle as shown. Mark the position and remove the brace. Then drill four holes to start the lag bolts which secure this crosspiece. The holes in each brace must be 1/4″ in diameter, while those in the handles should be slightly smaller. Use the same bits to prepare the 20″ front strut and the legs for their bolts. When the handles, legs, and braces are in position, drill the remaining four carriage bolt holes roughly 2″ to each side of the original pivot mount holes and fasten the frame together.

The body of the wheelbarrow is constructed from 10 feet of 1 X 12 for flooring and 8 feet of 1 X 10 for side boards. Saw four 28″ lengths of 1 X 12 and tack them into position along the handles and legs. Using a 3/32″ bit, drill and countersink holes for the 24 No. 8 X 1-1/2″ wood screws, and secure the planks to the handles and legs. Once the bed is attached, cut two 43″ pieces from the 1 X 10, hold one in position, and scribe the profile of a side board. Clamp the two boards securely together and saw them both along the scribed mark. Drill and countersink holes for 24 No. 8 X 1-1/2″ wood screws as shown and fasten the sides to the cart.

Finally, work the handle grips down to a comfortable size with a rasp and finish the wheelbarrow with a coat or two of paint. The result is a functional, easy-to-manage piece of equipment that will help to take the "chore" out of many yard and garden projects.

GARDEN HOE

Here's a triple-duty homemade implement that will make your cultivating chores easier. The business end consists of three replacement sickle-bar mower blades—available from a farm implement dealer—welded together so that the serrated edges face outward. A section of 3/8″ cold-rolled rod about ten inches long is welded to this head, then the shaft's opposite end is ground to a point which can be driven into an available tool handle. The metal collar on that staff (most old tool handles will still have this component in place) pinches the wood so the rod can't slip out and keeps the end of the handle from splitting. Depending on which edge faces downward, this handy item can serve as a hoe, a row marker, or a root cutter.

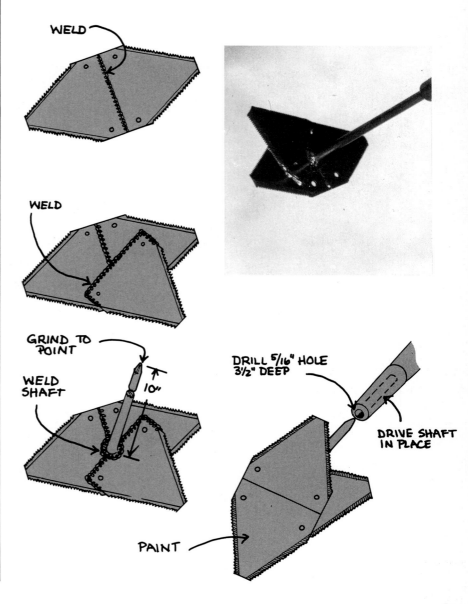

WELD

WELD

GRIND TO POINT

WELD SHAFT

10″

DRILL 5/16″ HOLE 3½″ DEEP

DRIVE SHAFT IN PLACE

PAINT

POSTHOLE DIGGER

Setting fenceposts to be sturdy supports for rails or wire ideally requires holes that remain about 6″ in diameter from the ground's surface to the bottom of the cavity. However, because the handles of a standard posthole digger must be splayed widely apart to close the jaws, the resulting holes become more and more funnel-shaped, thus requiring extra fill and making it more difficult to plant the posts securely and vertically.

By building an offset-handled posthole digger, though, that works with the same kind of action as does a pair of scissors, a homesteader can sink a deep, straight hole with a narrow, uniform diameter.

To fabricate this type of posthole digger, collect one 10-foot section of 3/4″ electrical metallic tubing (E.M.T.), four bicycle handgrips, a 2″-diameter steel ring, four 1/4″ X 1-1/4″ carriage bolts, a 5/16″ X 2″ machine bolt, two 5/16″ flat washers, and a 7″ length of 4″ E.M.T. A section of 4″ steel pipe can be substituted for this last piece.

The tools needed include a hacksaw, a drill, a 1/4″ and a 5/16″ bit, a ruler, a felt-tipped pen, a pocketknife, and a conduit bender. If no conduit bender is available, it's possible to give form to the handles by placing them inside a long, snug-fitting tension spring, or by filling them with sand and capping their ends, then carefully bending them around a convenient pipe or pole.

The first step is to make the 35° arcs in the handles as indicated in the illustration (each bar should be cut to a length of 60″, then bent into shape). This will give you a pair of offset shanks with 7″ grip ends, 9″-long upper offsets, 24″ midlengths, 3″ lower offsets, and 5″ of leg to serve as scoop mounts. Each bend takes up about 3″.

With the hacksaw, cut the section of 4″-diameter tubing in half lengthwise, and using the photo on this page as a guide, mark a cutting line at one end of each piece in preparation for forming the individual scoops. Each one has three teeth made by cutting 3/8″ equilateral triangles from the center of the business edge, and the corners are rounded to create a spade shape.

Before fastening the scoops to the legs, join the handles at the lower offsets with the 5/16″ bolt. When drilling the pivot holes, make sure the tubes are parallel and centered where the handles meet. Then mount the shovels by positioning them against the legs so the teeth are about 3″ from the ends of the tubes, and secure each scoop with carriage bolts that are positioned about 2″ apart.

The rest is easy: Cut the closed ends from one pair of handgrips, and after soaping the E.M.T. well, slide the grips over the metal handles to a point just below the upper offsets. Next, slip the 2″ steel ring over both tubes and cap the shafts with your remaining two grips. The restraining ring will prevent the steel shanks from separating and pulling against the pivot joint during digging and twisting, and the grips serve as insulation against electrical shock. The two lower sleeves simply act as stops to prevent the ring from sliding down the poles.

In most types of soil this tool will accomplish well its task of cutting a straight and narrow shaft. But, should you require more "heft" for tougher jobs, it wouldn't be too difficult to plug the handles at their bases and fill them with sand or wet concrete to give mass and rigidity to the implement.

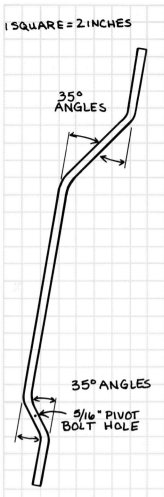

1 SQUARE = 2 INCHES

35° ANGLES

35° ANGLES

5/16" PIVOT BOLT HOLE

HAY RAKE

There's really no comparison between an ordinary mass-produced garden rake and the specialized haying tools used in Europe. French farmers handcraft these fine implements from three kinds of hardwood: hazelnut for the handle, aspen or ash for the head, and ash or rowan for the teeth. Here's how to incorporate some of that old world craftsmanship into your own hay rake.

When selecting the wood for the handle, try to find a hazelnut sapling 8″ to 10″ taller than your height and about 2″ in diameter. If hazelnut is unavailable, ash or spruce will do. Fix the pole in a vise and smooth off the bark and rough edges with a drawknife. When it's finished, the staff should be about 8″ taller than you are and about 1-1/2″ in diameter.

Next, use a saw to make a 17″ cut down the center of one end of the handle, and with a pocketknife, whittle these two ends into a pair of 3/4″-diameter circular prongs. Then wrap two or three strands of wire around the base of the cut, twisting the ends tightly together with a pair of pliers to prevent the sapling's splitting further.

For the rake's head, use a 1″ X 2″ X 28″ piece of ash. Clamp the board in a vise—with the 2″ side up—and drill two holes along the center line, one 12-1/2″ from each end of the plank. Make the holes just under 3/4″ in diameter and bore them clear through to the other side so the handle's prongs can be wedged in tightly.

To fashion the implement's 30 teeth, you'll need three ash boards, each 1″ X 2″ X 30″. After securing one board vertically in the vise, carefully split it down the middle—lengthwise—with a hammer and a hatchet. Then saw each half into five equal segments, leaving you with ten 1″ X 1″ X 6″ square pegs.

Cut the other two boards the same way. Then get comfortable and whittle the pegs into round teeth with a pocketknife. As you carve them down to 3/8″ in diameter and 5″ long, try to curve each tine slightly. Teeth that are curved in the direction of the pull make the rake a stronger and more efficient tool.

Drill 30 5/16″ holes evenly spaced along one of the 1″ faces of the head and angled slightly so when the teeth are installed the tines will tilt toward the user. Carry these holes all the way through the 1″ X 2″ X 28″ board so they come out on the opposite 1″ face. Hammer the teeth into these holes, tapping them until they are flush with the top surface of the rake's head and making certain that all the curves face in the same direction. To insure that the teeth are solidly fixed, secure each one in place with a 3/4″ nail on the handle side of the head. Each brad should protrude slightly, so that you can remove it if a tooth breaks and has to be replaced.

Finally, put the handle in the vise and match up the two holes through the 2″ faces of the rake's head with the prongs. Hammer the head onto the handle until the prongs are flush with the other side and fasten the fork in place with two 1″ nails, each driven in at an angle from the top of the head. Again, let the fasteners protrude a little for easy removal.

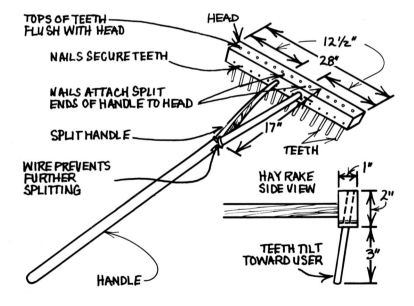

TOPS OF TEETH FLUSH WITH HEAD

NAILS SECURE TEETH

NAILS ATTACH SPLIT ENDS OF HANDLE TO HEAD

SPLIT HANDLE

WIRE PREVENTS FURTHER SPLITTING

HANDLE

HEAD

12½″

28″

17″

TEETH

HAY RAKE SIDE VIEW

TEETH TILT TOWARD USER

1″

2″

3″

BOW SAW

Any homesteader with an old 26″ bicycle rim, some scrap wood, and the usual workshop odds and ends can make a "brand new" bow saw for the price of the blade alone.

The outside diameter of a 26″ wheel rim is just shy of 24″. A bow saw similar to that in Fig. 1 can be made by cutting the rim in half and securing the bow between two 16″ wood handles combined with a cable or a rod tensioner. With a new blade, this bargain bow should cut as well as any store-bought model, but cost a fraction of the price. Just turn the blade to face out, and cut off both wooden handles flush with the saw's face. However, holding the bow ver-tically over the wood being cut soon makes for a tired wrist.

To make a bow saw that's less tiring to use than the traditional design, follow Fig. 2 in which the blade faces inward and one handle is 22″ long.

This way, the weight of the bow acts to keep the blade in a vertical position. To work on a log or limb that's too big or too unhandy to fit inside the saw's frame, simply reverse the blade to point outward.

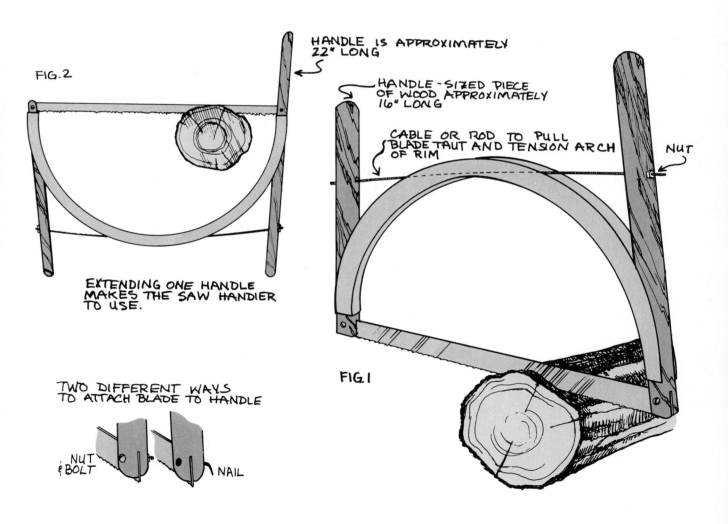

FIG. 2

HANDLE IS APPROXIMATELY 22″ LONG

HANDLE-SIZED PIECE OF WOOD APPROXIMATELY 16″ LONG

CABLE OR ROD TO PULL BLADE TAUT AND TENSION ARCH OF RIM

NUT

EXTENDING ONE HANDLE MAKES THE SAW HANDIER TO USE.

TWO DIFFERENT WAYS TO ATTACH BLADE TO HANDLE

NUT & BOLT

NAIL

FIG. 1

PUSH CULTIVATOR

As winter slowly melts into spring, most folks can't wait to get out into the garden again . . . to till, plant, weed, meditate, and enjoy one of the deep and subtle satisfactions of life.

And every summer, as hordes of undesired plants grow just as steadily as the intended crops, those same gardeners wish they had a good hand-powered push cultivator. However, the price of this classic garden implement usually overpowers the desire to own one.

Fortunately, there are enough similarities between that common weeding tool and the front wheel/main chassis of an ordinary one-speed bicycle that it's an easy job to convert a discarded two-wheeled transporter into a functioning garden cultivator.

First, cut off the tubing in front of both the bike's seat and its main sprocket, leaving the triangle that forms the back part of the frame intact. Replace the cycle's rear wheel with its front one and remove the pedals, crank, chain, front sprocket, and bearings from the bike's drive mechanism.

At this point, replace the bike's seat with a set of bolt-on cultivator tines—available at most hardware stores—and turn the trimmed-down unit over so the spikes point down.

To make the steering shaft, attach a section of threaded pipe by cutting a hole through the side of the former bike's pedal hub, thrusting one end of the pipe into this opening, and securing it in place with nuts on both the inside and outside of the hub.

Then use the handlebar's original collar clamp to secure the bike's grips to the other end of the pipe section.

So if you've ever dreamed of having your own big-wheeled garden tool, consider giving a discarded bicycle a new use in life. It may not look as classy as a store-bought model, but it really works.

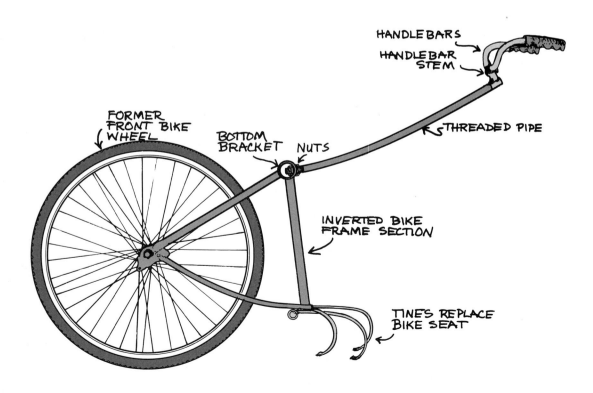

HANDLEBARS

HANDLEBAR STEM

THREADED PIPE

FORMER FRONT BIKE WHEEL

BOTTOM BRACKET   NUTS

INVERTED BIKE FRAME SECTION

TINES REPLACE BIKE SEAT

HAND HOE

This sturdy hoe can be fashioned in minutes from scrap materials. Take a piece of hardwood, perhaps 7/8″ thick and 1-3/4″ wide, and cut it to a suitable length, say 4 feet. Round the edges for a comfortable grip and attach an old bucksaw blade to the handle with bolts, as shown in the sketch. This handy-dandy hand hoe can't be beat for weeding and cultivating small garden plots, and it is especially useful with a crop such as onions.

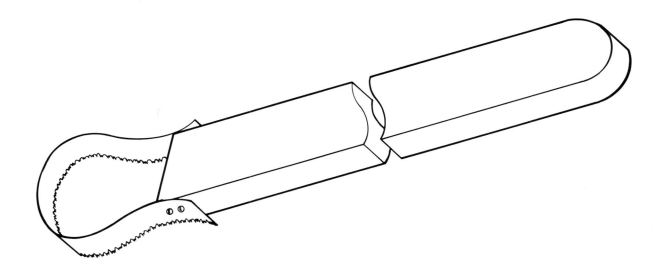

A WORD ABOUT WEEDS

The clean-as-a-whistle look is definitely out when it comes to weeds. Though it isn't necessary or even advisable to evict all those uninvited plants from your garden, this doesn't eliminate the need for tools such as this hand hoe and others traditionally used for keeping the soil around crops free of weeds. In fact, up to a point, you may want them there. After all, weeds—just like your planted crops—can help the soil retain moisture and keep it from eroding. In addition, their deep-reaching roots can pull nutrition up from the lower layers of the soil so that when you do need to pull some of those weeds, they'll add rich nutrients to the compost pile.

So, practice what might be called an "enlightened" approach to weeding. Remove and compost any specimens that are just too close to vegetables or flowers. Use the little hand hoe to slice them right off at the ground, especially any weed that's gone to seed. Also, you can really attack any grass plants that invade the garden. That prolific lawn cover spreads by underground roots and can be really difficult to abolish once it's taken hold.

If your garden is healthy, you shouldn't have much trouble with weeds anyway, for they thrive on neglect. Compost will nourish the earth and limit weed growth, mulch will help a great deal in their control, and a few minutes spent each day routing out the ones you really don't want should do the job.

BIKE SERVICE STAND

When most tools break, they're merely assigned to the scrap-heap. But before tossing out those old locking pliers because the teeth are too blunt, take a look at this service stand that will make almost any kind of bicycle repair or maintenance much easier. Its main component is a "biteless" pair of locking pliers, combined with about 10 feet of 1″ electrical metallic tubing (E.M.T.), a couple of scraps of 1″ angle iron, a small piece of 3/4″ pipe, and a few 1/2″ bolts and nuts.

This job shouldn't take much more than an hour to complete, and it requires only a cutting torch, a manual pipe-bending tool (heat *can* be used to bend the E.M.T.), a hacksaw, and a file or grinding wheel.

Start by shaping and assembling the conduit frame. A 64″ length of E.M.T., bent at a 60° angle in the center to form two 24″ legs, works well for the base, and a 46″ piece, curved to 80° at one end, will provide a suitable upright. Before brazing the vertical arm to the leg tube, shape the lower end of the pole—using your saw and file—so it matches the contour of the base tubing. You won't be able to produce a secure joint without making certain the pieces mate well.

The upright can be either positioned vertically or canted inward, 5° or so to provide additional clearance. If you plan to work on bikes in the 40-pound and up range, consider fastening a pair of 12″ struts between the stanchion and the tubular base for extra support.

To adapt the locking pliers for cycle-biting duty, first cut two 4″ lengths of 1/8″ X 1″ X 1″ angle iron, then trim away the ends of the tool's jaws so that the pair of angles will fit flush against the closed jaws when the adjusting nut is turned in. Make sure the angles form a square with each other and that the pliers are centered on, and perpendicular to, the irons. Braze each angle securely to its respective mount.

The clamp mechanism is extra-special because it features an all-position

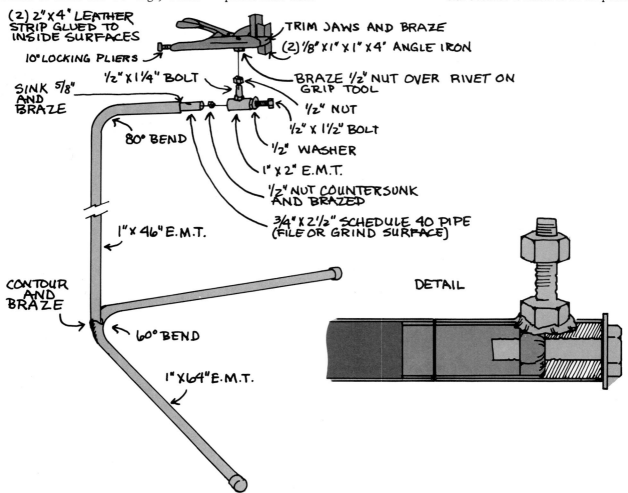

(2) 2″ X 4′ LEATHER STRIP GLUED TO INSIDE SURFACES

10″ LOCKING PLIERS

SINK 5/8″ AND BRAZE

1/2″ X 1 1/4″ BOLT

80° BEND

1″ X 46″ E.M.T.

CONTOUR AND BRAZE

60° BEND

1″ X 64″ E.M.T.

TRIM JAWS AND BRAZE
(2) 1/8″ X 1″ X 1″ X 4″ ANGLE IRON

BRAZE 1/2″ NUT OVER RIVET ON GRIP TOOL

1/2″ NUT

1/2″ X 1 1/2″ BOLT

1/2″ WASHER

1″ X 2″ E.M.T.

1/2″ NUT COUNTERSUNK AND BRAZED

3/4″ X 2 1/2″ SCHEDULE 40 PIPE (FILE OR GRIND SURFACE)

DETAIL

TOOLS FOR HOME AND GARDEN

swivel. To give the stand this capability, file or grind a section of 3/4" X 2-1/2" pipe until it slips easily into the open end of the upright stanchion, and braze a 1/2" nut inside this hollow plug in such a way that its outer face is flush with one end of the pipe (you may have to file the nut's corners slightly to make it fit properly). Sink the plug's opposite end 5/8" into the curved E.M.T. support, and braze it in place.

Cut a 2" length of conduit from your scrap and braze a 1/2" X 1-1/4"

bolt to its side, off center. Fasten a 1/2" nut to the upper jaw of the pliers, right over the rivet, in the same manner. By spinning a third 1/2" nut onto the exposed bolt and threading the clamp assembly onto the end of that stud, you can use the free nut to lock the grip in any position. To complete the swivel, just slip the clamp's collar over its pipe plug (with the flank bolt closest to the end) and run a 1/2" X 1-1/2" bolt with a washer into that stem's countersunk nut to serve as a lock.

Finish the project by giving the stand a coat or two of paint and gluing some 2" X 4" leather pads to the inside surfaces of the new angle jaws to prevent damage to the bike's finish. For safety's sake, slip some rubber caps over the legs' sharp ends. Since the modified locking pliers are still fully adjustable—and probably as tenacious as they were when you bought them—you may find that this homemade stand will serve many other useful purposes in addition to gripping bicycles.

BIKE SERVICE STAND

WOOD VISE

This vise isn't the usual jaw-and-turnscrew device found on most workbenches. Instead, the basic work-holder consists of three pieces of wood (Fig. 1): a 2 X 4 X 8″ end block, which is screwed securely in place, and two interlocking sections cut from a piece of 2 X 8. The larger of these is fixed to the same surface as—and aligned a short distance from—the end block, while the smaller component is used to wedge stock in place between the two fixed pieces.

The secret to the gadget's holding power is that the movable chock and its partner are made by slicing an 8″ piece of 2 X 8 pine lengthwise (with the grain) but on a slant (see Fig. 2), while the saw blade itself is set at a slight tilt rather than straight up and down. This technique produces a pair of angular, trapezoid-shaped pieces, each with a beveled edge. When the two cut sides are forced together, they mesh perfectly—the free one slightly under the fixed one—and their opposing angles prevent the wedge and the stock it's helping to grip from popping out.

In professional woodworking circles, the cut is called a "compound rip bevel", but it's easy to make using a table saw and a tapering jig. Simply set the blade at an angle of 35° to 40° and the jig at approx-

Many woodworking projects require that the stock being shaped, planed, sawed or smoothed be held firmly in place on the bench top. Commercially made wood vises tend to be expensive, but as a substitute, the home woodcrafter can fashion this sturdy homemade tool that will hold small or medium pieces of lumber steady.

imately 15°, and cut the 2 X 8 as shown in Figs. 2 and 3. Remember that the actual size of finished lumber is always smaller than its stated dimensions, and so a 2 X 8 in fact measures about 1-1/2″ X 7-1/4″.

If the saw being used for the project doesn't have a tapering attachment, you can make one (Fig. 3) by joining the ends of two 18″ lengths of 1 X 2 pine with a hinge. The right side of the contrivance can then follow your saw's rip fence, while the left is used to adjust for whatever degree of taper you want. A rigid crosspiece attached between the two arms will lock the setting in place, and it's also a good idea to nail a block of scrap wood at right angles to the lower end of the jig's left extension, to give some support to the stock being cut and to assure a square start. Of course, hand-held manual or power tools may be used to create functional—although somewhat less than per-

fect—components for your vise. Just follow the measurements shown in Fig. 2 and cut as carefully and accurately as possible.

Once the parts are shaped, position the large trapezoid (both stops can be trimmed, if necessary, to fit an easily moved mounting board). Then align the 2 X 4 end block so that its long sides are parallel to the angular section's uncut side and so the distance between the outside edges of the two stops is about 11″ (Fig. 1). Drill holes and use No. 10 X 2-1/2″ wood screws to secure the pieces.

To use the homemade vise, place the lumber to be worked on against the inside surface of the end block. Now slide the small trapezoid, narrow end first, into the remaining space and tap it hard with a hammer or mallet so that its beveled edge meshes with the cut side of the large angled block and it lodges firmly in place, holding the workpiece tightly.

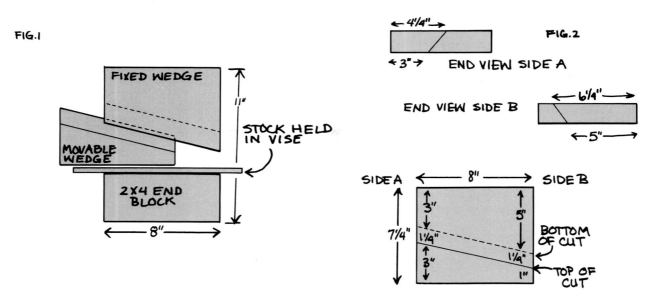

FIG. 3

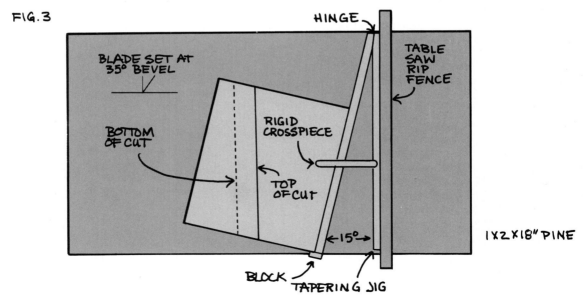

HINGE

TABLE SAW RIP FENCE

BLADE SET AT 35° BEVEL

BOTTOM OF CUT

RIGID CROSSPIECE

TOP OF CUT

15°

BLOCK

TAPERING JIG

1X2X18" PINE

WOOD VISE

81

FOLDING SAWHORSES

There's just no substitute for a sturdy pair of sawhorses when you need to cut up a batch of lumber or plywood. Unfortunately, until they're needed, these four-legged stands seem to be forever in the way. Whether they're stacked, hung, or stored on end, assembled sawhorses take up a lot of valuable space.

The solution is a set of folding sawhorses, which can be stored snugly against the wall when not being used. The legs of the wooden "steeds" that can solve your space dilemma work like a pair of scissors which, when locked in their upright position, firmly clamp a 2 X 4 crosspiece. Then once the cutting job is done and a homemade hinged bracket on the sawhorse is released, each pair of legs will collapse to a size barely larger than a single 2 X 4!

Building a folding sawhorse is slightly more complicated than nailing together a standard one, but the construction can still be accomplished using basic tools, including a handsaw, a saber saw, and a drill with a 1/4" bit. For each horse you'll need to collect an 8-foot length of 2 X 4, 30" of 1/8" X 3/4" steel strap, a foot of 1/4" cold-rolled steel rod, two 1/4" X 1" machine screws with nuts, a 2" X 4" piece of 16-gauge steel, and a small piece of 100-grit sandpaper.

Begin forming the legs by cutting two 31" lengths from the 2 X 4. This leaves a 34" section for the crosspiece. Next, rip each of the 31" boards down the 3-1/2" dimension to produce four legs, each approximately 1-1/2" square. At this point, you can trim one end of each support at a 75° angle so it will rest flush with the floor when the sawhorse is in use, but don't trim the other end until later.

Each set of legs is connected at points 3-1/4" and 11-1/2" from the top of each leg with brackets formed from 1/8" X 3/4" steel strap and held in place by 1/4" steel rod. The upper connection is a single 4" length of metal, and the lower bracket is formed from two 5" pieces that are overlapped and bolted together with

a 2"-square, 16-gauge steel stop folded over the pivot and sandwiched by the bolt and nut. This allows the legs to open and lock into position.

Slots must be cut into the inside of each leg at all four bracket mount points so the 1/8"-thick metal supports can be slipped in and pinned into place and so the bottom bracket can fold up. If you happen to have a table saw, the lower slots can be made by simply placing the wood over the retracted blade of the saw and then gradually raising the cutter to slice a groove slightly more than halfway through the board. The same basic cut can also be accomplished with a saber saw and some hand work.

However, each upper recess should be made by first drilling 1/4" holes in the center of the inside face, 3/4"

above and below the pivot point for the steel. Then cut out a slot between the two holes so the strap can be inserted and pinned into position.

Once you've bored the pivot holes in both the legs and the steel straps, hammer 1-1/2" lengths of 1/4" rod in place to secure the pieces. Now, lay the assembly flat on your workbench, place the legs at full extension, set the end of the 2 X 4 crosspiece against the legs at the upper pivot, and mark the cut necessary to pinch the board in the wooden "jaws". When you shape the upper angle, be conservative about the amount of material removed. The surfaces may then be filed down to achieve the proper fit.

To put the finishing touches on your hideaway sawhorses (they work best in pairs), cut a slot 2" from each end of the 2 X 4 crosspieces so that the top metal strap on each pair of legs can slide into a groove. Glue some sandpaper to the clamping surface of each support and lock the pieces into position. Now you're ready to trim wallboard, section plywood, or cut lumber with ease. And when the job's done, fold up the stands and stash them neatly away.

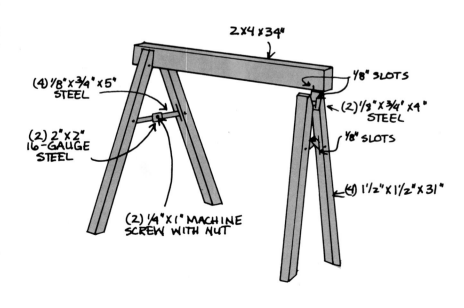

WOOD LATHE

Any aspiring woodworker eyeing the monotonously round or square legs on his or her homebuilt furniture has probably yearned to own a wood-turning tool. The trouble is, a lathe is hardly a priority purchase for a growing shop, as its cost usually isn't justified by its versatility.

However, by digging into those piles of scraps and spare parts, you may be able to pull out everything needed to build this excellent, useful power tool, with the exception of a ball bearing mandrel and a couple of spurs.

The finished lathe will accommodate wood chunks up to three feet long and over a foot in diameter, and handsomely carved legs and rungs can be turned on it.

LIST OF MATERIALS

54"	4" X 1-1/2" U-channel
10"	3" X 1-1/2" U-channel
18'	1-1/2" angle iron
9'	1-1/2" O.D. 11-gauge round, seamless, cold-finished, carbon-steel mechanical tubing
36"	1-3/4" O.D. 11-gauge round, seamless, cold-finished, carbon-steel mechanical tubing
16"	1/4" X 1" bar stock
24"	3/8" X 1" bar stock
14"	3/8" X 4" steel plate
42"	1/4" X 7" steel plate
12"	1/2" steel rod
5"	1/2" Schedule 40 pipe
3-1/2"	1/4" Schedule 40 pipe
56"	1 X 12 shelving
12"	2" angle iron
1	3-1/2" chain ring
12"	5/8" rod
6"	3/8" rod
36"	1/8" X 36" sheet steel
2	3-step pulleys
1	headstock spur
1	tailstock spur
1	5/8" arbor ball bearing mandrel
1	salvaged 1/2-HP washing machine motor
9	3/8" X 1-1/2" bolts
12	3/8" nuts
1	3/8" washer
1	3/8" wing nut
4	3/8" X 1-1/2" carriage bolts
1	5/16" X 4" bolt
1	5/16" nut
2	1/2" X 4" bolts
2	1/2" nuts
1	1/2" X 6" bolt
1	5/8" coupling nut
1	5/8" washer
2	3/4" coupling nuts
1	110-volt wall switch and wires

THE BED: The bed upon which the tool's working parts ride consists of angle iron, U-channel, and a piece of pine shelving, as shown in Fig. A. You'll find the components specified in the materials list, and the dimensions and weld points are indicated in Fig. B. The legs for the stand are bent to meet the U-channel squarely: a task that's much easier if the bend points are first heated with an oxyacetylene torch. In addition, the angle iron used for the braces—which span between each leg and the base—should be bent and ground so that no sharp edges protrude.

To avoid banging your shins on the 1 X 12 wooden support shelf, round the board on its "working side" and set its far edge against the opposite legs before drilling holes and bolting the shelf in place.

This full-capacity lathe is sturdily supported and can handle huge chunks of wood. The working parts of the lathe are set atop steel-box sections.

Since washing machine motors have different mounting configurations, the braces welding the left rear leg to the motor must be designed specifically to fit the bolt pattern on your unit. It's also a good idea to provide for a sliding mount so belt tension can be adjusted.

THE WAYS: The tailstock assembly slides on a pair of tubular steel tracks, enabling it to move and to clamp different lengths of wood between the lathe's centers (Fig. B). The runners—which slip along the lathe's ways—are made of larger tubing that provides a .005″ fit, and the tool rest

WOOD LATHE

slides on a foot made to exactly the same specifications. When centering the two tubes which form the ways, be certain that the "pipes" are parallel and that no parts become distorted by the welding heat. In addition, file off any welding spatter that might interfere with the smooth sliding of the parts.

THE POWER TRAIN: Any 1/2-HP washing machine motor can be coupled, using a pair of three-step pulleys and a V-belt, to the ball bearing mandrel in order to drive the lathe. If your motor is a single-speed unit (there are some two-speed ex-

amples available that can be incorporated into this lathe design), the spindle will turn at either 950, 1,725, or 3,125 RPM, depending on the belt's position on the pulleys.

SPINDLES: Most mandrels have a 3-1/4″ X 5-1/4″ bolt pattern and an overall shaft length of approximately 10″. Such a unit will fit neatly on top of the 3-3/4″ X 6″ plate that caps the headstock box.

The construction of the *tailstock* spindle, however, is more involved. When welding nuts to the various parts, install the bolts before tacking, so that the threads of the nut won't

be distorted by the heat. Note that the 5/8″ coupler nut must be driven into the two 3/4″ coupler nuts before it's welded in place.

HEADSTOCK AND TAIL-STOCK: The working portions of the lathe are set atop steel box sections, which have access holes cut for the clamping bolt on the tailstock and the switch and wires on the headstock. The spindles must be perfectly aligned to prevent wobble. One way to accomplish this is to weld the headstock into position first, and then align the tailstock to it. Slip one of the pulleys onto the spur end of the man-

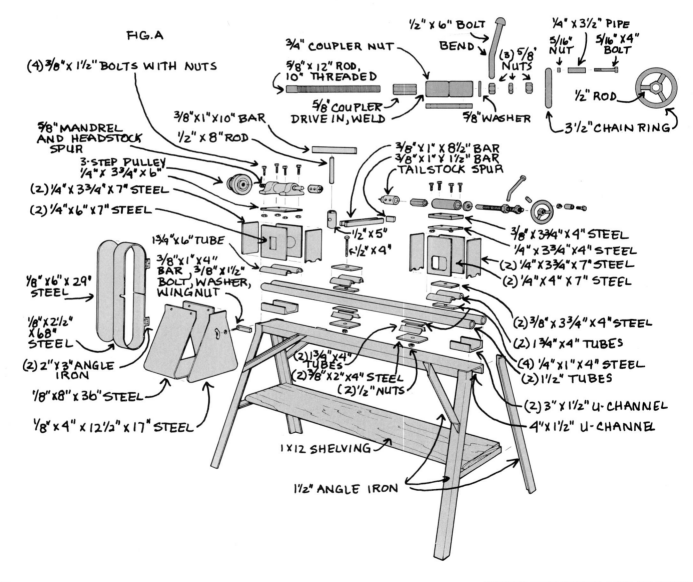

drel and slide the tailstock spindle shaft into the other end of the pulley. Then weld the tailstock box to its runner.

DETAILS: The lathe's switch is a common wall box set inside the headstock and is wired to interrupt the flow of power to the motor. To prevent wood shavings from getting into the brushes, the motor and the belt drive are enclosed in a sheet-metal box fitted with an access door. A coat of paint will finish the job, and you'll be ready to pick up some wood and start turning.

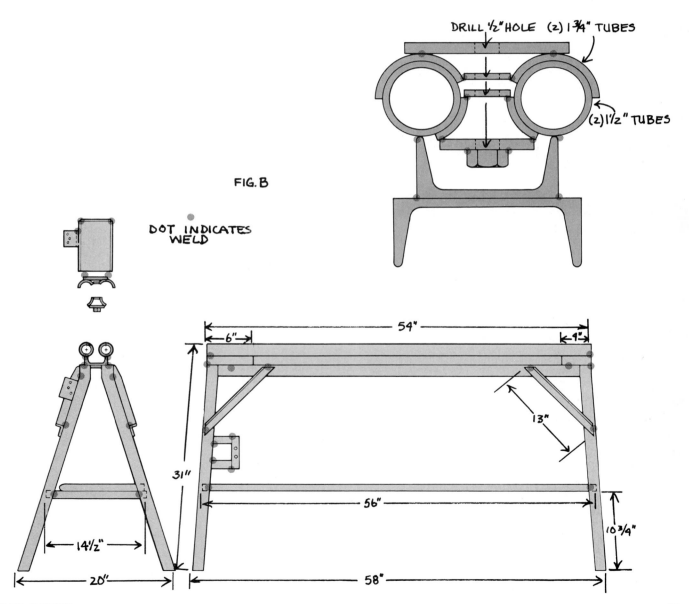

FIG. B

DOT INDICATES WELD

DRILL ½" HOLE (2) 1¾" TUBES

(2) 1½" TUBES

54"

6"

1"

13"

56"

31"

14½"

20"

58"

10¾"

HOMESTEAD WORKSHOP PROJECTS

HOMESTEAD RADIO

This handmade receiver can provide entertainment and information indefinitely with *no* operating costs. Additionally, it's the ideal receiver to use outdoors or—during emergency situations—anywhere at all . . . since it eliminates any dependence upon batteries or utility-company power.

WHAT'S INVOLVED: This homemade radio is actually a modified crystal receiver. The few parts needed to build it (see materials list) are readily available at electronic equipment supply stores. Better yet, find a broken radio or two, and you'll probably be able to build most of the receiver from recycled components. Little soldering is necessary to complete the project, and construction time is only about two hours.

Be sure to read all the instructions *before* you start building the radio, and don't be concerned if the electrical items you acquire look different from those in the photograph. As long as the parts match the designations given in the list, their appearance won't make a bit of difference!

COIL CONSTRUCTION: Even though constructing the coil is the most time-consuming portion of this project, it's really not a difficult task. Begin by foraging some material to serve as the radio's base (the one in the illustration is made of 1/8"-thick fiberboard) and a plastic container of approximately the dimensions suggested in the list of materials (the one shown is a cylindrical pill box).

Remove the cap from the container and center the lid, top down, about 1" from one end of the board. Drill a small hole through both the cap's center and the board, and fasten the two together with a nut and bolt.

Use a pair of pliers to heat a needle in a flame. Carefully push the hot needle through the plastic container to make Holes 1, 2, and 3 (Fig. 1.). As long as the openings are placed near the mouth of the container and about 3/16" apart, their exact locations aren't critical.

Next, thread the free end of the No. 24 copper wire through Hole 2 (outside to inside) and bring it back out through Hole 1, allowing about 6" to protrude. Now, slowly wind 25 turns of wire clockwise (as viewed from the "open" end of the vial) around the plastic. Make sure each wire coil rests snugly next to the preceding one, but don't let the wire cross itself at any point.

After making the 25 loops, cut the wire at a spot about 6" from the com-

(1) 3″ X 6″ piece of wood or plastic
(2) 1″ X 1″ X 3″ pieces of wood
(1) 2″ X 2-3/4″ to 4″ empty plastic pill container
(2) 5-way binding posts
(2) Fahnestock clips
(1) 1N34 diode
(1) 365-pF variable tuning capacitor
(1) 1-1/4″ angle bracket with mounting holes
(1) radio knob
(1) high impedance (2,000 + ohms) transistor radio earphones
(80′) No. 24 enameled copper wire
(16′) rubber-coated hookup wire
(4) small wood screws
(4) small nuts and bolts (electrical circuit type)

pletion of the last turn. Keep one hand on the coil so it won't unwind, and make Hole 4. Pass the leftover 6″ of wire, just cut, through that opening and back out through Hole 3.

Again using the heated needle, form Holes 5, 6, and 7 on a line about 3/16″ above the previously wound coil. Place one end of a *fresh* section of copper wire through Hole 5 and back out Hole 6, so that a 6″ length extends from that hole. Wind another 25 turns of wire and cut it, again leaving about 6″ of excess wire.

Then, while holding the wire taut so as not to lose the turns, make Holes 8, 9, and 10. Pass the unsecured 6″ wire piece through Hole 8 and back out through Hole 9. Thread the end of the unused wire through Hole 10 and back out Hole 9. There should now be *two* wires exiting from Hole 9, both of which are about 6″ in length.

Continue winding the remaining wire until you've completed 50 or 60 turns, starting from Hole 10. As before, cut the wire at a point 6″ from the completion of the last turn and, while holding the coil, make Hole 11. Pass the final 6″ of wire through the new opening and back out through Hole 7.

To complete the coil, wrap a piece of electrical tape once or twice around the upper few turns—to prevent them from slipping off the top of the form and undoing your work—

and connect the wrapped container to its cap.

OTHER COMPONENTS: The next step is to drill two holes in the mounting board, one each for the antenna post and the ground post. (Refer to Fig. 2 before starting.) Locate each 1/8″ opening about 1″ in front of the coil and about 5/8″ from the edge of the board.

Trim the wires coming from Holes 1 and 3 back to about 3-1/4″ in length and use medium-fine sandpaper to remove the enamel insulation from the last inch or so of each. Wrap the uninsulated portion of one of these wires around the threaded section of a 5-way binding post, press the threaded portion through one of the holes just drilled, and fasten the post in place with its small hex nut. Repeat this procedure for the other wire, hole, and post.

Shorten each of the two wires that exit from Hole 9 to about 4″ and strip the insulation from the final inch of each. Drill another 1/8″ hole about 1″ in front of the coil and midway between the two posts. Pass a small bolt through one of the Fahnestock clips, wrap the uninsulated ends of the wires extending from Hole 9 around the bolt threads, and secure the assembly to the board with a nut.

At this point, remove the plug from the end of the transistor earphone cord and carefully separate

about 4″ of the double wire, leaving the insulation intact. Then, using wire cutters or a penknife, strip the insulation from the last inch of each of the rubber-coated pieces.

Another 1/8″ hole should now be drilled, about 2″ from the coil and 3/4″ from the left side of the board (as viewed with the coil's holes facing you). Assemble the second Fahnestock clip and bolt, and secure one of the uninsulated earphone wires to the clip in the same manner in which you attached the wires from Hole 9 to the first fastener. Secure the assembly to the board with a nut.

By pressing down on the end of the Fahnestock clip, you can now insert one end of the diode wire through the hook in the clip's center. Repeat this process with the other end of the diode and the other clip, making certain that the diode tip with the colored band on it is closest to the clip that's most distant from the coil.

Mount the angle bracket at a point that's the same distance from the coil as is the foremost Fahnestock clip, and on the opposite side of the board (as shown in the photograph). Removing the two hex nuts from the shank of the tuning capacitor, insert that shaft into the hole in the angle bracket, and refasten the two nuts. Fit a knob to the end of the tuning shaft to make tuning your homemade radio easier.

Cut each of the remaining two wires (from Holes 6 and 7) to about 4-3/4″, strip the insulation from the final 1-1/4″ of each, and wrap the uninsulated portion of the remaining earphone wire around the left terminal of the tuning capacitor. (If your capacitor has both terminals on the same side, it makes no difference which one is used.) Encircle the terminal with the uninsulated portion of the wire from Hole 7, forming a double layer of wires. They may now be soldered, crimped, or taped to the terminal.

Finally, twist the wire from Hole 6 around the other terminal of the tuner, and solder, tape, or crimp the connection. Complete the assembly of your homemade radio by fastening the two small wooden blocks to the underside of the mounting board.

ANTENNA ASSEMBLY: For the best performance from your radio, connect it to a good antenna/ground system. To prepare for such a hookup, attach sections of rubber-coated wire, each 40″ to 80″ in length, to the antenna post and to the ground post. It would also be convenient to fasten alligator clips to the ends of both of these wires.

If you live in or near a city with a radio station, simply connect the antenna to the metal finger-stop on your telephone and the phone lines as an antenna. If, however, you don't own a phone—or if you do, but reside well out of town—it'll be necessary to string up an outdoor antenna. The

same No. 24 wire that you used to make the coil will do a good job.

Ideally, the antenna should be between 80 and 115 feet in length and as high as is practical. For optimum performance, insulate each end of the antenna from its respective mounting and connect the radio to the antenna, using the shortest piece of rubber-coated wire possible. Last of all, secure the ground wire to a water pipe or to a metal rod driven well into the earth.

After all those connections have been made, you'll be able to pick up stations simply by adjusting the variable tuning capacitor.

WHAT YOU'LL GET: You now possess a radio that won't stop playing as long as there's a signal strong

enough for it to pick up, and one that requires no maintenance, as long as you don't play catch with it.

Don't be surprised, though, if you hear some rather strange sounds emanating from your earphone from time to time. The radio should receive stations across the entire AM band, as well as some signals on the low end of the shortwave band. You might even be able to pick up broadcasts from the LORAN beacon, which provides navigational aid to ships at sea.

Even if you seldom actually use the homemade receiver, you'll be glad to know that you'll always have access to the airways, come what may, and that the device will play almost forever, for free!

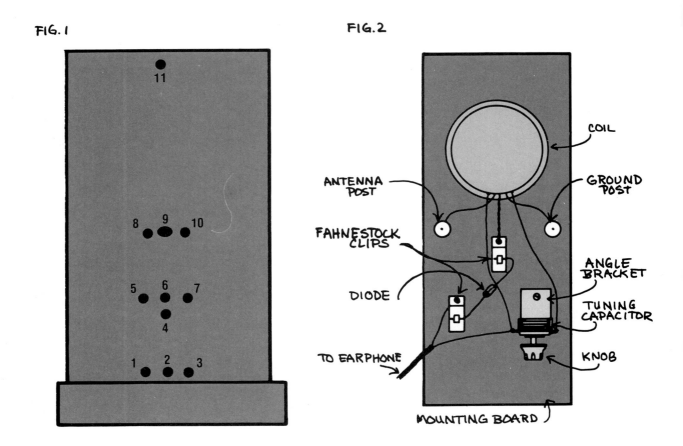

FIG. 1

FIG. 2

HOMESTEAD WORKSHOP PROJECTS

CEMENT MIXER

Numerous jobs regularly appear around the home or farmstead that require mixing up a small batch of concrete or mortar. Done by hand, this is an unpleasant and backbreaking task, and purchasing a power cement mixer to turn out bucket-sized loads is impractical. However, by using the drum of a discarded top-loading washing machine as the mixing vessel and mounting it on a mobile pipe frame, you can outfit yourself with a versatile hand-powered mixer that's ideal for most of the jobs you'll want to tackle on your own.

You should be able to construct the entire mixer, using only a pipe wrench, a drill with 3/32″ and 1/4″ bits, a screwdriver, a hacksaw, and an adjustable wrench. You'll also need to gather the materials shown in the accompanying illustration, plus a quart of auto body putty.

Start by fabricating the three paddles that will be mounted inside the drum. If you're fortunate, you'll be able to find some brackets, corner supports, or angle-iron scrap that can simply be trimmed and mounted with a minimum of fuss. If not, however, you'll have to cut the blades from 18-gauge sheet metal, bend them, and drill two 1/4″ holes in each section, as shown in the diagram. Then bore matching holes in

the tub and secure the agitators in position, using 1/4″ bolts. Once that's done, you can also liberally apply body putty to the bottom and sides of the vessel's inside to seal the holes.

Assemble the frame by threading together pieces of galvanized iron pipe. Mount the smaller (rear) rollers by sliding a bolt through the disks and the tee fitting and fastening it with a nut. Attach the main wheels by slipping the axle shaft through its tubular housing and putting on the wheels and washers. To make them secure, mark and drill the cotter pin holes as close as possible to the disks, remove the washers and wheels, grease and reassemble the front axle and roller unit, and fasten it together with two cotter pins.

The mixing drum rotates on the shaft fastened to the central pipe cross and is bushed with a 10″ section of 1-1/4″ electrical metallic tubing (EMT). Grease the pipe "axle", slip the conduit over it, and lubricate the assembly again. Then slide the tub over the shaft, and thread on the pipe cap to hold the components in place. It's a good idea to put some lubricant on the frame's "spine" bar at the points where it contacts the vat to aid the rotation process.

Finally, you can paint the assembly, and once you attach a set of bicycle grips to the handles, your mixer will be ready to use!

This machine can hold one full 40-pound bag of ready-mix without any problem. For most people, it's easy enough just to grab the rim of the tub and pull it around by hand to stir up the "mud". When the drum is rotated in the correct direction, the angled paddle blades should bite into the gritty substance, and each blade should drop its load as it reaches the top of the drum. Optional handles can be attached to the outside of the drum by mounting them to the 1/4″ bolts that hold the paddles, though longer bolts may be needed. If these grips are added, be certain they clear all parts of the frame.

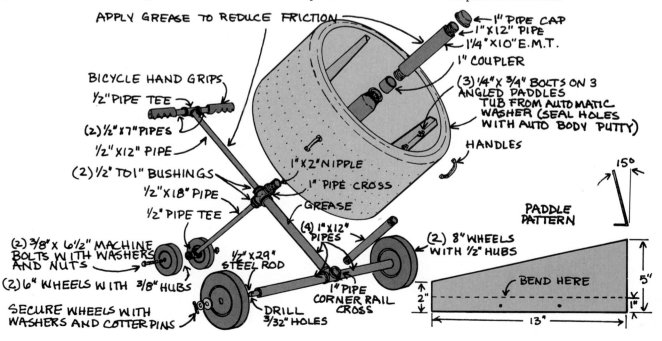

APPLY GREASE TO REDUCE FRICTION

1″ PIPE CAP
1″ X 12″ PIPE
1¼″ X 10″ E.M.T.
1″ COUPLER
(3) ¼″ X ¾″ BOLTS ON 3 ANGLED PADDLES
TUB FROM AUTOMATIC WASHER (SEAL HOLES WITH AUTO BODY PUTTY)
HANDLES

BICYCLE HAND GRIPS
½″ PIPE TEE
(2) ½″ X 7″ PIPES
½″ X 12″ PIPE
(2) ½″ TO 1″ BUSHINGS
½″ X 18″ PIPE
½″ PIPE TEE

1″ X 2″ NIPPLE
1″ PIPE CROSS
GREASE
(4) 1″ X 12″ PIPES

(2) 3/8″ X 6½″ MACHINE BOLTS WITH WASHERS AND NUTS
(2) 6″ WHEELS WITH 3/8″ HUBS
SECURE WHEELS WITH WASHERS AND COTTER PINS

½″ X 29″ STEEL ROD
DRILL 3/32″ HOLES

1″ PIPE CORNER RAIL CROSS
(2) 8″ WHEELS WITH ½″ HUBS

15°
PADDLE PATTERN
BEND HERE
5″
2″
1″
13″

CIDER PRESS

A century ago, the home cider press was a familiar sight in rural America. Today, however, you're not likely to encounter one anywhere but in antique shops, *unless*, that is, you choose to go ahead and build your own. This design combines an apple grinder and a press, to get as much delicious juice from the harvest as possible.

GATHERING YOUR MATERIALS: Start by collecting the necessary hardware. The only item you're likely to have difficulty in locating is a pressing screw, which may be bought, or else reclaimed from a discarded office chair. The other metal parts include the chain, crank, chainwheel, and bottom bracket assembly from a scrapped bicycle, plus a 3/4″ X 12″ shaft to serve as an axle, two 3/4″ brass bushings, a 1/4″ X 2″ roll pin, a 3/4″-bore sprocket with a diameter about 2/7 that of the chainwheel, and a 20-pound pulley or flywheel that fits on the steel axle. You'll also need a section of 3/4″ pipe that's about 20″ long, two pipe caps, an 8″ length of 1/8″ X 1″ X 2″ X 1″ channel iron, a 1/4″ X 1-1/2″ X 8″ metal plate, 16-gauge flat stock measuring 3/4″ X 220″ (it's best to buy a full 20-foot piece to avoid paying a cutting charge), and the assorted fastening hardware that's specified in the diagram on page 94.

Next, select the lumber to be used. The press's framework can be made of yellow pine, but the two bottomless tubs (in which the ground apples are first caught and then pressed), the hopper, grinding drum, drum housing, screw guide, and trough walls are made of oak, which is sturdy and doesn't affect the cider's flavor. An 8-foot length of 2 X 6, a 33″ piece of 2 X 8, and two sections of 2 X 4—one 8 and the other 10 feet long—will be enough pine to complete your frame, and about 24 feet of 1 X 6 oak should be adequate to supply all the hardwood components. You'll also need a few scraps of pine to use when making the hopper cover, its handle, and a pressing foot support, as well as a section of plywood, measuring 3/4″ X 14″ X

42″, from which to fabricate the trough base and the pressing foot itself.

To avoid halving a component that should have remained whole, plan your cuts *before* making them. As an example, you should cut the two 34-1/2″, the 17-1/2″, and the 6-1/2″ frame sections from the 8-foot 2 X 4. Also, order the oak in two lengths —10 and 14 feet—then cut all the 3/4″ X 1-1/4″ X 12″ tub staves (20 for each tub) from the smaller of the pieces. Once you've trimmed everything to the sizes indicated in the diagram, go ahead and complete the cross-lap and dado joints as shown, and cut the notches in the trough rails to the proper dimensions. Remember, too, that the trough walls must be grooved to accept the 3/4″ plywood base.

PUTTING IT TOGETHER: You may find that two components of the press are a little tedious to assemble. The first is the tapered hopper, which requires that you make a compound joint, one that connects two angled pieces of wood. If you've never had experience with this admittedly difficult carpentry task, the bin *can* be fashioned much more easily by simply butting the sides and ends together and securing them with screws to produce a box-shaped hopper.

The other time-consuming chore is assembling the grinding drum. Begin this job by cutting part of your flat stock into 48 small bars—1-1/2″ long apiece—and bending each one, in a vise, to form an L shape with 1/4″ and 1″ legs (the remaining quarter-inch will be used up in the bend).

Next, take your six 5″-diameter disks and drill eight evenly spaced 1/8″ holes through each wooden

plate at points 3/4″ from the outer edge. Then use a coping saw to cut two slots—one 3/4″ and the other 1/4″ long—outward from each of the 1/8″ holes and at right angles to each other so that the longer of the two, following the radius of the circle, slices through the edge of the disk. When all 48 L-shaped slots are formed, take a small hammer and tap the angled metal bars firmly into place within their respective "cradles". The bars will protrude from the slots approximately 1/4″ to become the apple-grinding teeth.

Finally, complete your drum by gluing all the toothed disks together (let the teeth form a random pattern, as shown in the illustration), drilling a 3/4″ bore through the *exact* midpoint of the resulting wooden cylinder, and making a second hole— 1/4″ in diameter—perpendicular to the axle bore and going *through* one side of the drum and partially into the other. Before inserting the axle shaft and its roll pin, however, revolve the grinding assembly slowly, and true its teeth as necessary—with a file or wheel—to prevent a lateral wobble when the machine is in use. With this done, you can slip the axle shaft through the bushings and drum, align it properly, and then drill on through the axle and pin the shaft in its place.

The metalworking portion of this project is fairly straightforward. What's left of the flat stock is used to band the tub staves together (the oak slats ought to be about 1/4″ apart, and the straps' ends should overlap an inch or so), and installing the screw and pressing foot support bracket involves nothing more than bolting them in place.

To make the drive mechanism, just cut the bottom bracket assembly (the part that holds the pedals and sprocket) from the bike, and grind what's left of the frame tubes flush with the cylinder to produce a smooth surface. Then lop off the pedal crank *opposite* the chainwheel, remove the rubber and frame from the remaining pedal, and weld the crank's circular housing to the surface of the 1/4″ X 1-1/2″ X

8″ bar, close to the end. Next, temporarily place the bar on top of the press frame's single leg, and wrap the bicycle chain around the large and small sprocket to determine where it should be cut in order to fit. After rejoining the ends with a connecting link, move the crank mount until the chain is taut, and secure the assembly to the frame.

SOME FINAL WORDS: The last step is to finish the wooden parts. With the exception of the pressing foot and the inner surface of the juice trough, everything should be given a coat of polyurethane varnish. Since the excepted components will be repeatedly exposed to the squeezings, they must be covered with two layers of fiberglass resin.

When the mill is complete and fully "cured", you're ready to make cider. Since the job is much less messy when you use a filter, take the trouble to line your tubs with several layers of cheesecloth or with some clean *white* pillowcases before you begin. In choosing your apples, remember that using several varieties tends to make the best cider. And even though minor bruises and dents in the fruits won't harm the flavor of your final product, be certain to remove rotten or moldy spots before you run the apples through the grinder.

If you feel energetic, feed whole apples into the hopper. On the other hand, you might want to halve or quarter them prior to grinding, both to make the mechanism a bit easier to turn and to assure that the "meat" is well chopped. In either case, crank with one hand and press down firmly on the hopper lid with the other. Once you've run a bushel or so through the grinder (the hopper holds about half a peck), you can slide the first tub under the press and have a friend start grinding anew, using the second oak "bucket" as a receptacle. Meanwhile, *you* can begin to squeeze out the juice (which will run into a pail under the trough's spout). Be sure to really lean into the screw handle, too, so you don't leave any of the precious liquid in the pulp. Depending on how earnestly you grind and press (and on the quality of the fruit), the little mill will yield anywhere from three quarts to more than two gallons of apple cider per bushel.

When you've used up your supply of apples (utilize the leftover pulp as compost or livestock feed), hose down the press. Then you can relax and quench your thirst with the fruity ambrosia!

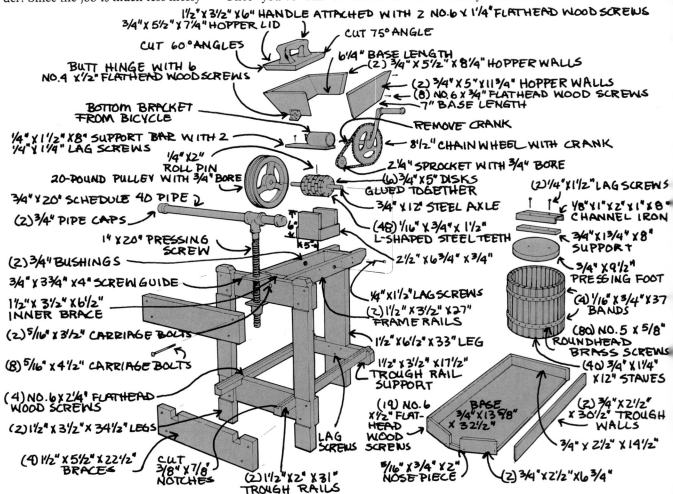

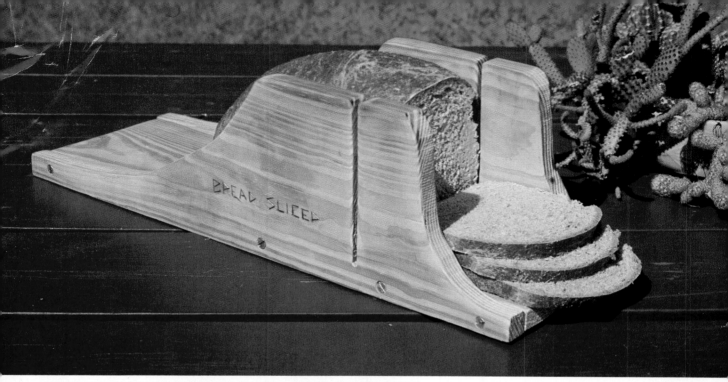

BREAD SLICER

Anyone who makes or loves to eat homemade bread—but who has never been able to cut it into straight and even slices—will really appreciate this combination bread slicer/cutting board/serving tray. With it, loaves of bread can be cut into perfect slices, as thin as you wish.

This handy gadget works on the same principle as a carpenter's miter box, and though it was designed with bread in mind, it's also suitable for cutting eggplant, squash, cheese, or almost any other sliceable food that fits into it. Just slide the item into place, position the blade of a long, sharp knife in the slots, and the slices come out straight and true.

The whole slicer can be made from one piece of wood measuring 3/4″ X 6″ X 54″. The plank is cut into three 18″ lengths, two of which are shaped as sides before being fastened to the third, which forms the bottom of the slicer.

The model shown here is big enough to handle loaves made in most bread pans, but it can be easily scaled up to slice larger baked goods.

Feel free to shape the sides according to your own taste. Regardless of the design chosen, it'll be easier and quicker to clamp the two pieces of wood together and cut and slot both sides at the same time. And those slots, of course, should be cut down far enough so that—on assembly—they'll come out just even with the base's top surface.

Sand the surfaces of all three pieces of wood untill they're clean and smooth. Then assemble the unit with eight 2″-long wood screws, four on a side. For an even tighter fit, run a bead of good wood glue down the faces of each joint before screwing the sides of the slicer to its base. The completed bread slicer may be left unfinished, rubbed with vegetable oil, or stained and coated with a hard, oil-resistant finish.

For a decorative touch, drill a hole in one end of the slicer's base so it can be hung on the wall when it's not in use.

This useful tool will be a welcome addition to your own kitchen and a great help for the bread lovers on your gift list, too!

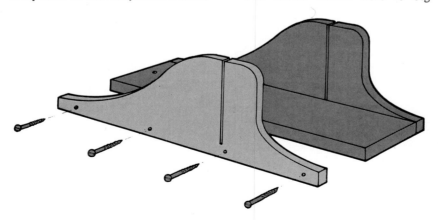

WINCH

Around every home there are lifting, hoisting, or pulling chores that crop up and are difficult for a person to tackle without mechanical assistance. For many of these jobs, a winch capable of lifting a ton without strain is the most practical tool. By following the steps outlined here, you can build a versatile model that's well suited to numerous tasks.

LIST OF MATERIALS

Base	(1) 3/16″ X 2″ X 7″ X 2″ U-shaped channel	31″ long
Anchors	(4) 1/8″ X 2″ X 2″ angle	3″ long
Support brackets	(4) 3/16″ X 3″ X 10″ X 3″ U-shaped channel	7″ long
	(8) 5/16″ X 1-1/4″ hex bolts, nuts, washers	
	(8) existing transmission mounting bolts	
	(1) 7″ X 10″ piece of rubber inner tube	
Drum	(1) 4″-diameter Schedule 40 pipe	9-1/2″ long
	(1) 3/4″ Schedule 40 pipe (drum axle)	14″ long
	(1) 1″ Schedule 40 pipe (spacer)	1″ long
	(2) 7″-diameter disks of 16-gauge sheet metal	
	(1) 4″-diameter spur gear	
	(1) 6″-diameter V-pulley	
	(1) U-joint splined hub (compatible with transmission shaft)	
Crank	(1) 3/4″ Schedule 40 pipe	8″ long
	(1) 3/4″ Schedule 40 pipe	16″ long
	(1) 3/4″ Schedule 40 pipe	2-1/2″ long
	(2) 3/4″ pipe elbows	
	(1) clutch plate (compatible with transmission shaft)	
Brake and pawl	(1) 1″ X 5/16″ flat plate (brake handle)	18″ long
	(1) 1-3/8″ X 5/16″ flat plate (pawl)	8″ long
	(2) 1-3/8″ X 5/16″ flat plate (support brackets)	4-1/2″ long
	(1) 1/2″ steel bolt (pivot pin)	5″ long
	(2) 5/16″ X 2″ bolts, nuts, flat washers	
	(5) 1/2″ flat washers	
	(1) 1/8″ X 1″ cotter pin	
	(1) extension spring with 3/8″ flat washer for mount	
	(3) 5-44 X 1-1/4″ bolts with washers and nuts	
	(1) 40″ X 1/2″ V-belt	
Cable	(1) 50 feet of 3/16″ steel cable	
	(1) steel hook with pin and clamps	
Miscellaneous	(2) rubber handgrips	

FINDING PARTS: Start the project by locating a discarded manual shift car or truck at a local scrap iron dealer or an auto wrecking yard. Almost any make or model of manual gearbox will do, but the type with the gear-changing mechanism built right into the transmission's cover plate works best, because there's no shift linkage outside the box to mess with.

Also needed are a number of channel, angle, and flat iron pieces to make the base and various supports for the winch. The remaining components include the pulley and belt, both of which can be salvaged from an old washing machine, the automotive parts, and the pipe.

BEGIN BUILDING: Remove the tailshaft housing, which holds the speedometer cable and is bolted to the rear of the gearbox, from the transmission and cut out a scrap of rubber inner tube the same size and shape as the box's rear plate. This piece of rubber will serve as a gasket between the transmission and the cut-down U-channel which supports that end of the gearbox. When cutting out the gasket, locate and make holes in the rubber for the mounting bolts and the transmission's main shaft, all of which will pass through the gasket.

All four of the 3/16″ X 3″ X 10″ X 7″ main support brackets are cut from one 28″-long piece of 3/16″ X 3″ X 10″ X 3″ U-shaped channel. If you don't own a gas torch, a local welder can do all the necessary metal cutting for you.

Lay down the 31″-long section of 3/16″ X 2″ X 7″ X 2″ channel that serves as the base and place the transmission on it. Then turn two of the main support brackets up on edge with one of the 3″ side lips flush against the base, and set them against the gearbox's main shaft, one in front and the other at the rear of the transmission. Cut these brackets off about 1-1/2″ above the top of the shaft, drill a 1-1/16″ hole through each plate where it touches the shaft's end, and then trim both brackets down to form the tapered shape shown in the illustration. These will be the crank and drum brackets.

Follow the same procedure with the two channel-iron brackets that fit right up against the faces of the gearbox itself. This time, however, it will be necessary to drill holes in the plates to match the bolt patterns on the front and rear of the transmission. You'll also have to cut out a slot on the front bracket large enough to

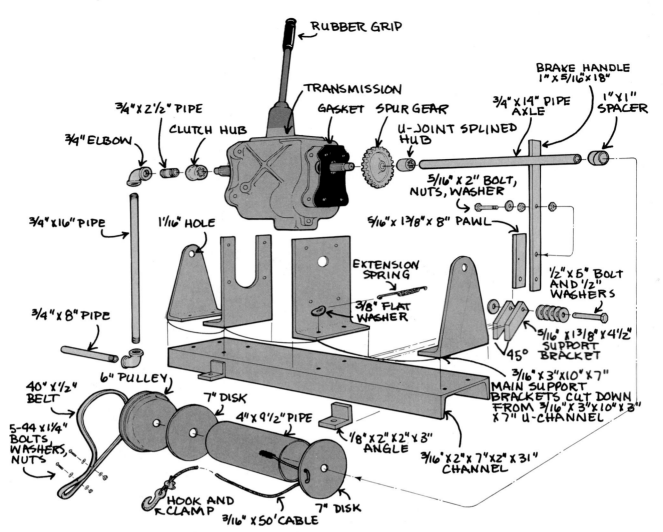

RUBBER GRIP

BRAKE HANDLE 1" x 5/16" x 18"

3/4" x 2 1/2" PIPE

CLUTCH HUB

3/4" ELBOW

TRANSMISSION
GASKET SPUR GEAR

3/4" x 14" PIPE AXLE

1" x 1" SPACER

U-JOINT SPLINED HUB

3/4" x 16" PIPE

1 1/16" HOLE

5/16" x 2" BOLT, NUTS, WASHER

5/16" x 1 3/8" x 8" PAWL

EXTENSION SPRING

1/2" x 5" BOLT AND 1/2" WASHERS

3/4" x 8" PIPE

3/8" FLAT WASHER

5/16" x 1 3/8" x 4 1/2" SUPPORT BRACKET

45°

40" x 1/2" BELT

6" PULLEY

7" DISK

4" x 9 1/2" PIPE

1/8" x 2" x 2" x 3" ANGLE

3/16" x 3" x 10" x 7" MAIN SUPPORT BRACKETS CUT DOWN FROM 3/16" x 3" x 10" x 3" x 7" U-CHANNEL

5-44 x 1 1/4" BOLTS, WASHERS, NUTS

3/16" x 2" x 7" x 2" x 31" CHANNEL

HOOK AND CLAMP

3/16" x 50' CABLE

7" DISK

allow the gearbox's case to mount flush against the support. Once the two brackets have been trimmed to size and drilled, slip the newly made rubber gasket onto the rear of the transmission and bolt the supports firmly to the gearbox using the original bolts if possible.

The transmission should now be positioned on the channel-iron base so that its front is about 8" from one end. Drill a couple of holes through the foot of each of the brackets attached to it and through the base channel. Then bolt the box in place with four 5/16" X 1-1/4" bolts, nuts, and lock washers. Note that an additional 3/8" flat washer with an edge bent up and drilled is slipped under one of the bolt heads before it's cinched down. The tension spring for a ratchet pawl will hook into the

drilled hole later, during the final assembly of the winch's accessory parts.

HANDLE WITH CARE: Naturally, the longer the handle on a winch, the greater the leverage and the ease in pulling or lifting a heavy load. This winch is fitted with a handle approximately 1-1/2-feet long. Since the radius of the circle defined when the handle is turned is greater than the distance from the transmission's shaft to the base of the winch, the unit must be mounted to allow clearance for a full turn of the handle, or another arrangement must be made. The design includes a locking ratchet so the handle is not constantly under load and a splined connector where the handle meets the shaft so the crank can be pulled free of the shaft, turned to a new position, and

reengaged to do more work.

The splined connector requires a cast-off clutch plate whose hub has splines that will mate with those of the transmissions's input shaft. Cut out the hub and weld it to the 2-1/2"-long 3/4" pipe nipple. Then slip the nipple through the 1-1/16" hole at the top of one of the triangular support brackets, making sure the fit is loose but not sloppy, and thread a 3/4" pipe elbow onto the nipple's other end. Position the bracket so it's easy both to slip the hub onto and to pull it off the transmission's shaft, then drill two 5/16" holes and bolt the support securely to the base.

Finish the crank by threading the 16" length of 3/4" pipe into the open end of the just-mounted elbow, put another 90° elbow on the pipe's other end, and screw the 8" length of

3/4″ pipe into that. Be sure to weld all the threaded joints together so they'll never come apart during the winch's use.

HELP WITH HOISTING: The hoist's business end is made by cutting the splined hub from an old universal joint and welding it to a spur gear about 4″ in diameter. The gear's hub size isn't critical, as long as it fits over the splined shaft that comes out of the transmission. Weld a 14″-long piece of pipe to the other end of the U-joint's splined hub, allowing the pipe to extend about 1/2″ into the hub for extra strength, slip a 6″-diameter V-belt pulley over the axle, cutting some material out of the pulley's hub if necessary, and weld the pulley to the splined hub, too.

Cut two 7″-diameter disks from some scrap 16-gauge sheet metal and drill a 1-1/16″ hole in the center of each of these drum end plates. Slip the first one over the axle and weld it securely to the pulley. Then center a 9-1/2″-long section of 4″ pipe (the drum itself) on the plate, slide the second end plate down the axle until it touches the drum's other end, and weld the assembly securely together. It is important that the section of pipe is true on the end plates so the finished drum won't be off-center as it rotates. One good way to true up this assembly is to cut four pieces of wood to the same width and then

squeeze them, equally spaced around the axle, in between the 3/4″ shaft and the 4″ drum before it's welded to the end plates.

Slip an inch-long piece of 1″ pipe over the 3/4″ pipe shaft, slide this spacer up against the drum assembly, loop the brake belt over the V-pulley, drill two 5/16″ holes through the foot of the last main support bracket, push the bracket up loosely against the spacer, and bolt the support to the base.

For the brake and pawl assembly, cut a 45° angle onto one end of each of the two 5/16″ X 1-3/8″ X 4-1/2″ brake- and pawl-support brackets. Weld the supports to the side of the base directly under the drum assembly's spur gear, with the 5/16″ X 1-3/8″ X 8″ pawl stock positioned between the two brackets so that it contacts the spur gear's teeth squarely.

Then drill a 1/2″ hole through the support brackets, the pawl, and one end of the 5/16″ X 1″ X 18″ brake handle. Two 5/16″ holes should also be drilled through the brake handle at this time. Drill the first 4″ above the 1/2″ hole and the second 6″ above the first. This is also a good time to drill a 1/4″ hole through the pawl about 4″ down from its top for the tension spring to hook into.

After that, run a 1/2″ X 5″ bolt through a flat washer, the butt end of the brake handle, four more washers,

the first support bracket, the butt end of the pawl, the second support, and another washer. Drill a 1/8″ hole through the bolt's end and secure the whole assembly with a 1/8″ X 1″ cotter pin. Hook one end of the spring to the 1/4″ hole in the pawl arm and the other end to the hole in the bent-up washer bolted to the main support bracket. Place a 5/16″ X 2″ bolt in each of the brake handle's two 5/16″ holes, using two nuts, one on each side of the bar, to firmly cinch each bolt in place. These will secure the brake band.

Weld four 1/8″ X 2″ X 2″ X 3″ angle-iron brackets to the base and drill 3/8″ holes through them so you can bolt the hoist down so it won't move under a load. Then take the whole unit outside, wash it down thoroughly with solvent, and give it a couple of coats of a bright industrial paint.

AND YOU'RE READY TO GO: It's now a simple matter to slip a couple of rubber handgrips over the winch's bare metal handles. It's also easy to slide the V-belt into the pulley's groove, wrap it around the brake handle's lower bolt, and then hook the belt up over the handle's top bolt as shown. Hold the belt in place by drilling two or three 1/8″ holes through both sides of the loop and fastening the sides together with 5-44 X 1-1/4″ bolts.

Finally, the 3/16″ steel cable is permanently fastened to the winch's drum by passing it through two 1/4″ holes drilled approximately 1-1/4″ apart in the "outside" drum end plate. Loop the cable through the holes as illustrated so that 4″ lies on the drum, and braze it in place. The other end of the cable is formed into a loop, and a hook is attached to it with standard cable clamps.

Bolt your winch down, hook the cable to anything that it'll hold, select a gear (reverse can be used, but the crank must be turned the opposite direction), and crank away. The ratchet and pawl will prevent the cable from suddenly paying out when you let go of the crank, and the brake can be hand-operated (with light loads) when the pawl's released.

MOUSETRAPS

The two devices shown here look very different: One is sleek and functional and the other quite basic. But they both will handily trap a hungry mouse, holding it captive till you release it to an appropriate place.

You probably have on hand the few materials needed, and the only tools required for making both catchers are a coping saw, a ruler, a hammer, a nail set, a pair of wire cutters, and a drill with an assortment of bits.

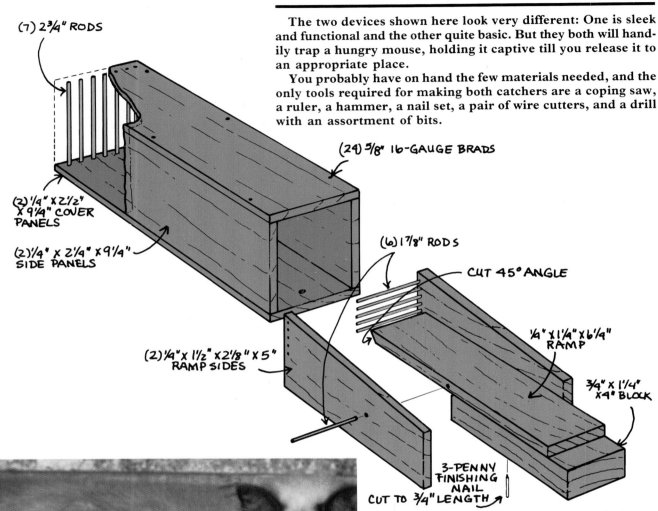

(7) 2¾" RODS

(24) ⅝" 16-GAUGE BRADS

(2) ¼" X 2½" X 9¼" COVER PANELS

(2) ¼" X 2¼" X 9¼" SIDE PANELS

(6) 1⅞" RODS

CUT 45° ANGLE

¼" X 1¼" X 6¼" RAMP

(2) ¼" X 1½" X 2⅛" X 5" RAMP SIDES

¾" X 1¼" X 4" BLOCK

3-PENNY FINISHING NAIL CUT TO ¾" LENGTH

WOODEN CELL: Begin by cutting a strip of pine that's 1/4" X 2-1/2" X 54" to produce the pieces called for in the illustration. Once this is done, use a No. 48 bit to drill lines of holes—keeping the individual bores about 5/16" apart—with each series parallel to and 1/4" from one of the ends of each 1/4" X 2-1/2" X 9-1/4" panel and the wide end of each 1/4" X 1-1/2" X 2-1/8" X 5" panel. Drill yet another hole through each of the smaller panels, at a point 1" from the straight edge and 3-1/4" from the wide end. (To keep the openings lined up, it's best to clamp the matching pairs of pieces together, then bore the holes. Note that the lines of openings in the

HOMESTEAD WORKSHOP PROJECTS

ends of the two wedge-shaped panels don't extend all the way across the pieces, but terminate 1-1/4″ down from the peaked corners.)

Next, clip apart a coat hanger to form bars of two different lengths. You'll need six that are 1-7/8″ long and seven that are 2-3/4″ long. With this done, tack the box together using some 16-gauge, 5/8″ wire brads, making sure that the walls are positioned *between* the top and bottom boards and that the bar holes in the upper and lower panels are at the same end of

the box. Then tap the seven hanger rods into place and drill a 1/8″ hole through the bottom board, being certain it's centered and is 3/4″ from the end opposite the bars.

Assemble the ramp mechanism by tacking the narrow ends of the wedge-shaped pieces to the sides of a 3/4″ X 1-1/4″ X 4″ softwood block. The lower edges of the 1/4″ walls should be flush with the bottom of the block, and the joint should be 1-3/4″ long. Then tap five more bars into the aligned openings. Fashion a security

pin by cutting a 3/4″ piece from the finishing nail and drive it into the bottom of the softwood block at a point 1″ from its inside edge.

Finally, trim one end of the remaining 1/4″ X 1-1/4″ X 6-1/4″ wooden slab to a 45° angle, then drill a 3/32″ hole through its width, 2-3/4″ from the angled tip. Secure the piece between the walls of its housing by running the last 1-7/8″ hanger rod through the side sections *and* the bore in the ramp.

To use the trap, just set some bait inside near the bars, and place the ramp assembly—grille first—into the tunnel's open end till the finishing nail falls into the locking hole. Your "prey" will enter the opening at the end of the trap, and its weight will cause the ramp to fall, allowing the critter to get at the food. But once the mouse steps off the ramp, that offset part will fall back into place and block the only route to freedom.

SOLITARY CAN-FINEMENT: This tin-can calaboose is very down-to-earth and not too attractive, but it really does work. If you'd like to try it out, simply find a wire coat hanger, a soup can with a lid, and two thin rubber bands. Then, using a 1/8″ bit, drill 12 holes into the can and the lid at the places indicated in the drawing.

Next, cut the coat hanger to form five rods of the following lengths: one 3″, two 4″, one 6″, and the last 9″. Then, using a pair of needle-nosed pliers, start to bend the pieces to the shapes illustrated. (The best way to do this is to form the rods to near completion, but in each case leave a straight section so you can slip them into their respective openings, then *finish* the bending process once they're in the holes.) Rubber bands, stretched between the hooks on the door and the back of the legs, snap the cover shut when the latch is released.

The gizmo is set by first wrapping bait around the "crank" of the catch rod, then securing the door's latch arm under the catch's elbowed tip. When the tiny pest tugs at its dinner, the lid "pulls to", and the mouse will be securely canned until you're ready to grant a reprieve.

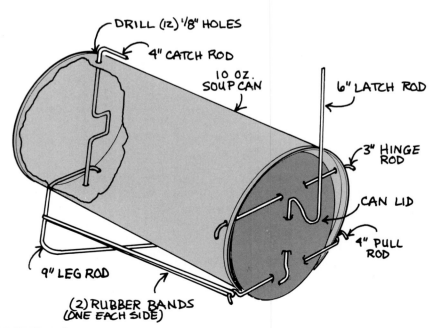

DRILL (12) 1/8″ HOLES

4″ CATCH ROD

10 OZ. SOUP CAN

6″ LATCH ROD

3″ HINGE ROD

CAN LID

4″ PULL ROD

9″ LEG ROD

(2) RUBBER BANDS (ONE EACH SIDE)

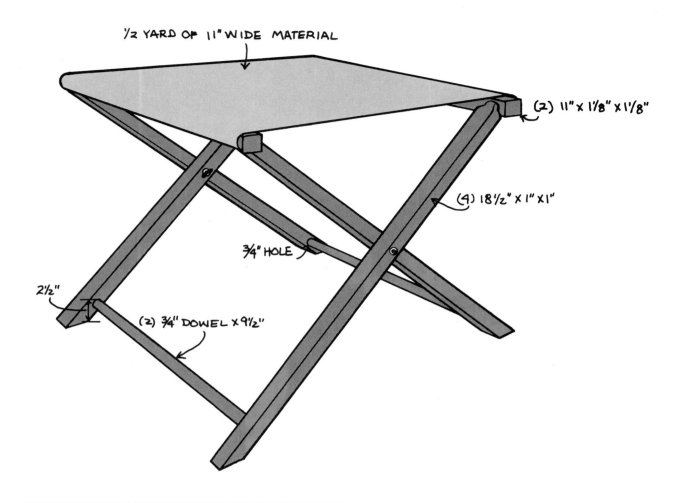

½ YARD OF 11" WIDE MATERIAL

(2) 11" X 1⅛" X 1⅛"

(4) 18½" X 1" X 1"

¾" HOLE

2½"

(2) ¾" DOWEL X 9½"

CAMP STOOL

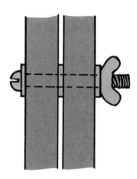

A sturdy fold-up stool could be one of the easiest-to-build— and certainly one of the handiest—pieces of camping equipment to come from your workshop.

While hardwood is best for this folding seat, any sturdy wood is suitable. Using the stock you have available, make four 1″-square, 18-1/2″-long legs; two 1-1/8″-square, 11″-long top bars; and two lower rails cut from 3/4″ dowel, each 9-1/2″ long.

Shape the upper ends of the legs as shown in the sketch so they'll fit into 5/8″ holes bored in the top bars. The centers of the holes should be 7-5/8″ apart in one bar and 9-5/8″ apart in the other. The lower rails of the stool should be fitted into 3/4″ cavities drilled 2-1/2″ from the bottom of each leg.

Join the two stool supports by boring a hole in the middle of each leg. Insert a bolt through each pair of crossed legs, with a washer on either side of the legs and another placed between them (see sketch), and secure the bolt with a wing nut.

Finally, stretch 1/2 yard sturdy 11″-wide material over the top of the stool and nail the cloth securely to the underside of the upper bars. The wood may be finished if you like.

TOYS FOR ALL AGES

TABLE SOCCER GAME

Why spend a fortune on a professionally built table soccer game when you can build one fit for an arcade for one sixth the commercial model's price? In exchange for some workshop time and scrap materials, you can have a game that develops eye-hand coordination, strong wrists, and team spirit. All that, plus hours of good plain fun, can be yours.

COLLECT MATERIALS: A miniature soccer field can be constructed with the materials specified in the accompanying illustrations and the use of the following tools: a circular or table saw, a drill with an assortment of bits, a coping saw, a hammer, a screwdriver, some finish-grade sandpaper, a pair of wire cutters, a hacksaw, a compass, and a tape measure.

Major components of the project can be cut from a 33" X 48" sheet of 3/8" plywood, a 40" X 48" sheet of 3/4" plywood (or, better yet, one 10-foot and two 8-foot lengths of 1 X 6), a pair of 12-foot 2 X 4's, three 3-foot lengths of 1" dowel, four 10-foot sections of 1/2" electrical metallic tubing, a 36" X 66" section of white plastic laminate, and a 30" X 89" piece of the same material with a wood-grain surface. The wood-grain veneer used to cover the outer walls of the playing box and its support frame is optional. By omitting it and staining these surfaces instead, you can cut the cost of the project by a quarter.

BUILD: The game is basically a box centered on a tablelike frame. Begin by constructing the four sides of this frame and fastening its four corner braces and three horizontal supports, as indicated in the diagram. Be sure to set these components flush with the upper edge of the sides.

If you've chosen to use the wood-grain veneer, now's the time to attach it to the frame with contact cement. The next step is to shape and mount the legs and finish up the game's underpinnings by installing the two cross braces between the vertical supports at the ends.

Begin assembling the playing box itself by trimming all the components to the sizes indicated. Miter the wall sections' corners to form a rectangle with 26-1/4" X 46" outside dimensions, and cut a 3/8" X 3/8" rabbet into the lower inside face of each of the four boards. Next, clamp the two long side walls evenly together and drill the two 1-3/4" ball-feed holes and the sixteen 3/4" control-rod holes through both boards simultaneously to insure that the sides match exactly. Using the same method, cut identical 2" X 5" ball-return openings in the end panels. Complete the structure by gluing and screwing the mitered joints together and fastening

the plywood floor to the box with glue and 3d finishing nails. Secure the tray to the legged frame by countersinking three No. 6 X 1" flathead wood screws through the plywood into each horizontal support.

The actual playing field—and the *inside* walls of the tray—should be covered with the white plastic laminate to insure a consistent game. After trimming the sheets to size and painting the pattern on the base segment, mark the side panels for drilling and the end pieces for cutting. Next, glue the sheets in place and smooth the edges of the openings. If the outside of your table will be covered by wood-grain plastic, place the long sides, followed by the top strips, in position at this time.

To make the ball-return racks and housings, drill and countersink a 1/8" hole, longitudinally, through each of the four 5/8" X 1-5/8" dowel stubs. Then bore 3/8" cavities in the sides of the stubs, each 1/4" deep and 1-1/4" from one end. Slip the 3/8" X 10-1/4" dowel sections into these shoulder openings to form two simple ball racks, and center one rack outside each end of the table's supporting frame, positioning the right peg 2-1/4" and the left peg 2" from the lower edge of the frame in each case. Complete this step by gluing a cap—or a thin section of dowel—over each of the screwheads.

Repeat the procedure to make the scoring bars, working with 1" lengths of 5/8" dowel joined by 5/16" X 10" shafts, which should allow the macramé beads with 3/8" holes to slide easily. Before you mount the

counters, complete the housings. These goal cages are constructed by cutting the parts to size (don't forget to make the 3/8″ step in the side pieces, 3-3/8″ down from the upper edge), gluing and tacking them together, and adding corner braces for extra support.

To attach the assembled ball-return enclosures to the table, first fasten some small blocks, approximately 3/8″ X 1/4″ X 2-1/4″, to the end boards of the playing box (remembering to install the laminated trim first) about 11-1/4″ apart and equidistant from both sides of the ball-return openings. Then slip the completed housings over these vertical supports and run some No. 4 X 3/4″ flathead screws through the casings and into the blocks. Finish by covering the housings, mounting the scoring bars with screws, and capping the ends of

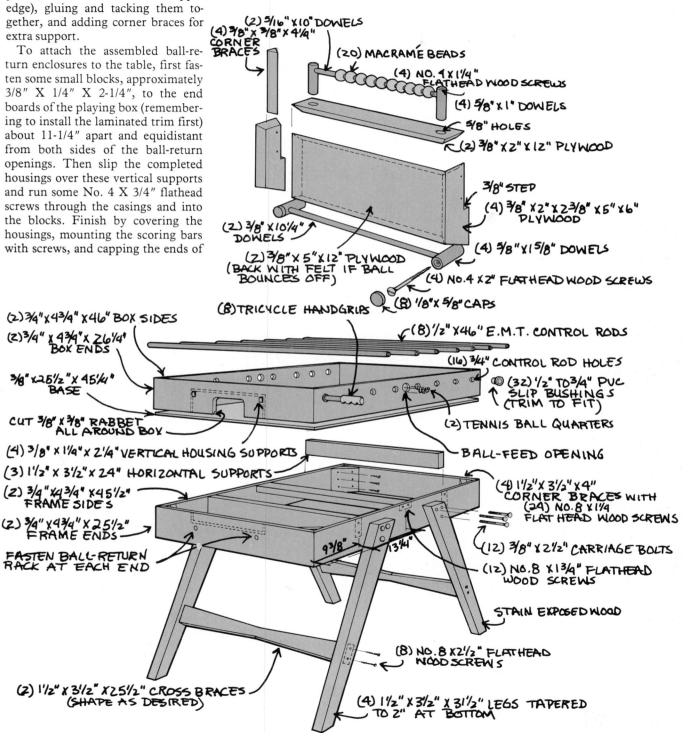

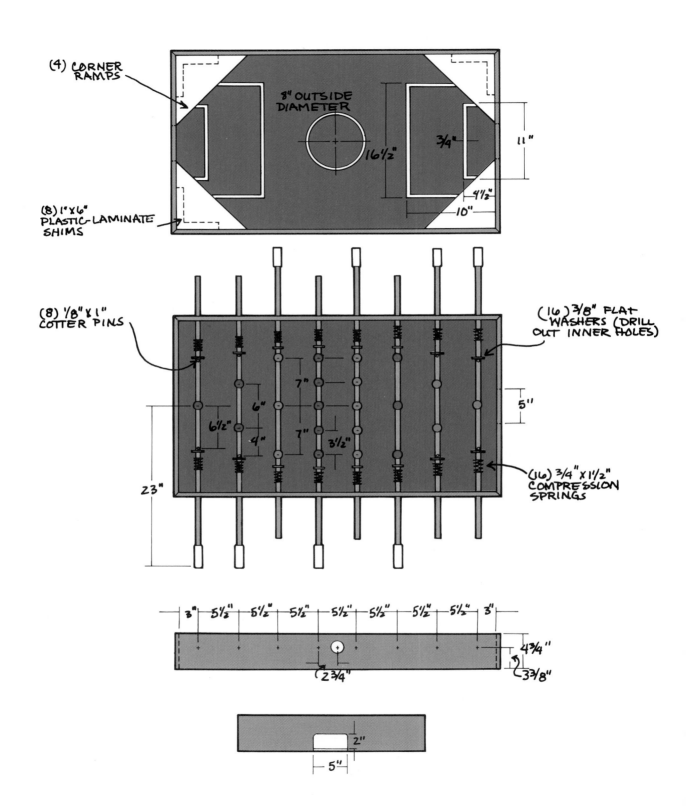

(4) CORNER RAMPS

8" OUTSIDE DIAMETER

3/4"

11"

16½"

4½"

10"

(8) 1"x6" PLASTIC-LAMINATE SHIMS

(8) ⅛"x1" COTTER PINS

(16) 3/8" FLAT WASHERS (DRILL OUT INNER HOLES)

7"

6"

6½"

4"

7"

3½"

5"

23"

(16) 3/4"x1½" COMPRESSION SPRINGS

3" 5½" 5½" 5½" 5½" 5½" 5½" 5½" 3"

4¾"

3⅜"

2¾"

2"

5"

106

the ball return rod's support pegs.

Now, it's time to make the players and fasten them to the control rods. Begin by fabricating a jig from a 6" scrap of 2 X 4 as follows: Cut a lengthwise 90° V-notch, about 3/4" deep, from the center of the block, then trim the resulting wedge section down to approximately 2" in length. Next, using a thin 1" screw, lock this piece back into the groove, leaving a distance of 3-1/2" between the open end of the notch and the nearest edge of the tapered insert.

Cut the 1" doweling into 22 sections 3-1/2" long (the players). One at a time, place them snugly into the block's gutter and—using an 11/16" spade-type bit—drill through them at a point 2-3/4", on center, from their lowest edge. Enlarge the bores slightly by running a scrap section of 1/2" E.M.T. (with one end cross-cut and slightly spread) through them once or twice, using a rotary motion. Then form each contestant's legs by shaping the dowels—fore and aft—at the lower end and sanding any rough surfaces smooth. If you wish, you can also round the upper edges of the dowels to simulate shoulders, and provide mounts for macramé-bead heads by drilling shallow 3/8" holes into the tops of the pegs and gluing 3/8" X 1-1/8" dowels in place to form necks. For a finished look, paint faces on the beads.

Before installing the player-control rods, set the 1/2"-to-3/4" PVC slip bushings in place. Trim each one to a total length of about 1/2", carefully enlarge the inner diameters with a rat-tail file (just enough to insure that the 1/2" E.M.T. will slide through without binding), and glue a bushing into each side of every control-rod opening. (Suggestion: Of the several cements tried in building the prototype shown here, the only stickum to form a permanent bond was 3M's Super Weatherstrip Adhesive, which is available in most hardware and automotive supply stores.)

Slip the eight 46" rods into their respective openings, taking care to slide the players, washers, and springs over the conduit sections in the order indicated in the diagram. Sixteen 3/8" washers must be drilled out to fit the tubing's outside diameter, and the same number of compression springs—each 3/4" X 1-1/2" in size—should be cut from the internal tensioners of discarded pole lamps.

With all the parts installed and the control rods staggered as shown, carefully position the wooden athletes according to the specifications given in the drawing. Then drill a 3/32" hole through each dowel and into the conduit beneath it, and install a No. 4 X 3/8" panhead sheet metal screw to hold the peg firmly in place. Fix the washer stops, as indicated, on the two outer rods at each end of the field and lock them in place by drilling 1/8" holes through the E.M.T. and inserting 1/8" X 1" cotter pins. Wrap up this step by gluing a tricycle handlebar grip to the control end of each rod.

All that's left to do is to attach ball-feed chutes, which are used to put the "puck" in play, and the four corner ramps. The chutes are made by cutting a tennis ball into quarters, then screwing and gluing a 1/2"-thick C-shaped wooden spacer between one of the curved sections and the lower outside edge of the large centered hole in each side of the table. The ramps are merely triangular plates of laminate with feathered leading edges, positioned with the corners meeting the sides of the goal openings and sloped toward the center of the field to return corner balls. They are glued at each of the tray's corners over plastic-laminate spacer strips that raise the rear of the triangles slightly.

AND HAVE A (FOOS) BALL: An ordinary table-tennis ball is far too light to react properly when struck by a player's foot, and any attempts to weight the hollow spheres will just result in an eccentric roll pattern. Regulation Foosballs work best and can be purchased from local suppliers of table games.

Once you've gotten the hang of twisting the handles and shifting the players to and fro, you'll be amazed at how adept you'll become at controlling your team. And—win or lose—you and your friends can enjoy a good evening's entertainment on a reasonable budget.

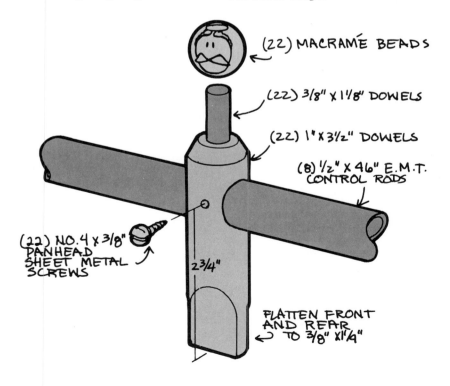

(22) MACRAMÉ BEADS

(22) 3/8" X 1 1/8" DOWELS

(22) 1" X 3 1/2" DOWELS

(8) 1/2" X 46" E.M.T. CONTROL RODS

(22) NO. 4 X 3/8" PANHEAD SHEET METAL SCREWS

2 3/4"

FLATTEN FRONT AND REAR TO 3/8" X 1 1/4"

MOUTH BOW

The mouth bow is among the oldest of musical instruments. It was depicted in drawings by cave dwellers, and some 15,000 years later, modern man is still charmed by the humming, twanging sounds of this stringed resonator.

In its most traditional style, the mouth bow is similar to the simple hunting bow and is little more than a springy bough with a length of twine, leather, or gut strung between the two ends. The so-called Appalachian mouth bow is a variation of this theme, having a flat strip of wood tapered on each end, rather than a rounded branch. Its design is clean and uncomplicated, and lends itself to artistic woodworking or painting.

GATHER THE MATERIALS: There's no "correct" way to assemble this easy-to-play folk instrument, so let your own creativity guide you. The particular design shown here calls for a strip of hardwood measuring 3/16" X 1-1/4" X 32", a guitar string (a heavy-gauge steel second or third B or G string works well) preferably with a ball end, a *wooden* violin tuning peg, two No. 2 roundhead brass screws, each 1/2" or 3/8" long,

and—if your guitar string has a "loop" end rather than a ball—an 18-gauge wire brad.

The tools you'll need are a jigsaw, a drill with assorted bits (1/16" to 1/2" or so), a small screwdriver, a hammer (if you use the brad), a power sander (optional), sandpaper in various grades, and—if you want to add a finish to your musicmaker—some tung oil or boiled linseed oil, fine steel wool, and several clean rags.

Probably the most difficult task involved in making the mouth bow is finding the right sort of resilient hardwood (walnut, maple, cherry, ash, or white oak are all popular and provide a nice range of colors). The variety you do get will depend, of course, on what's available from lumber suppliers, local sawmills, cabinetmakers, friends, or even your own scrap pile. Most lumberyards deal primarily in softwoods such as fir (fir, pine, or cedar), though some carry hardwoods. Companies that specialize in unusual and exotic woods can provide you with clear, straight-grained pieces that have just the strength and flexibility you'll need for your project. Such pieces are also more expensive. Since the necessary "cutting to size" will be difficult, even with the best hand equipment, it might be worthwhile to have the wood milled to size at a local sawmill or lumberyard.

If you have suitable tools however, and wish to cut the slat yourself, get a piece of stock that's at least 2" X 2" X 36", which will produce strips for more than one bow. Allowing for the loss of some wood in sanding, slice off a strip a little more than 3/16" thick, then trim it to slightly more than 1-1/4" in width and 32" in length.

SHAPING AND STRINGING: Once the slat has been cut, form a gentle point at each end, starting the taper about 6" from the tip. Try to make both ends symmetrical.

Now, smooth the slat. Use a mechanical sander to take down any

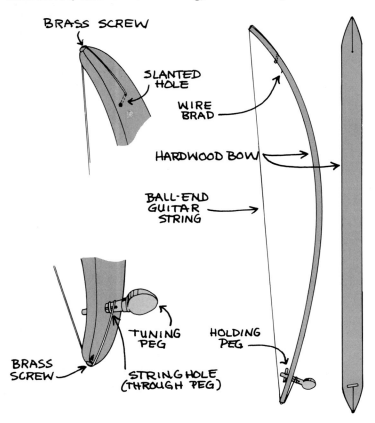

BRASS SCREW
SLANTED HOLE
WIRE BRAD
HARDWOOD BOW
BALL-END GUITAR STRING
TUNING PEG
HOLDING PEG
BRASS SCREW
STRING HOLE (THROUGH PEG)

The mouth bow is tuned by flexing the wooden slat to take the tension off the wire and either tightening or loosening the violin key to raise or lower the pitch, respectively. After tuning, one end of the bow is placed against the player's cheek, and the string is plucked while the shape of the mouth is changed to vary the sound produced.

a 1/16″ hole is drilled through the tuning peg, close to the point at which it enters the slat. The end of the guitar string is then threaded through this hole and bent, and the string wrapped around the peg.

ASSEMBLE IT: Before giving the bow a finish, assemble it to make sure it needs no revising. Thread the string through the slanted hole and wrap the far end around the tuning peg. Then run the string around both tip ends and through the screw slots. Flex the slat into a bow—one that's perhaps 4″ to 5″ deep at its midpoint—by standing the tip on a stable surface and applying a little pressure. Take up slack in the guitar string by wrapping more of it around the tuning peg, and thrust the peg firmly into its hole. Finally, hold the bow well away from your face and pluck the string with your finger or a pick. If everything holds together, you're ready to finish the job.

The instrument can be left as is, stained, or oiled. Don't use a heavy finish such as varnish, as it interferes with the resonance of the wood. Leave the screws in place—and the brad, too, if used—but do take off the string and tuning peg before applying the finish. When it's well rubbed in and thoroughly dry, reassemble the instrument, set the tension, and get ready to play.

CHEEKY DOINGS: Playing the bow is just a matter of using your mouth as a sounding box while the slat lies against your cheek (see the photographs to learn the correct way to hold the instrument). Grasp the center of the bow with one hand and pluck the string with the other. Then open and shut your mouth, and stretch and alter its shape to change the resonating sounds. It's a lot like humming, and with a little practice you should soon be able to play Jimmy Driftwood and Johannes Brahms with equal ease.

The mouth bow is an ancient instrument, and maybe that's why its sound seems so refreshing and comforting in this modern world. Just gather with your friends for an evening of music, and you'll see!

really rough spots, but be careful to move the tool lightly and evenly over the wood so it isn't scraped down too far. Further hand sanding with fine sandpaper, and even with fine steel wool toward the last, will make the slat as smooth as glass.

When the slat is finished, drill a 5/64″ hole into each tip to accommodate the two No. 2 brass screws. Turn the screws into place, making sure that the slots in the heads are positioned so that the string can run through them when it's fitted on the bow.

Drill a 1/16″ hole about 1-1/2″ from one end of the slat, centered and slanting upward toward the tip (see the diagram). The ball will then

anchor the string. If the string that you've chosen has a loop end, nail the brad in at an angle, 1″ below and leaning away from the new hole. The loop will hook over the brad, and the string can then be threaded through the hole.

On the opposite end of the slat, drill a 5/16″ hole—or whatever size is needed to accommodate your violin tuning peg—straight through the slat at a point about 3-1/4″ from the tip. The tuning peg is tapered and should fit snugly in the hole, with an available portion of from 1/2″ to 3/4″ long—between the fingerhold and the slat—upon which the string will be wrapped. Note that your instrument will be much easier to string if

BONKER BOX

If you've ever tried making your own musical instruments, you probably know the feeling of accomplishment that comes when you coax the first sounds from one of your creations, and the sense of satisfaction that develops as you fine-tune those tones through gentle experimentation. On the other hand, if you've never had a go at handcrafting your own musicmakers, a perfect way to start is with a bonker box.

This ancient Aztec instrument—also known as a tongue drum, tune box, or slit drum—uses the percussion principle to create mellow, bouncy tones that even the rankest novice couldn't corrupt.

Ideally, you'd want to make a bonker box out of a stable softwood like mahogany, but ash (the wood used in the instrument pictured), spruce, redwood, and cedar all produce pleasant sounds of varying characters. However, some money can be saved by using quality wood for the top only and by building the sides from pine or plywood.

To make your own tune box, you'll need a 1" X 7-1/4" plank that's 5-1/2 feet long (if full-inch-thick wood isn't available, you can get by with 3/4" material), a piece of 3/8" X 18" hardwood dowel, a 1/4" X 14" piece of dowel, and two 1"-diameter hard rubber balls.

Although it's possible to construct a bonker box with the simplest of hand tools, it is easier to get tight joints and superior sound if a table saw and jointer are used.

THE BOX: If you're using wood a full inch thick, begin by cutting your five main wooden components to the dimensions shown in our diagram. If, however, you're using 3/4" material, increase the width of the end blocks 1/2" so they measure 3/4" X 5-1/4" X 6" to make up the difference in thickness and thus insure a proper fit.

After everything's cut to size, slice your 3/8" dowel into fourteen 1-1/4" pieces, and—with the box temporarily clamped together—mark the spots selected for these wooden pins on the instrument's outer surface. Next, by "splitting" the side edges of each end block and the top edges of all four "walls" with pencil lines, and using this half-width dimension as a guide for determining the drilling points in the top and side boards, you can accurately make the twenty-eight 25/64" bores necessary to lock the sound box together. (Remember to drill only halfway into the thickness of the slabs, and make your deeper holes running into the boards from the edges.

Using yellow carpenter's glue in the holes and along all the joining surfaces, clamp the ends and sides of the box together with the eight dowels in place, then set the assembly aside while you work on the top.

THE SOUNDING BOARD: The tongues themselves aren't at all difficult to cut if you use a coping saw, but you must make well-defined lines and guide the blade accurately along them to create an attractive surface. Begin by drilling the eight 7/16" starting holes through the top plank as shown. The holes should be 1-1/4" apart on center, and you'll want the end openings in each group to be 1-3/4" from the side edges of the board. By the same token, there should be 2-1/2" of wood between the centerline of each series of holes and the end of the board, or 13" between the centers of the two groups of holes.

When you've finished drilling, you can mark the separations between the six tongues. Use a straightedge to make the four parallel lines between the hole sets, then scribe the rounded tongue ends (at the locations indi-

cated) with a compass or a smooth-edged disk. Make your straight cuts first, then go back and trim out the curves.

With the tongues cut and shaped, it's time to rout or chisel a groove 1/4" to 1/2" wide and a little less than half the thickness of the wood deep on the underside of each key. Begin these cuts at a point even with the outer edges of the starter holes and work toward the tips of the tongues. The grooves will give the keys some additional freedom of movement and will also affect the tuning of the drum. The tone of a tongue may be raised by routing deeper beneath its tip, and lowered by increasing the depth of the groove at the base of the key. Test your tuning by holding the drum top near your ear and rapping the tongue with a knuckle.

Complete the box by gluing the top to the sound box, clamping it in place, and allowing the assembly to dry for 24 hours.

THE BONKERS: While you're waiting, put the beaters, or mallets, together by first cutting the 1/4" dowel in half and drilling a 1/4" hole halfway through the center of each ball. A small amount of epoxy placed in each hole will keep the handles in place once you have pressed them in. (The balls are fairly brittle, so you might want to buy several in order to have a spare on hand in case one splits.)

FINISHING TOUCHES: Once the drum is ready, start sanding it with a coarse paper and work your way up to a fine grit. For an added touch, consider rounding the box's edges. When the surface is smooth, rub in a coat or two of tung oil or linseed oil and let it dry.

Then just let fly with your mallets and enjoy the sounds! You'll no doubt discover that you can't produce a bad note, but you will be able to find the live spot on each tongue (near the free end) that creates the most resonance. By experimenting with different woods, box sizes, tongue lengths, and thicknesses of wooden parts, you can discover a whole new world of sound.

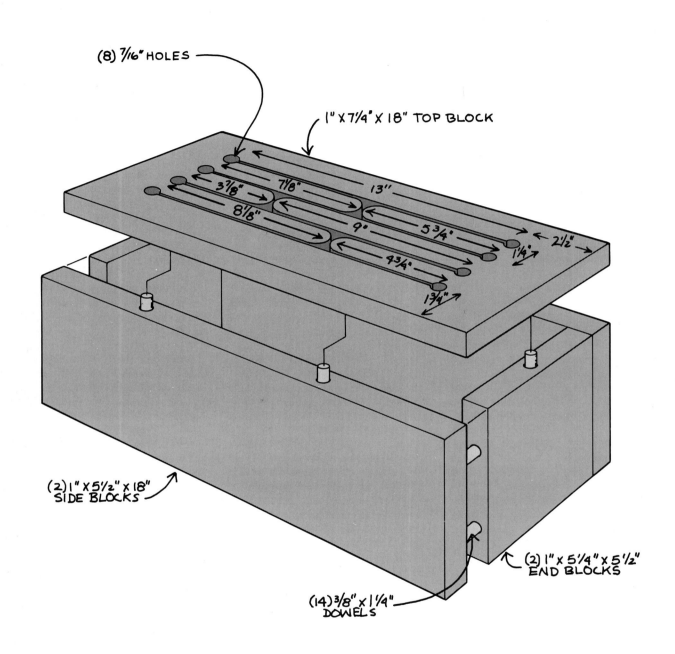

(8) 7/16" HOLES

1" X 7¼" X 18" TOP BLOCK

13"

7⅛"

3⅞"

8⅞"

9"

5¾"

2½"

1¼"

4¾"

1¾"

(2) 1" X 5½" X 18"
SIDE BLOCKS

(2) 1" X 5¼" X 5½"
END BLOCKS

(14) 3/8" X 1¼"
DOWELS

GAME OF SKILL

Here's a challenging game for one person to play, as you know if you've ever whiled away a rainy summer afternoon or long winter evening with this easily made little puzzle that takes a lot longer to solve than it does to make!

The only materials needed are a 3/4"-thick scrap of lumber (softwood will work, though hardwood is better) large enough to cut out an equilateral triangle with 5" sides, and a bag of golf tees. A drill with an 11/64" bit and a handsaw are the required tools.

The playing board for the game consists of 15 holes, each 5/8" deep, laid out in rows on a triangular pattern. First, cut out the board. Then lay out the positions of the holes by lightly penciling an equilateral triangle with its sides 1/2" in from the edges of the board, marking off these lines at 13/16" intervals, and connecting those points, as shown, with light pencil lines. Drill the holes wherever two lines intersect. For a fancier design, rout or scallop the upper edges of the wooden block. Then finish it with linseed oil, polyurethane varnish, or the stain of your choice.

To play, just put a tee in every hole but the one at the apex of the triangle, then jump the tees like checkers—one at a time, removing each one that's jumped over—until only one remains. That, of course, sounds ridiculously simple, but just give it a try. There are only a small number of "winning" jump combinations. Most folks who have won this game can't ever remember how they did it!

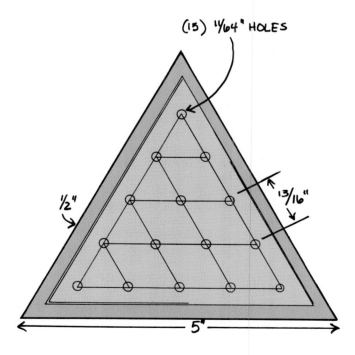

(15) 11/64" HOLES

1/2"

13/16"

5"

PIPE XYLOPHONE

Many children first experience making "music" while banging on the tinny, off-key bars of a toy xylophone. This may be stimulating for the youngsters, but it can be a real headache-producer for their parents. However, you can inspire your young musician's creativity and soothe your own nerves with the homemade musicmaker pictured here.

A shopping trip for materials (requiring a lot less cash than would be needed to purchase most manufactured toys) and an hour or so of assembly time will produce an exciting learning tool for your child. Furthermore, you'll be amazed by this xylophone's pleasing tone, and if you have a good ear, you can even adapt the design to vary the range and/or the pitch of this pipe xylophone.

HOW IT'S PUT TOGETHER: The simple xylophone is made from easily located materials. For the pipe you'll need one standard 10-foot length of electrical metallic tubing (E.M.T.), usually sold in hardware or building supply stores. The 1/2" size, which has an outside diameter of almost 3/4", will produce a 13-pipe xylophone like the one shown in the photo: It will have three notes *below* the standard eight-tone octave and two *above* it.

The instrument's base is a wide piece of 3/4" shelf board about 11" X 24". Rather than resting directly on the wood, the pipes are supported and cradled by an assembly of long strips and small blocks of polyurethane foam, cemented in place with ordinary white household glue.

PIPES: To begin, use either a pipe cutter or a hacksaw to divide the conduit as indicated in the chart. Start with the longest one. The length of each pipe determines its pitch, so try to match the measurements as precisely as possible. Allowing a little extra when you cut, however, will permit fine-tuning adjustments. Check each chime against the preceding one; the new note should be the next tone higher in the scale. Remember that the changes from "ti" to "do" and "mi" to "fa" are half steps, while the other intervals are whole steps. If the pitch is flat (too low), you can saw off a little more to correct it, and very small dis-

crepancies can be fixed later by extra filing. It's a good idea to err on the side of too long, obviously, since it's impossible to add length to a pipe. If you do find that the pitch is sharp (too high), cut a new piece of pipe for that tone and shorten the "mistake" even more to use for the next lower note in the scale.

Most simple xylophones (including this one, which is approximately in the key of G) have pipes representing only notes of the major scale, but you *can* estimate and "whittle" more half notes or even additional octaves to expand the instrument's versatility. If the xylophone is to be played with a piano, the pipes will need to be cut and adjusted to match that instrument's notes.

After the pipes have been sawed to the specified lengths and tuned, their cut ends should be ground smooth. Use a round metal file inside the mouth and a flat file for the outside surface. Then finish those areas with fine black (silicone carbide) sandpaper to remove dangerous rough edges.

FOAM: In order for the pipes to resonate clearly, they must rest on an absorbent yet resilient foundation: Polyurethane foam is an ideal material for that purpose. Cut strips of foam from an old mattress, or else pick up odd pieces of foam at fabric outlet stores.

First, take a sharp knife (or an electric carving knife or band saw) and

cut two 1-1/4" X 17-1/2" strips. These supports should be at least 3/4" thick so that the pipes won't hit the board when struck. You can, if necessary, use 3/8" foam and double the layers, as shown in the diagram.

Laying the foundation strips in a V-shaped formation on the wooden base (see photo), adjust the angle so the space between the inner edges of the cushions measures 1-5/16" at the small end and opens up to 8-3/4" at the wide end of the "V". The pipes will then be supported at the points that create the least interference with the music. Attach the pieces of foam to the wood with plenty of white glue, as the spongy material tends to absorb the adhesive readily.

Next, cut 28 small blocks of 3/8" foam, each about 5/8" X 1-1/4" (try slicing them in the shape of parallelograms so they'll align with the slanted supports), and glue the first pair, one on top of each foam strip and flush with the end of the strip, just to the outside of the spot where the longest pipe will be. Lay that tube in place—barely touching the blocks—glue on the next pair, and so forth. It's a good idea to arrange *all* the pipes across the supports and to pencil in the spots where the rest of the foam pieces must be attached, to insure coming out even at the other end of the support blocks.

When the glue has set, nestle each section of conduit in its own cradle and make certain that it protrudes an

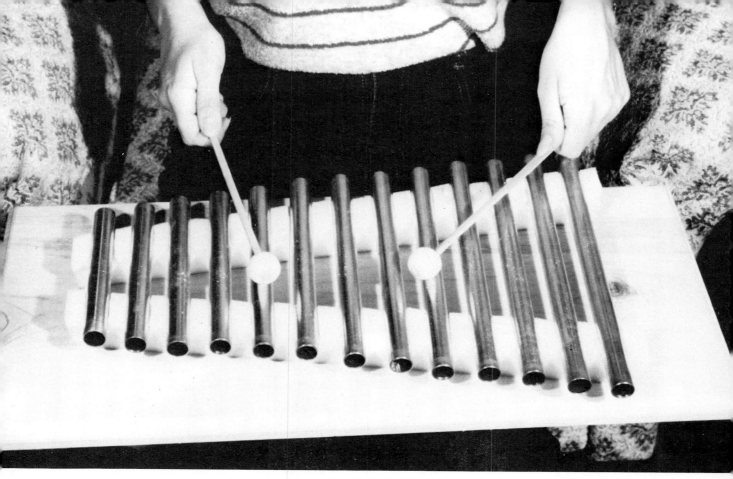

equal distance at each end. This will assure that it rings with the clearest possible sound when struck.

MALLETS: Now, all you need is a pair of mallets to make your xylophone sing! Note that different strikers will give the instrument a slightly different tone. To achieve a sweet muted sound, use rubber vibraphone mallets purchased from a music store. Wooden drawer knobs attached to foot-long pieces of 3/8″ dowel, or even tinker-toy wheels with sticks, will produce louder tones. If the musicmaking becomes too clangorous, simply muffle the noise by stretching a wide rubber band around the head of each mallet. The idea is to unleash your imagination and experiment with whatever happens to be readily available. The model shown here uses chopsticks, inserted and glued into large wooden macramé beads!

Once you and your young ones give it a try, you'll find that playing the pipe xylophone is easy and pleasurable. Thanks to its simplicity, this homegrown instrument is perfect for improvisation and creative harmonizing. You don't need an instruction book or a teacher, either. Just pick up the mallets—or hand them to an eager young tunesmith—and enjoy some ear-pleasing melodies!

HOW TO PITCH YOUR PIPES

	NOTE		INCHES
	sol	5	11-3/4
	la	6	11-3/32
	ti	7	10-7/16
	do	1	10-1/8
	re	2	9-9/16
	mi	3	9-1/16
BASIC OCTAVE, G MAJOR SCALE	fa	4	8-3/4
	sol	5	8-7/32
	´la	6	7-13/16
	ti	7	7-1/4
	do	1	7-1/16
	re	2	6-5/8
	mi	3	6-7/32

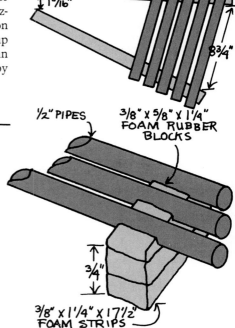

1⁵⁄₁₆″

8³⁄₄″

½″ PIPES

3/8″ X 5/8″ X 1¼″ FOAM RUBBER BLOCKS

3/4″

3/8″ X 1¼″ X 17½″ FOAM STRIPS

PIPE XYLOPHONE

BOOMERANG

A boomerang is a bent or angular throwing stick that typically is flat on one side and rounded on the other, enabling it to soar or curve in flight. Lately there has been a growing interest in the Australian sporting boomerang, which is the lightweight kind designed to return near the thrower, as opposed to the heavier, nonreturning type used for hunting.

Here are some tips for making and controlling your version of a well-tested model. It should perform beautifully. All it takes is a little practice in the sport of boomeranging for many happy returns!

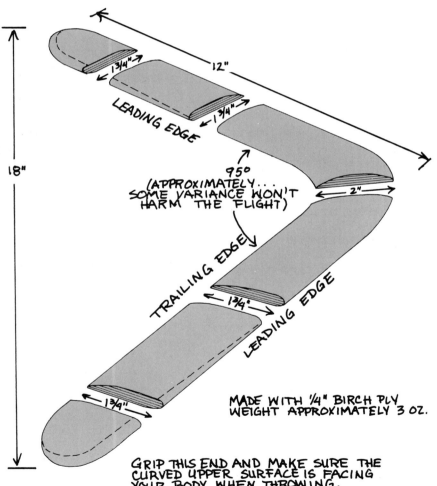

DESIGNED BY HERB A. SMITH
OF SUSSEX ENGLAND

18"

12"

1 3/4"

1 3/4"

LEADING EDGE

95°
(APPROXIMATELY...
SOME VARIANCE WON'T
HARM THE FLIGHT)

2"

TRAILING EDGE

LEADING EDGE

1 3/4"

1 3/4"

MADE WITH 1/4" BIRCH PLY
WEIGHT APPROXIMATELY 3 OZ.

GRIP THIS END AND MAKE SURE THE
CURVED UPPER SURFACE IS FACING
YOUR BODY WHEN THROWING.

HOMING INSTINCT: To begin, draw the accompanying pattern—full size—on a sheet of stiff cardboard. Note that this design will produce a *right-handed* boomerang. Southpaws must make a mirror image of the plan, shifting the leading and trailing edges accordingly. When the template is sufficiently symmetrical and pleasing, check your wood for warps. If any exist, lay out the pattern in such a way that the finished boomerang's top (rounded) surface will be formed by the concave warp of the wood. That is, the wings of the finished flier should either be absolutely level or turn up slightly at the tips.

With your boomerang-to-be traced on the board, you can cut out the pattern by using a jigsaw or scroll saw (a finishing blade will leave much smoother edges). Then use coarse sandpaper to remove a small wedge-shaped portion from the bottom of the leading edge of each wing, as shown in the dotted lines in the drawing. This is the *only* shaping that will be done to the underside of the boomerang.

Once that's done, take your wooden blank and—with a pencil—mark the to-be-shaved-away areas on the top of the boomerang as follows: The leading edges should extend 1/4" into the upper surface of the wood, the trailing edges should be smoothed back 1/2", and both should be worked to a thinness of no less than 1/8". Next, using a fine-toothed wood rasp, gradually remove the extra material as indicated by your penciled guidelines. Use the wood's plies, as each is revealed in turn, to help you produce a uniform bevel.

At this point, the boomerang will be in its final shape and can be smoothed, first with medium, then with fine, sandpaper. Be sure to round off all sharp edges! The finished projectile may be decorated any way you wish, but do waterproof the wood with a couple of coats of clear lacquer or polyurethane varnish.

A SNAPPY COMEBACK: To take your wooden bird on its maiden flight, wait for a day with no wind or with just a slight breeze. (A light boomerang such as this one is impossible to control in winds over five miles per hour). Then find at least 40 yards of open space where you won't be likely to damage anyone's property or hit an innocent spectator with a wild throw. Now, stand facing the wind, turn about 45° to your *right*

(with the breeze on your left shoulder), and holding the boomerang vertically so that its curved surface is toward your body and the "hook" is pointing forward, throw it at an imaginary target about 40 yards away and approximately 15 feet above the ground. Snap your wrist upon release (similar to the motion used to pitch a baseball) to spin the curved stick end over end. If all goes well, it should first fly straight out, then bank upward and to the left (again, a left-handed boomerang will be thrown, and will fly, in the opposite direction . . . so all of the instructions here should be *reversed* by lefties) before leveling out a bit and returning to hover and touch down near you.

If the device lands to your right, turn a little bit more to your left for the next throw. Should it land to your left, however, face slightly more to the right, or lean the boomerang a tad toward the right horizon before

throwing it again. Practice. Remember, each stick has its own personality with which you must become familiar in order to succeed consistently. The final trick is to catch the returning boomerang by making a sandwich of it between the palms of your hands. For safety's sake, try this only when the stick is in its gentle final hover.

TALKING BACK: Once you've mastered the pattern given here, you may want to step out on your own a bit by duplicating it in 3/16" plywood. The result is a more delicate thrower that will be easier to hurl and therefore better suited to young boomerangers. If you're feeling really adventurous, try some designs of your own. You'll undoubtedly make a few failures along the way, but by following the basic design parameters of this boomerang, you're sure to come up with some exciting and rewarding performers!

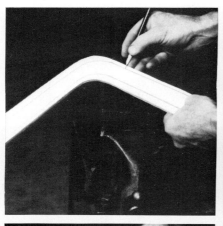
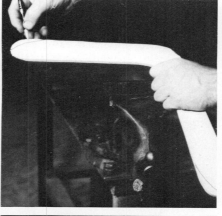
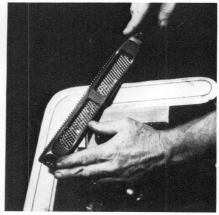
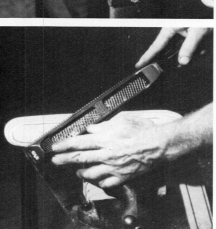

After sketching the rasping lines on the blank, the undercuts are filed away on the bottoms of the leading edges. Then the tops of the wings are tapered and curved with a rasp and the apex where the arms meet is shaped. The boomerang is then ready to be sanded smooth, decorated, and thrown.

The necessary tools include a small welder and two different tubing benders (to handle 1/2" and 1" E.M.T.), as well as a hacksaw, an electric drill with bits, a screwdriver, a round file, a measuring tape, a pipe wrench, and a coping saw. If you're purchasing new electrical conduit (in 10-foot lengths), you'll need two complete 1" sections, one 3/4" piece, and three 1/2" lengths to handle most of the job. Also required are an additional 2 feet of the 1/2" size and an 8" length of 1-1/4" tubing. The two-piece seat can be cut from a single 20" X 28" slab of 1/4" plywood.

The chassis is made from two 58" lengths of 1" conduit which are bent to the same contour, then joined to form a sort of paddle shape. To curve these sections properly, choose one, and—starting at either end—measure off 4". Make a 90° bend at that point, which should take up about 10". Mark off 5 more inches, start a 45° arc (this one uses up 5"), leave an 8" straight section, form the final 45° curve, and then determine the length of the remaining leg (it should be about 21").

Once you've curved a pair of the tubular side rails, join them by temporarily placing your 1-1/2" pipe coupling between the parallel front tubes as a spacer, then welding the butted rear tips to each other. Use a scrap of 1"-diameter mechanical tubing (or filed-down 3/4" pipe) inside both parts to serve as a bridge.

The rear axle housings are welded to the chassis next, and these should be positioned so they intersect the right-angle bends at midpoint and are equally divided by the joint. A 2-1/2" section of 1/2" conduit holds each one to the frame at the inner ends, but since the goal is to mount the housings true for proper wheel alignment and camber, these stubs may have to be made slightly longer or shorter to suit your homemade chassis.

The rest of the frame components are made from 1/2" E.M.T., which can be fine-trimmed as necessary. A 20" crossmember fastens between the side rails at a point 10-1/2" in

FOUR-WHEEL FUN

Two-wheelers don't have to be the only game in town. This isn't news to those who spent their fun-filled youth pumping the daylights out of a pipe-and-wheel contraption that was called an "Irish Mail". Well, here's a modern version of that pump scooter, and it can be built with electrical metallic tubing (E.M.T.) and some odds and ends.

front of the butt joint at the rear. Then two 90° pieces—one 9" and the other 24" in total length—are similarly arranged to help support the plywood seat.

To form the seat-back frame, bend both a 30-1/2" and a 35" conduit section into the shapes indicated, then weld the wider piece to the upper surface of the frame rails (1" forward of the crossmember) at an angle of 60°. The narrow hoop mounts atop that at an 85° bias to the chassis. Then the seat-back strut, along with the 41-1/2" rear support, is fastened in place to lock the axle housings to the seat structure.

At this point, complete the steering hub and pump handle. Both of these parts have to be adjustable, so they're designed to slide within the parallel front frame rails as necessary, and can be held in place with hose clamps. The hub is simply the 1-1/2"

pipe coupling welded to each half of a longitudinally split section of 1-1/4" E.M.T., then capped at each end with 1-1/2" to 3/4" pipe bushings. The threads within the center hole in each reducer must be filed out if it's to accept the shank of a 3/4" nipple. The handle is nothing more than a section of 1" conduit equipped with a 3/4" X 14" upper grip bar and a 1" X 7" pivot shaft—at the lower end—made from a scrap of mechanical tubing (this piece can be replaced with a length of 3/4" pipe if you don't mind filing its outer surface a bit). A 3/16" X 1-1/2" X 7" hunk of flat metal welded perpendicularly to the midpoint of the pinion functions as the drive lever, and the 1" shaft rides inside a pair of 1" X 2-1/4" E.M.T. stubs. These stubs are clipped to the chassis rails with half-sections of 1-1/4" conduit and hose clamps.

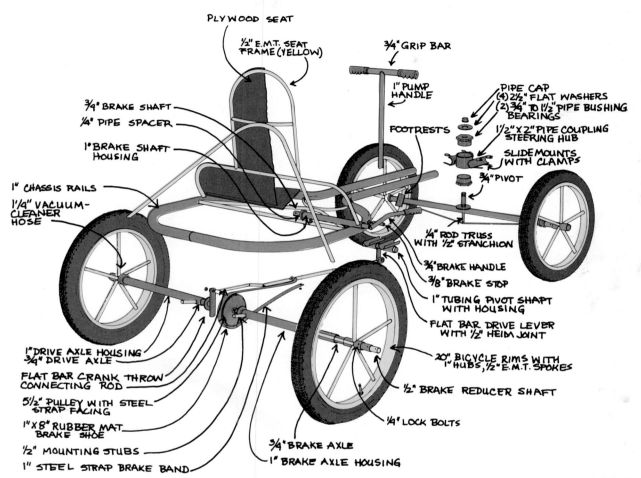

PLYWOOD SEAT

½" E.M.T. SEAT FRAME (YELLOW)

¾" GRIP BAR

1" PUMP HANDLE

PIPE CAP
(4) 2½" FLAT WASHERS
(2) ¾" TO 1½" PIPE BUSHING BEARINGS
1½" X 2" PIPE COUPLING STEERING HUB
SLIDE MOUNTS WITH CLAMPS
¾" PIVOT

¾" BRAKE SHAFT
¼" PIPE SPACER
1" BRAKE SHAFT HOUSING

FOOTRESTS

1" CHASSIS RAILS
1¼" VACUUM-CLEANER HOSE

¼" ROD TRUSS WITH ½" STANCHION
¾" BRAKE HANDLE
⅜" BRAKE STOP
1" TUBING PIVOT SHAFT WITH HOUSING
FLAT BAR DRIVE LEVER WITH ½" HEIM JOINT

1" DRIVE AXLE HOUSING
¾" DRIVE AXLE
FLAT BAR CRANK THROW CONNECTING ROD
5½" PULLEY WITH STEEL STRAP FACING
1" X 8" RUBBER MAT BRAKE SHOE
½" MOUNTING STUBS
1" STEEL STRAP BRAKE BAND

20" BICYCLE RIMS WITH 1" HUBS, ½" E.M.T. SPOKES
½" BRAKE REDUCER SHAFT
¼" LOCK BOLTS

¾" BRAKE AXLE
1" BRAKE AXLE HOUSING

A buttress front axle allows easy foot steering, and it's made by welding a 3″ piece of 1/2″ E.M.T., then a 2-1/2″ washer and 3/4″ X 3-3/4″ pipe nipple combination, to the center of, and perpendicular to, the 1″ X 30″ conduit axle. A 27″ length of 1/4″ reinforcing rod trusses the assembly, and two angle iron sections, fastened to the ends of the housing and tilted toward the rider, form modest footrests. The axle itself is merely a 40″ stretch of 3/4″ conduit run through the housing. The front wheel hubs ride on that shaft and are held in place with 1/4″ bolts pinned through the tube's ends.

To attach the front assembly to the steering hub, just slip the 3/4″ pipe center pivot through the two bushings in the coupling and lock it in place with a large washer and 3/4″ pipe cap.

The drive and brake mechanisms also work on a sleeve-within-a-sleeve principle. The 3/4″ X 17-1/2″ drive axle shaft utilizes a 3/16″ X 1-1/2″ X 5″ flat metal crank throw (a 2-1/2″ washer, welded in place 1″ from that bar, makes a good walk stop). The braked (right side) wheel is fastened to a 3/4″ shaft that houses—and is bolted to—a 1/2″ X 17-1/2″ pipe, which is then connected to a 5-1/2″

pulley. The right axle shaft uses an antislide washer, as does the drive axle, and it's carried inside the axle housing as well.

A one-wheel brake is all that's needed for this simple "pump-about", and that can be worked out by tacking a 1″ X 9″ E.M.T. housing to the upper part of the chassis just behind the crossmember. Two more conduit sections, welded at a right angle, provide a brake handle and shaft. Once this control is slipped into place and a small spacer and stop are installed, a 27″ length of strapping band is fastened between the brake shaft and crossmember, with the pulley nestled in the loop created. In practice, this arrangement works reasonably well, since a good deal of tension can be drawn on the strap through the mechanical advantage of the small pivot. But the system performs even better if the pulley groove itself is covered with a steel band, and the inner side of the steel loop is then faced with a strip of "grabby" rubber matting to act as a brake shoe.

All the cart's wheels can be fabricated from E.M.T. scraps and discarded bike rims, since regular spoked wheels probably couldn't stand up to the side thrusts placed upon them by a "four-footer". To make sturdy units, use 1" X 4" conduit hubs, centered within the rims. For each one, cut five 1/2" spokes to length (from 7" to 7-1/8" long, depending on the rim). Lay the rim on a slab of plywood, mark its circumference, and then bore a hub-holding hole dead center. By using spacer blocks to lift the rim and spokes to the hub's midlevel, you can tack all of your parts in place first and can finish welding them when you're satisfied with the assembly.

As soon as the wheels are bolted on the axle shafts (short lengths of vacuum-cleaner hose make nice grease covers to fit over the axles between the hubs and the housings), you can complete the pumper by fastening the seat boards and the connecting rod in place. To keep the driving force aligned along the axis of the cart, the 1/2" X 29-1/2" rod has a small offset in it about 4" from the crank (rear) end. A 1"-long piece of 1/2" conduit welded to the end of the connecting rod serves as a wrist sleeve through which the driving mechanism can be bolted to the crank throw. At the front end of the rod, a 1/2" nut allows for the installation (and adjustment) of an eyebolt, or—if you have expensive tastes—a Heim joint.

With everything welded, bolted, and screwed in position, you can paint your chariot. The final step can be tricky: trying to keep the children off this four-wheeler until the paint dries!

WHIRLIGIG WIND VANE

There comes a time in even the busiest of days when we must —no matter how important the task—rest our backs and our minds. Creative use of this "puttering time" has been responsible for many a cherished wooden toy, hand-whittled kitchen implement, and piece of heirloom furniture.

By combining charm with practicality, a wind vane is a welcome addition to any home. Each of the three spinners illustrated here can be constructed in an hour or two, depending on the manual skill and whims of the builder, from nothing more than a little imagination and a few scraps off the workshop floor.

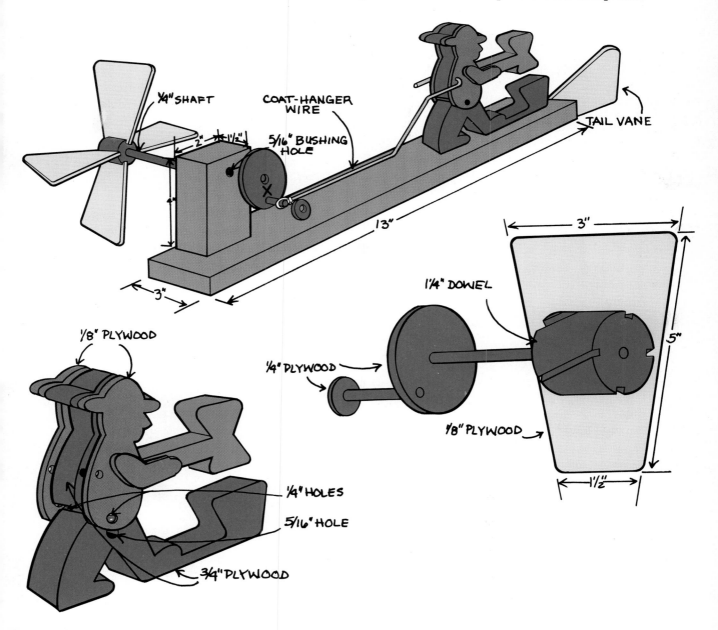

¼" SHAFT

COAT-HANGER WIRE

5/16" BUSHING HOLE

TAIL VANE

2"

1½"

13"

3"

3"

1¼" DOWEL

¼" PLYWOOD

⅛" PLYWOOD

5"

1½"

⅛" PLYWOOD

¼" HOLES

5/16" HOLE

¾" PLYWOOD

USE SMALL DOWEL OR NAIL SO SAW PIVOTS FREELY

DRIVE AND BEND FINISHING NAIL AS GUIDE

NO TEETH ALONG MIDDLE

SHORT PIECE OF 1" TWIG

Construction of each of these whirligigs is largely self-explanatory with lots of room for artistic expression. Besides, giving *exact* patterns for all of the parts would result in an uninteresting gaggle of identical wind vanes. The object is to build a vane according to your own skills and inclinations. After all, it's the "original touch" that turns spare time and ordinary materials into treasures.

THE WOODCHOPPER AND THE SAW WIELDER: These stout fellows pursue their activities atop wind-quartering vanes operated by the breeze blowing *across* the blades, rather than through them. With this novel arrangement, a relatively small fan is enough to drive the whirligig mechanism. And, although only a zephyr is necessary to start the figures chopping or sawing, the spin-

ners don't speed up appreciably in *stronger* gusts, thus extending the life of the wooden axles.

Construction of each vane begins with the assembly of the small fan, whose blades are cut from 1/8" plywood (cut the tail vane at the same time). In the hub, which is a short section of thick dowel, cut four slots at about a 15° diagonal, glue the blades in place, and insert a 1/4" dowel to serve as a drive shaft. Be sure to coat the shaft generously with soap (which will lubricate the action for months) *before* slipping it through the 5/16" bushing.

The next step—which is the key to the operation of any similar whirligig—is to build a simple cam consisting of a small wooden disk into which a short dowel is eccentrically set. The distance from the center of the disk to the dowel will determine how active the figure becomes. The "X" on the sketch of the woodchopper represents this distance and equals an inch, which gives the little man plenty of action. When it's com-

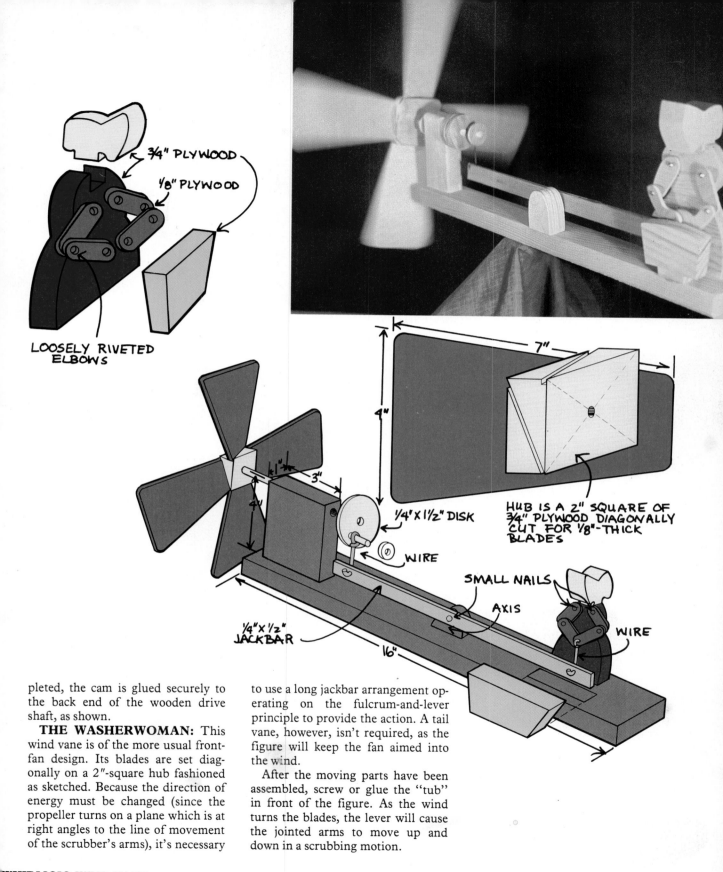

¾" PLYWOOD

⅛" PLYWOOD

LOOSELY RIVETED ELBOWS

7"

4"

HUB IS A 2" SQUARE OF ¾" PLYWOOD DIAGONALLY CUT FOR ⅛"-THICK BLADES

1"

3"

¼" X 1½" DISK

WIRE

4"

SMALL NAILS

AXIS

¼" X ½" JACKBAR

16"

WIRE

pleted, the cam is glued securely to the back end of the wooden drive shaft, as shown.

THE WASHERWOMAN: This wind vane is of the more usual front-fan design. Its blades are set diagonally on a 2"-square hub fashioned as sketched. Because the direction of energy must be changed (since the propeller turns on a plane which is at right angles to the line of movement of the scrubber's arms), it's necessary to use a long jackbar arrangement operating on the fulcrum-and-lever principle to provide the action. A tail vane, however, isn't required, as the figure will keep the fan aimed into the wind.

After the moving parts have been assembled, screw or glue the "tub" in front of the figure. As the wind turns the blades, the lever will cause the jointed arms to move up and down in a scrubbing motion.

WHIRLIGIG WIND VANE

SCRAPYARD STALLION

Although many toys found on store shelves are downright clever, the *cost* of that ingenuity is often discouraging. But even in a world of alkaline batteries and high-impact plastic, there's still room for an honest-to-goodness old-fashioned hobbyhorse. The materials won't cost much, and this lively bronco will thrill any young range rider.

This stallion's bounce comes not from curved rockers, but from a junked automobile leaf spring, which can be found in almost any scrapyard. It doesn't matter what sort of vehicle "donates" your spring, as long as it's in one piece and at least 4 feet long from eye to eye. Try to find one with at least one rubber end bushing intact, since this will help dampen the shock of each bouncing stroke.

Besides the main leaf, you'll need a piece of 3/4" plywood measuring 31" X 33" and another that's 7" X 11-1/2", an 11-1/2" X 15" section of full-inch-thick board, a 26" length of 1" dowel, a scrap of 2 X 4 that's about 6-1/2" long, a 7/16" X 40" hank of rope, and a 1-1/2" length of 2-1/4"-diameter round banister handrail.

The metal components include a piece of 3/16" X 1-1/2" X 1-1/2" X 5" angle iron, a 2-1/2"-long section of channel bar measuring 3/16" X 1-1/2" X 3", and an 8" length of 1-1/4" square tubular steel. For hardware, you'll need a 1/2" X 6" machine bolt with two nuts, a 3-1/2" bolt of the same diameter, a 5/16" X 2" carriage bolt, two No. 8 X 1/2" roundhead wood screws, and an assortment of 5/16" machine fasteners: two 1", four 1-1/4", two 1-1/2", and two 2" in length.

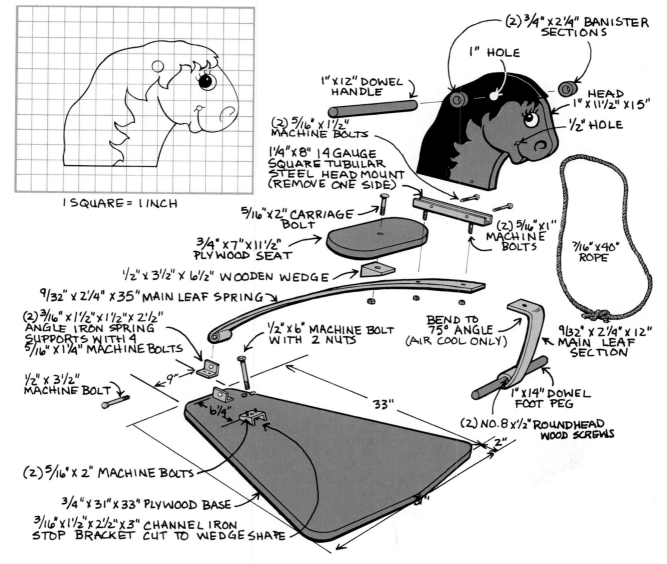

1 SQUARE = 1 INCH

(2) 3/4" x 2 1/4" BANISTER SECTIONS

1" HOLE

1" X 12" DOWEL HANDLE

HEAD 1" X 11 1/2" X 15"

1/2" HOLE

(2) 5/16" X 1 1/2" MACHINE BOLTS

1 1/4" X 8" 14 GAUGE SQUARE TUBULAR STEEL HEAD MOUNT (REMOVE ONE SIDE)

5/16" X 2" CARRIAGE BOLT

3/4" X 7" X 11 1/2" PLYWOOD SEAT

(2) 5/16" X 1" MACHINE BOLTS

7/16" X 40" ROPE

1/2" X 3 1/2" X 6 1/2" WOODEN WEDGE

9/32" X 2 1/4" X 35" MAIN LEAF SPRING

(2) 3/16" X 1 1/2" X 1 1/2" X 2 1/2" ANGLE IRON SPRING SUPPORTS WITH 4 5/16" X 1 1/4" MACHINE BOLTS

1/2" X 6" MACHINE BOLT WITH 2 NUTS

BEND TO 75° ANGLE (AIR COOL ONLY)

9/32" X 2 1/4" X 12" MAIN LEAF SECTION

1/2" X 3 1/2" MACHINE BOLT

9"

33"

1" X 14" DOWEL FOOT PEG

(2) NO. 8 X 1/2" ROUNDHEAD WOOD SCREWS

2"

6 1/4"

(2) 5/16" X 2" MACHINE BOLTS

3/4" X 31" X 33" PLYWOOD BASE

3/16" X 1 1/2" X 2 1/2" X 3" CHANNEL IRON STOP BRACKET CUT TO WEDGE SHAPE

SCRAPYARD STALLION

Begin by cutting the wooden parts to shape. Use the grid diagram to recreate the outline of the head and to drill the 1/2″ and 1″ holes where indicated. Then trim the seat and the five-sided base, saw a 12″ piece from the dowel, and cut the 2 X 4 to form a broad wedge.

To fasten the foot-long handle to the head, first bore a 1″ hole through the core of the banister rail and cut that piece in half to form two wooden rings. Then, using yellow carpenter's glue, cement the dowel into its opening in the head and the two rings to both the head and the handle. When the glue is dry, paint the head one base color. Later, you can add the black outlines and perhaps finish up the mane with a few deft strokes from a can of spray paint.

The next step is to form the spring. First, cut it into two lengths—one 35″ and the other 12″—then bend the shorter section to a 75° angle so the leg with the eye is about 9″ long. Both these procedures require the use of a cutting torch. Drill four 11/32″ holes through these metal parts: one into the middle of the short leg on the angled bar, and the other three through the main leaf spring. Position these about 6″ from one another with the first at a point 1″ from the leaf's cut end. Since spring steel is rather hard, drill small pilot holes first or use a drill press.

To mount the main leaf, place it on the plywood base in such a way that the core of its eye is centered about 1-3/4″ from the narrow end of the platform. Mark this spot—along with the width of the eye—and cut the angle iron section into two equal pieces and the channel iron into a solid-topped wedge shape forming an angle of 22°. While you're cutting metal, slice one side from your length of square tubular steel to produce an 8″-long U-shaped section.

Bore the holes in these metal pieces to accept the various 1/2″ and 5/16″ fasteners. Use the predrilled openings in the long leaf to position the holes in the newly made "U" piece. Then, with the angle and channel mounts as templates, drill the six 5/16″ holes

through the platform, being careful to center the 1/2″ hole in the spring stop bracket 6-1/4″ from the midpoint of a line drawn between the holes in the angled "holders".

Now, fasten the supports in place, using 5/16″ bolts as illustrated (you may want to countersink the heads to keep them from marring the floor), and double-nut the 1/2″ X 6″ stop bolt firmly to its mount. Slip the 1/2″ X 3-1/2″ bolt through the angle brackets' shoulders and the end of the leaf spring, then bolt the 8″ length of modified square tubular steel to the spring and to the smaller angled leaf. Fasten the base of the wooden head inside the groove of the exposed tubular steel section; you'll need to cross-drill two more mounting holes and remove some wood at its lower

edge to allow a flush fit. Then slip the remaining 14″-long piece of dowel through the bushingless eye and lock it there with two No. 8 X 1/2″ wood screws.

Finish the project by fastening the seat to the main leaf with the wooden wedge between, using the carriage bolt, and tying the bridle rope into a loop through the 1/2″ hole in the horse's mouth. Optional dressing up might include the addition of leather ears, a sisal mane, or a more elaborate paint job.

No matter how you deck it out, though, children are sure to enjoy the horse's lively spring. And as long as the young riders are under 50 pounds, this bronco will be bucking for quite a few years to come.

Hi-ho, Silver . . . awaaay!

RING TOSS GAME

Here's a traditional toy that's easy to make and that will keep children happy for hours, especially on days when they must play indoors.

To make the ring posts, cut two 3/4″ X 5″ X 5″ pine bases. Drill a 1/2″ hole into the center of each square and glue a 1/2″ dowel 6″ long into the hole. Sand the rod tips and block edges to a safe, half-round bevel, and finish the two ring posts with a light coat of varnish or wax.

Fashion six rings from pieces of 1/8″ hardboard. Using a jigsaw or coping saw, cut 5-1/2″-diameter disks with 3-1/2″ center holes. After sanding the rough edges, set the two ring posts 5 yards apart and let your youngsters test their skill!

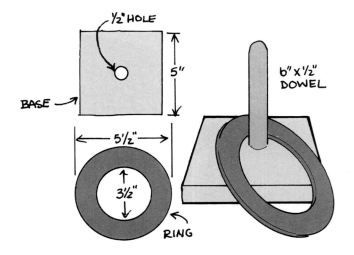

BUZZ BOMBER

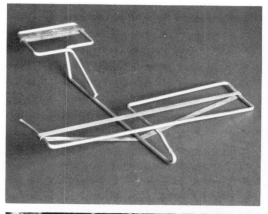

Like the traditional bull roarer, this little gadget is made to be swung around in a circle on a tether. The wind passing over rubber bands on its wings and tail produces an impressive scream.

To make the toy, take a section of 1/8" copper-coated welding rod (it comes in 36" lengths) and a pair of broad-nosed pliers, and simply bend the "airframe" to the configuration shown in the photo, using the grid diagram as a dimension guide. Trim off the 3" or so of metal that's left.

Once you've completed the frame, stretch a wide rubber band across the wings and another over the tail. Then tie about five feet of cord to the front corner of the craft's *left* wing and a wooden bead to the string's free end. The plane is now ready to take to the sky.

Be sure to warn children that the flier can cause injury if it strikes a bystander and that the craft's aerobatic antics should be limited to outdoor areas away from trees, buildings, and other obstructions.

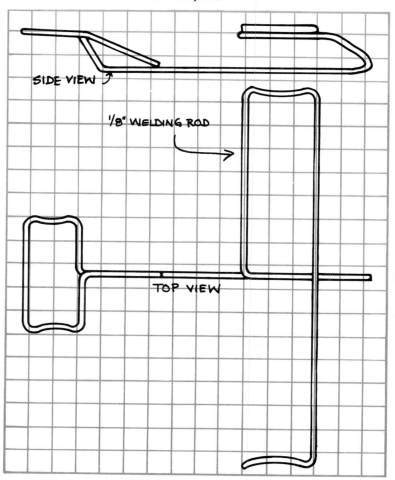

1 SQUARE = 1/2 INCH

SIDE VIEW

1/8" WELDING ROD

TOP VIEW

Begin by cutting a piece of 1/2″— or thicker—plywood into a 16″ X 24″ rectangle. Then, centered at each 16″ end, draw and cut out a 1-1/2″-high triangle with a 1-1/2″ base. These openings are the goals that the coin puck will fall into when the players score. With that done, fasten strips of 1 X 2 along the sides of the board, using nails, dowels, wood screws, or other fasteners. These wooden walls define the playing field and serve as a backstop for the goals.

That finishes the carpentry. To complete the board, draw a red centerline with a felt-tipped marker and, if you wish, varnish the surface. A nice finishing touch is to line beneath the goals with triangles of cloth or cardboard to catch the coin when a score is made.

A nickel and a pair of homemade hockey sticks are all that you need to complete the game. Carve (or cut with a jigsaw) the little swatters from 1/8″-thick pieces of wood. Get creative with the shape if you like, but it's best to standardize the length of the stick's "blade" at 1-1/2″. Obviously, a larger stick would give a player quite a defensive advantage.

RULES FOR THE UNRULY: In its first few weeks of use, your hockey board will probably be subjected to an incredible amount of punishment. So here are some simple rules to keep the game—and that occasional weekend houseful of rowdy guests—under control:

Play begins with the flip of a coin. The winner of the toss then opens the game by shooting from anywhere on the near side of the red centerline, while the other player, staying on the opposite side of the line, defends with the stick. After a goal has been made, the player who didn't score puts the puck into play.

There are only two infractions that carry penalties. The first is placing a defensive stick within the goal "pit", and the second is allowing one's stick to cross the red line. Either of these fouls results in the other player's getting a free shot. This can be taken from any point on the free shooter's side of the board, while the unlucky

NICKEL HOCKEY

You can throw together a rough-and-tumble nickel hockey board in ten minutes or so. Or you can make as fancy a playing "field" as your scrap lumber supply and woodworking skill allow. In either case, the design will be about the same.

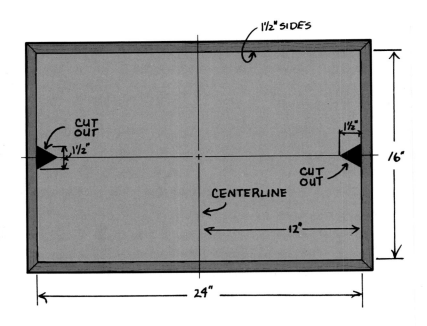

opponent's stick must be held motionless at the apex of the defended goal. Free shots thus require banking the coin off the wall and are far from being the "sure scores" they might seem to be.

If the puck is knocked clear off the board, the player who's not responsible for the overly eager swat is allowed to shoot the nickel, just as in the opening move. Should the coin stop on the centerline, the shot goes to the player who reaches the puck first. In this free-for-all, it's very easy to go past the line in pursuit of the elusive five-cent piece.

SNOWBOUND STRATEGIES: Probably the most difficult nickel hockey skill is keeping cool when you're on the defensive. It's pretty hard to remain calm when your op-

ponent has the puck whizzing about like an enraged bumblebee. It's tempting to leave your goal to chase after the nickel, but an undefended goal can easily lead to a quick defeat.

In fact, many nickel hockey enthusiasts figure that the most important tactics to master are those that can help one move to the front of the line of people waiting to play, and therefore back into the game as rapidly as possible. Announcing that there are fresh doughnuts in the kitchen is a good ploy.

The enthusiasm this game generates is as much fun as the play itself, and if you can find the few minutes necessary to put together your own nickel hockey board before next Saturday night, you'll understand what all the ruckus is about!

The accompanying photos show how the fuselage and wings are made. Lay out a pattern along the fold of a manila envelope and cut through both thicknesses to yield three folded pieces. Sharp scissors or a razor knife will do the trick. While manila is a perfect material for lightness and strength, paint doesn't adhere to its surface, making decoration a problem. The brightly colored model shown here was made from a file folder and then painted. It flies reasonably well, but it isn't capable of the extended journeys that a manila aircraft can achieve.

To avoid stalls and add stability, sandwich a ball of modeling clay about 3/8″ in diameter into the nose. You can experiment by varying the weight to change the flight pattern. Slightly less ballast will make the glider perform loops and returns. And though this lightweight sailplane is intended primarily for indoor use, folding the lower wing up—by pushing in the center of the bottom airfoil with a pencil—to form a monoplane helps increase the craft's stability in a light breeze.

It's surprising how well the biplane glides and does stunts. Indeed, this simple toy should provide hours of fascination for anyone who fancies a temporary (and admittedly vicarious) flight.

BIPLANE GLIDER

Inexpensive, simple-to-assemble gliders are available in nearly every toy shop, but it's infinitely more satisfying to fly a craft you've constructed yourself. Here's a design for a homemade, high-performance miniplane that flies as well as any of the commercial models. After flying it, you may think up some innovative designs of your own.

THE GLIDER CAN BE MADE THIS SIZE
OR CAN BE ENLARGED.

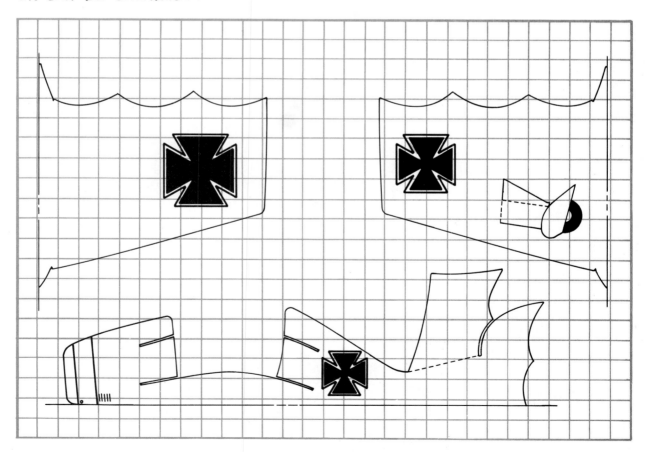

BIPLANE GLIDER

BOTTLE ROCKET

You can keep your budget intact and still provide the youngsters with hours of safe, exciting fun with this water-powered skyrocket. The two-stage missile uses nothing more than compressed air and water to reach altitudes of well over 100 feet. When the "booster" has expended its fuel supply, the top section separates and deploys its payload: a nose cone that with the help of a small parachute floats safely back to earth.

The propulsion unit is a two-liter plastic soft drink bottle. The jug's polyethylene skin is capable of withstanding a water pressure of nearly 200 pounds per square inch before bursting, though you'll only be feeding it a fraction of that amount. Just paint or tape the body to simulate one of the "big jobs", but leave an untouched strip the length of the bottle so you'll be able to see how much water "fuel" it contains.

The nose cone is made from the neck and upper portion of a second container; just cut around the bottle at the line where the taper meets the straight midsection. Later, the threaded part of the neck can be adorned with a piece of foam rubber cut in a conical shape.

A parachute can be fabricated by cutting a circle of lightweight plastic 2 feet in diameter from a dry-cleaning bag and by using small tabs of adhesive tape to attach eight 18″ pieces of string spaced equally around the chute's circumference. The free ends of the cords are then gathered together and tied to a hole in the side of the cone.

The launching platform is a 12″-square piece of 1/2″ plywood trimmed to form an octagon. The control shack consists of one 6″-long 2 X 4 braced perpendicularly with another that's 4″ in length (both members should be beveled and shaped to approximate the silhouette of a real blockhouse). Fasten this onto the platform, using five countersunk No. 8 X 1-1/2″ wood screws. Three 3/4″ X 3/4″ X 4″ wood strips are screwed to the bottom of the base to serve as legs. Opposite the control shack, a 3/8″ hole is bored through the platform and the leg beneath it to accommodate an anchoring nail or gutter spike.

The plumbing fittings function as both a support for the rocket and a means of delivering the pressure necessary to launch it. Assemble them by first threading the inside of the ribbed end of a 1/2″ ABS female pipe-to-barb 90° elbow with a 3/8″ pipe tap. Then screw a 3/8″ brass hose barb into that opening, and fit the elbow's other end with a 2″ nipple of Schedule 40 1/2″ PVC pipe. Fasten the air-supply hose—a 12-foot piece of 3/8″ plastic tubing fitted at one end with the valve stem from an old inner tube—as indicated. After drilling a 1-1/8″ hole in the center of the launching pad, mount the plastic elbow to the underside of the plywood with a pair of 1/2″ copper pipe clamps and No. 4 X 1/2″ wood screws. Make sure the PVC pipe nipple protrudes squarely from the pad's central hole.

Force a garden hose gasket over the nozzle support, temporarily slip the bottle onto the nipple, and carefully mark a line on the 2 X 4 block directly across from the collar molded into the container's neck. Bore a pair of 1/8″ parallel holes at this line and far enough apart to equal the outside diameter of the neck itself, which should be about 1-1/8″. (If you must remove the control shack blocks from the platform in order to align these holes properly, by all means do so.)

Finish the release mechanism by bending a 10″ piece of 1/8″ welding rod into a "U" so the ends align with the holes, slip the wire prongs through the block, and bend their tips outward so they'll slide over the neck collar easily. A 12-foot length of cord equipped with a dowel handle can then be tied to the welding rod to serve as a remote-control launching "trigger".

Select a location free of trees and overhead wires and anchor the board to the ground with a spike. Before launching, it'd be a good idea to coat the PVC nipple with plumber's grease. Put enough water in the bottle to fill it a little more than halfway, nimbly invert the booster so it rests atop the nipple, and shove and lock the welding rod clip over the bottle's neck collar, forcing the container down against the hose gasket.

Lightly fold and pack the parachute and its cords into the cone and place that cap over the booster's blunt nose. With everyone standing well away from the rocket, one person plugs the air valve into the bicycle pump and proceeds to build up pressure, and another stands with release cord taut, watching the platform for signs of pressure-induced leakage. When the seepage occurs (usually in the range of 40 to 50 PSI), the launch technician yanks the release . . . and w-h-o-o-s-h, the rocket blasts off with all the excitement of a real space mission!

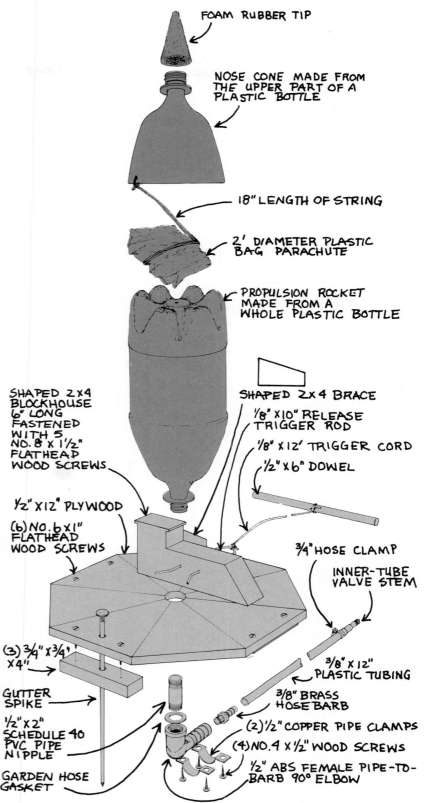

FOAM RUBBER TIP

NOSE CONE MADE FROM THE UPPER PART OF A PLASTIC BOTTLE

18" LENGTH OF STRING

2' DIAMETER PLASTIC BAG PARACHUTE

PROPULSION ROCKET MADE FROM A WHOLE PLASTIC BOTTLE

SHAPED 2×4 BRACE

1/8" ×10" RELEASE TRIGGER ROD

1/8" ×12' TRIGGER CORD

1/2" ×6" DOWEL

3/4" HOSE CLAMP

INNER-TUBE VALVE STEM

3/8" ×12" PLASTIC TUBING

3/8" BRASS HOSE BARB

(2) 1/2" COPPER PIPE CLAMPS

(4) NO.4 ×1/2" WOOD SCREWS

1/2" ABS FEMALE PIPE-TO-BARB 90° ELBOW

SHAPED 2×4 BLOCKHOUSE 6" LONG FASTENED WITH 5 NO. 8 ×1 1/2" FLATHEAD WOOD SCREWS

1/2" ×12" PLYWOOD

(6) NO.6×1" FLATHEAD WOOD SCREWS

(3) 3/4" ×3/4" ×4"

GUTTER SPIKE

1/2" ×2" SCHEDULE 40 PVC PIPE NIPPLE

GARDEN HOSE GASKET

BOTTLE ROCKET

HIGH STEPPERS

Every youngster who's seen a clown striding about on stilts has undoubtedly wished to own a pair. Here are two solutions to the problem faced when your young one asks you to make some . . . right away! For a quick-fix solution, reach for a couple of large vegetable or juice cans and follow the easy instructions below. While your child is happily clattering along on his tin can stilts, you'll have time to build the more durable—and much quieter—wooden stilts, also described.

TIN CAN WALKERS: Take two No. 10 (or larger) cans and cut one end out of each one, leaving the other end intact. Then using a large can opener or screwdriver, cut or punch two holes in the sides of each container, directly opposite one another and just below the rim of the closed end.

Make a handle for each stilt by threading a piece of rope about 4 feet long through the holes and tying the ends into a loose knot. Standing on the cans with arms straight down, a youngster should be able to grasp a knot in each hand and pull the ropes fairly taut. When the knots are at the right length, tighten them and cut off the loose ends.

WOODEN STILTS: These "high steppers" are not only easy to build, but because they don't have offset footrests as conventional stilts do, they're easier to use. The child's weight rests directly above the center support of each staff, resulting in a freer movement that eliminates many of the problems in learning to "walk tall".

It doesn't take much more than a supply of scrap wood to construct the stilts. You'll need two 60″ lengths of 1 X 2, two 16″ pieces of 2 X 2, two 1 X 2 spacers (each about 4″ long), four 5-1/2″ pieces of 1 X 6, 40 No. 8 X 1-1/2″ flathead wood screws, and a small amount of carpenter's glue.

With the exception of the 1 X 6 gussets, all the wooden components for this project can be trimmed from a 5-foot length of 2 X 4, if desired.

After cutting the handles, gussets, spacers, and support legs to the dimensions shown in the illustration, temporarily assemble each stilt and drill holes for the fasteners. The easiest way to do this is to position one handle, leg, and spacer assembly on a flat surface so that the upward-facing edges of the components are all flush and so that the sides of the handle and leg overlap. Next, place one gusset on top of this timber trio, making sure all the pieces are positioned according to the drawing, and drill holes where indicated through both the gusset and the wooden pieces beneath it. This procedure will be simplified if you use a No. 8 combination drill and countersink tool.

Spread some glue on the contact surfaces, including the joint between the handle and foot, and thread your fasteners loosely into their holes. Flip the assembly over and repeat the procedure on the other side, being careful not to drill the complementary series of holes directly opposite the initial ones. Then bore two holes through the handle and into the foot, and install a screw at each of these locations to insure a solid connection. Finally, tighten the remaining 18 fasteners in each stilt assembly and cover the new "timber limbs" with a coat or two of good outdoor paint. Tack patches cut from an automobile tire on the bottoms of the stilts and on the upper surface of the footrests to prevent slips.

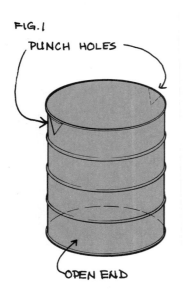

FIG. 1

PUNCH HOLES

OPEN END

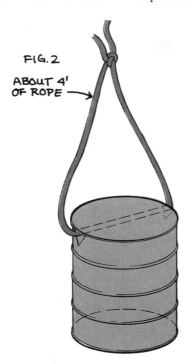

FIG. 2

ABOUT 4′ OF ROPE

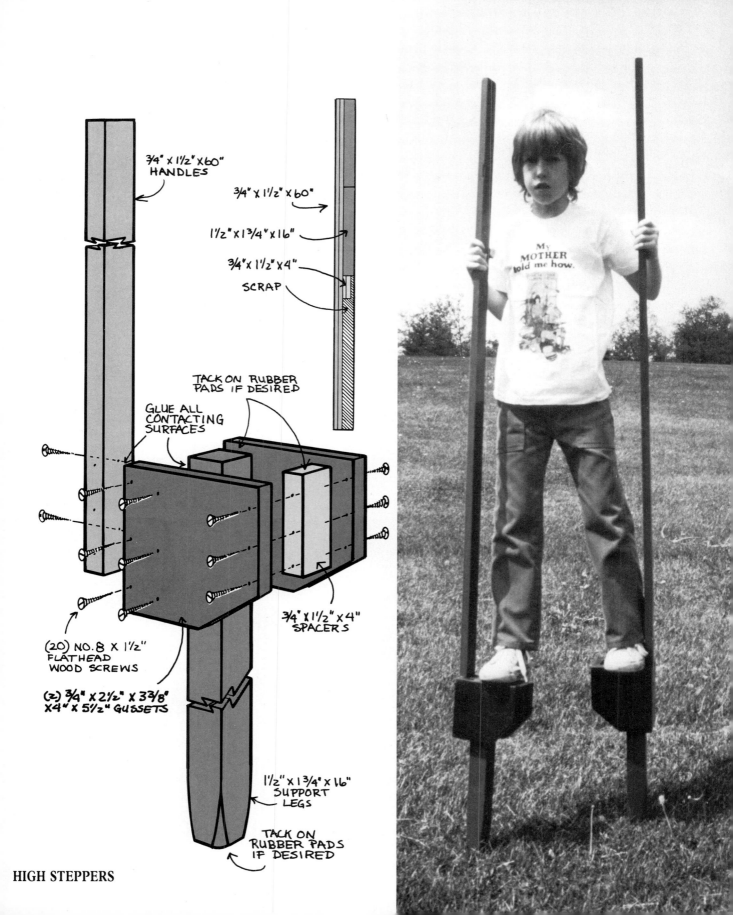

3/4" X 1 1/2" X 60"
HANDLES

3/4" X 1 1/2" X 60"

1 1/2" X 1 3/4" X 16"

3/4" X 1 1/2" X 4"

SCRAP

TACK ON RUBBER
PADS IF DESIRED

GLUE ALL
CONTACTING
SURFACES

(20) NO.8 X 1 1/2"
FLATHEAD
WOOD SCREWS

(2) 3/4" X 2 1/2" X 3 3/8"
X 4" X 5 1/2" GUSSETS

3/4" X 1 1/2" X 4"
SPACERS

1 1/2" X 1 3/4" X 16"
SUPPORT
LEGS

TACK ON
RUBBER PADS
IF DESIRED

HIGH STEPPERS

Because the blade's shape determines how well it will fly, it's important that the wood be of the proper dimensions. The width of the finished blade should be a little more than twice its thickness, and the length must be at least ten times the width. The prop-up pictured here has a 3/8″ X 1″ X 10″ propeller. Vary the size of the blade if you wish, but be sure to maintain the thickness-to-width-to-length ratio.

Start with a cut-to-length rectangular scrap of lightweight (*heavier* than balsa) lumber such as white pine. Measure the wood lengthwise and mark the midpoint on both sides. Then draw a line completely around the middle of the propeller block, connecting the two dots and dividing the wooden piece into two 5″ sections in the process.

In order to fly, the prop-up must be carved into a characteristic propeller shape. With the block positioned so that the long edge is facing you and the inch-wide surface is on top, imagine the right-hand 5″ half of

WHITTLED PROP-UP

Fashioning a high-flying propeller on a stick that will soar into the air like a helicopter when given a sharp spin requires only a piece of lightweight wood, a pocketknife, a cylindrical wooden rod roughly the thickness of a pencil, some glue, and a marker. It's made up of only two glue-joined parts: a propeller blade and a launching stick.

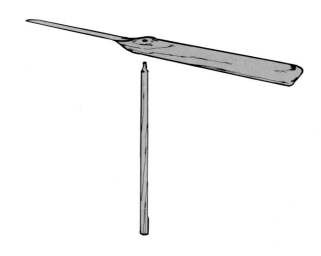

the blade sloping up and away from you while the left-hand portion slants up towards you.

Beginning at the middle line and working toward one tip of the piece of wood, whittle from the top of one edge to the bottom of the opposite side. Turn the wood upside down and repeat the process on the underside of the carved piece, forming a blade that follows the diagonal of the wood piece's cross-section.

Shape the other end in exactly the same manner but angle it in the opposite direction. Both sides of the propeller should be made as thin as possible; otherwise, the blade will be too heavy and the prop-up won't fly. Streamline the spinner further by tapering the blades from their centers to the edges and by rounding off the corners. Sand the whittled wood to give your aircraft a smooth surface.

Now all your tiny helicopter needs is a launching stick. Measure the propeller again to find the exact midpoint and mark this spot. Then carve or drill a hole large enough to allow your launching rod to fit snugly into the center of the blade. Use any thin, wooden, cylindrical rod for this part. A 9″ "all-day sucker" stick is ideal for the task, but a pencil or piece of dowel will serve as well. Apply glue to one end of the rod, insert that tip in the center hole of the propeller, and let the adhesive dry.

With the building phase completed test flights can begin. Hold the toy so the propeller is on top and give the rod a twirling flip between the palms of your hands. When the rod is released, the prop-up should spin rapidly and climb far above your head. If, however, it dive-bombs to your feet you'll know it was twirled the wrong way. Spin the launching rod in the opposite direction the next time, and it will take off.

The handmade helicopter can be flown indoors (with care), but it's best to fly it outside where it can soar as high as 50 feet in the air. If it's released with a slight tilt, it can be flown from person to person, and it can even be caught by the stick with a little practice.

WILLOW WHISTLE

This willow whistle is fun to make and will provide many hours of musical entertainment. It can also be used as a signaling device in an emergency and to train a dog to respond only to the distinct tone of its owner's whistle.

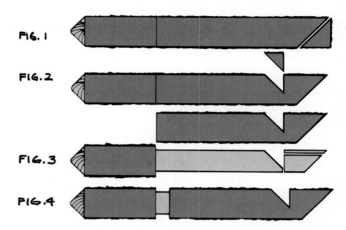

Find a tree or shrub with suitable bark. A weeping willow is a sure thing, but any woody plant with a bark that's fairly tough and smooth will do the job fine.

Locate a 4″ knot-free section of branch about as big around as a finger. Then cut off the branch 4″ to 6″ longer than the segment you've tagged for your whistle. Note that the additional length need not be smooth or knot-free.

Next, trim any subsidiary twigs from the branch and—at the point where you want your whistle to begin—score completely through the bark all the way around the stick. Lop off the tip of the other end of the piece of wood at about a 45° angle (see Fig. 1).

After that, loosen the bark by taking the handle of your knife and beating vigorously around and along the entire length of the whistle section. These blows should be fairly hard, but be careful not to overdo them or the bark will split. Now, grasp the whistle portion in the palm of one hand and the "extra" inches in the palm of the other hand and—ever so gently—twist. If nothing happens, beat the bark some more and try to twist it again. Sooner or later, the

sheathing will separate from the wood with a snap.

Bark loose? Good. Slide it back into its original position over the bare wood. Then—on the long side of your 45°-angle tip about 3/4″ in from the point—cut a small horizontal slit through the bark deep enough to score the wood below. Now make an angled cut about 1/4″ farther down the whistle from the scored slit and remove a triangular wedge of bark as in Fig. 2.

Gently remove the tube of bark and look for the scored line (about 3/4″ in from the tip) on the wood underneath. Then cut off the end of the wood, and slice a thin vertical slab away from its longer side (see Fig. 3). Reinsert the tip of wood into the slanted end of the tube of bark, slide the rest of the skinned branch into the cylinder's other end (see Fig. 4), and there you have it: a completed whistle!

Blow through the angled end and adjust the whistle's tone by moving the long wooden plunger in and out (if it sticks, just wet it a bit). With a little practice, you can do the same all over again with a larger branch, then cut some finger holes and—presto!—you've made a recorder.

CLIMBING BEAR

Here's an old-time folk toy that can be whipped up in a jiffy for any of the little people on your gift list. They'll spend many an enjoyable moment making the bear climb the "ropes" and watching it slide back down.

It's a project that leaves plenty of room for creativity, so you might, for instance, prefer a climbing squirrel or monkey. As long as you do one critical thing properly—drill the holes through the paws at the correct angle—almost any size and shape of animal cut from almost any thickness of shop scrap will work. But be sure that a climber fashioned for a very young child is made from a light piece of wood. That way, it won't hurt if the toy accidentally hits the youngster in the head when it drops from the top to the bottom.

First, sketch a bear (or whatever) on a sheet of paper and transfer it to a scrap of leftover board that's somewhere between 3/8" and 3/4" thick. Draw an animal from 3" to 6" tall—depending on the size of the child you intend to give it to—and saw it out. Then make a little "yoke" like the one shown in the photos, and drill three holes in it.

The next step is the critical part: The holes through the bear's paws *must* be drilled at an angle as close to 45° as possible, and *not* straight up and down.

The size of the holes isn't critical as long as the hard-braided cotton cord that the bear climbs on can slip through the openings easily enough to allow the bear to slide back down. The bear shown here climbs ordinary heavy-duty cotton packaging cord, and the 5/32" holes in the animal's paws seem to work just fine.

Decorate your bear with nontoxic paint (remember, little folks tend to chew their toys), and thread 45" to 50" of twine through each of its paws. Tie a couple of knots in, or fasten a large bead to, the tail end of each string so the animal won't come off, and secure the tops of the cords through the ends of the yoke. A third "hanging" string is then fastened through the center of the yoke.

Tie the center string to anything handy that's high enough to hold the bottoms of the "working" cords at a comfortable height. Just alternate pulling on one cord and then the other and watch that bear climb! When it reaches the top, relax your grip on the strings, and your climbin' critter will slide right back down, all ready for its next trip.

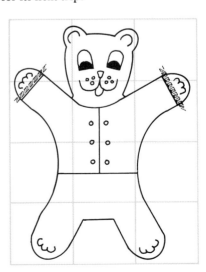

1 SQUARE = 1 INCH

TOYS FOR ALL AGES/CLIMBING BEAR

POCKET SUNDIAL

You can build the pocket timepiece shown in the accompanying photo for the price of a small tin box of aspirin! To make this a truly "no cost" project, first raid the medicine chest for one of the little flat metal boxes. Then put the tablets in a labeled bottle, and if you have a yen for the decorative, paint the box.

Now, trace the full-sized patterns provided here. Use those sketches to reproduce the faceplate and the gnomon (or pointer) on thin cardboard and cut out both pieces. Make the slit indicated by the solid line in the center of the plate before fitting the cardboard into the bottom of the metal box, securing it with adhesive if necessary.

The next step is to transfer the dial pattern to paper, coloring it if you wish, and to glue the dial onto the cardboard so the slits match.

Finally, glue the directional arrow into the lid of the aspirin container so that it points in the same direction as the 12 on the clock face.

To read the time, simply open the box up flat in your hand, point the arrow to the north, and insert the gnomon so that its tallest edge will be nearest the number 12. The shadow will point to the approximate time, except when daylight saving time is in effect; then the timepiece will be about an hour slow.

There you have it: a handy "pocket watch" that's shock, crush, and dust resistant. In fact, the only real drawback to this little gem is that it isn't waterproof, but then you wouldn't use a sundial in the rain anyway!

SUNDIAL PARTS - ACTUAL SIZE

GNOMON

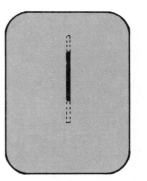

CARDBOARD FACEPLATE

DIRECTIONAL ARROW

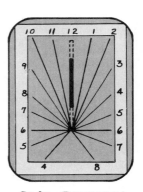

DIAL PATTERN

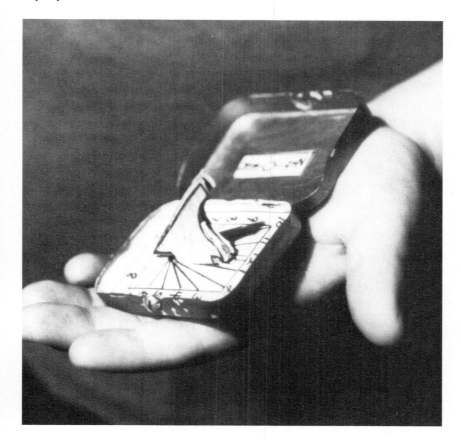

DOLL CRADLE

Here's a toy created entirely from shop scraps. Using the grid drawings as a reference, fabricate cardboard templates. After tracing the outlines on appropriate pieces of wood, cut those boards to shape. Fluting the bedposts' corners with a router is an optional but attractive finishing touch.

Half-lap the 65° joints between the legs and the rockers, cut a 1/4″ X 13/16″ X 4-1/8″ rabbet into the upper inside edges of each upright, and glue the joints together. When they've dried, cement the bottom boards in place and then glue and brad the side and end panels in their proper positions.

Finish by painting or staining the wee bed, then go make some child very happy.

1 SQUARE = 1/2 INCH

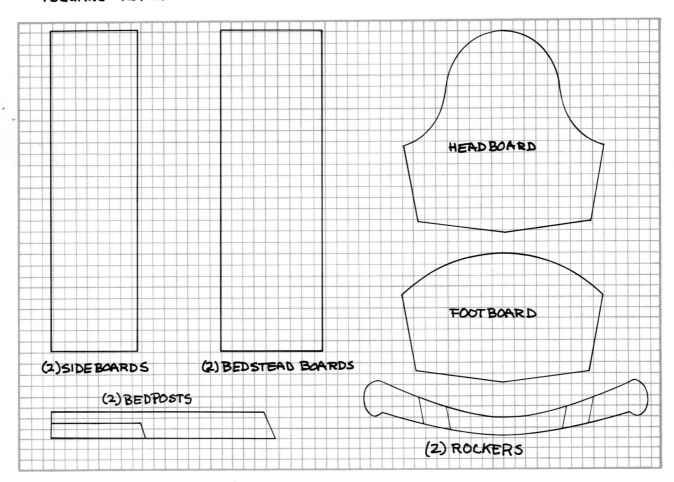

(2) SIDE BOARDS

(2) BEDSTEAD BOARDS

(2) BEDPOSTS

HEADBOARD

FOOTBOARD

(2) ROCKERS

ROCKING HORSE

The body of this range-ready rocking horse is formed from a single thickness of 1″ lumber, while its head and tail are laminated with two more thicknesses of the same lumber cut with the grain running at a right angle to that of the body. Though the pieces of 1 X 12 can be glued together in advance and cut as one, using a band saw, there's an advantage to sawing each of the layers separately: Because the horse's back arcs downward significantly and because the critter's tail rises pertly in the air, there'll probably be enough wood left over after cutting out the main body to form the laminations for the head and tail.

The runners for the rocker can be profiled to suit the age and coordination of your child. The curve on the design shown here is a bit on the conservative side and limits the forward and backward movement to prevent head-over-heels disasters. If you do decide to shorten or raise the ends of the rockers, it might also be a good idea to choose a sound hardwood—such as maple or ash, which can stand up to the additional stress—rather than pine or another softwood.

The saddle design is, of course, a matter of personal preference. This one is English, but you might opt for Western for your underage cowpoke. In either case, secure the stirrups to the saddle's under-the-belly "cinch" with a brass paper-fastener so that the fabric can be removed and cleaned easily.

1 SQUARE = 1 INCH

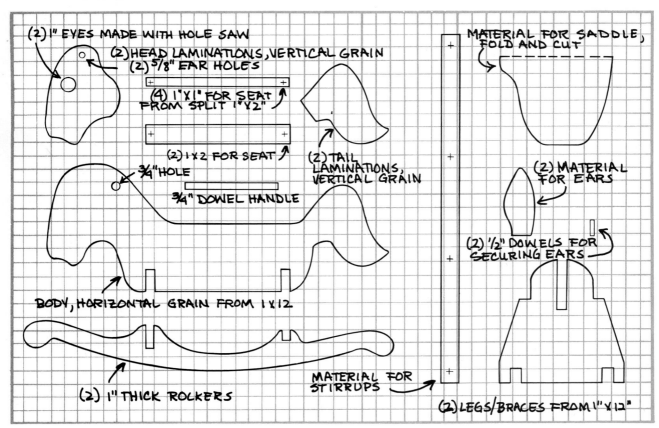

(2) 1″ EYES MADE WITH HOLE SAW
(2) HEAD LAMINATIONS, VERTICAL GRAIN
(2) 5/8″ EAR HOLES
(4) 1″X1″ FOR SEAT FROM SPLIT 1″X2″
(2) 1X2 FOR SEAT
3/4″ HOLE
3/4″ DOWEL HANDLE
(2) TAIL LAMINATIONS, VERTICAL GRAIN
BODY, HORIZONTAL GRAIN FROM 1X12
(2) 1″ THICK ROCKERS
MATERIAL FOR STIRRUPS
MATERIAL FOR SADDLE, FOLD AND CUT
(2) MATERIAL FOR EARS
(2) 1/2″ DOWELS FOR SECURING EARS
(2) LEGS/BRACES FROM 1″X12″

WOODEN TOP

Amidst the gadgetry and gimcrackery of modern toys, a plain old-fashioned plaything is especially appealing. And it would be hard to imagine a more traditional toy than this homemade wooden top.

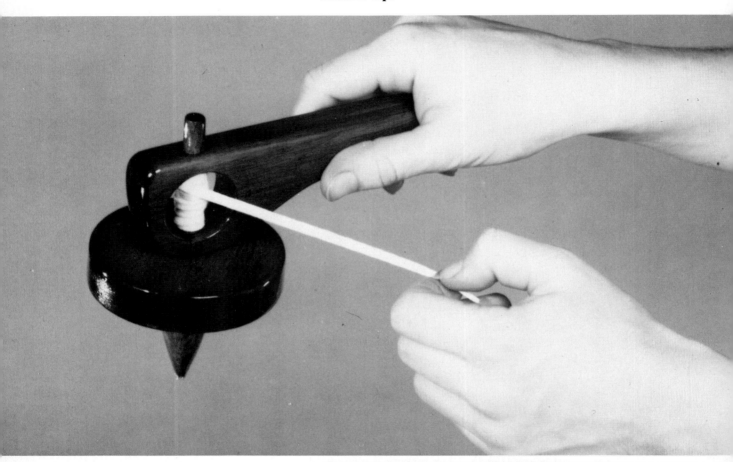

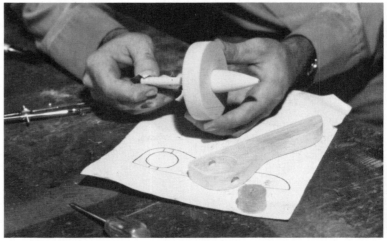

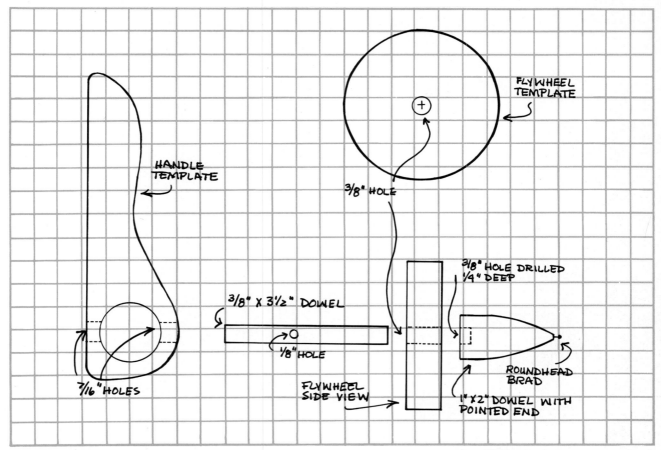

HANDLE TEMPLATE

FLYWHEEL TEMPLATE

3/8" HOLE

3/8" HOLE DRILLED 1/4" DEEP

3/8" X 3½" DOWEL

1/8" HOLE

7/16" HOLES

FLYWHEEL SIDE VIEW

ROUNDHEAD BRAD

1" X 2" DOWEL WITH POINTED END

1 SQUARE = ½ INCH

The little spinner can easily be built by the most inexperienced woodworker and requires nothing more than a coping saw, a drill with 1/8", 3/8", and 7/16" bits, some sandpaper, a small round-head finishing brad, carpenter's glue, a 3-1/2" length of 3/8" dowel, a 2" section of 1" dowel, an old shoestring, and a piece of scrap wood that measures about 3/4" X 5" X 7". It's possible to fashion the top in as little as half an hour.

The accompanying drawings can be transferred to your working material, but first they must be enlarged to fit a grid with 1/2" squares; then the design can be traced onto your lumber scrap. Be sure to retain the center-point mark on the circular piece as you enlarge and transfer the plan.

Cut the wood to size, then drill a "pilot" hole through the handle and saw out the round opening that will serve as the top's string housing.

With that done, "guesstimate" the center of the just-cut opening and bore two 7/16" holes—on a vertical line that intersects the central point—through the upper and lower "walls". Next, carefully drill a straight 3/8" hole exactly through the midpoint of the toy's flywheel to serve as the axle mount.

Now, take the piece of 1" dowel, find its center, and drill a 3/8" hole about 1/4" into one end. Using a coarse piece of sandpaper or a file, fashion the opposite end of the peg into a point as shown, and tap your brad right into the tip. To complete the spinning part of the top, lightly coat one end of the 3/8" dowel with glue and push it through the wooden disk until a 1/4" nub protrudes. Cover the nub and a small area around it with adhesive and fasten the metal-tipped

peg to the flywheel and its axle. Then temporarily slip the shaft into the handle's two holes and bore a 1/8" hole through the rod, as illustrated, to serve as a catch for the string.

Finally, sand all parts of the top to a smooth finish (you might want to round the edges), and stain the toy or give it a coat of polyurethane varnish.

To set the gyro spinning, merely slide it into the handle, thread one end of the cord through the axle hole, carefully wind the remaining string around the shaft, and then pull hard on the string's free end. The whirling part of the toy will drop from the handle and dance merrily, spinning along any hard, smooth surface. There's little doubt that your home-built top will fascinate the youngsters on a rainy spring day, and you, too, may be tempted to give it a whirl.

SHINGLE ROCKET

Back in the days when the Iowa plains were covered with prairie grass instead of corn, pioneer children used to fling shingle rockets high into the air. Watching the rockets in flight and dodging them as they fell to earth brought excitement to the lives of these often isolated youngsters.

Even if you've never touched knife to wood, you can spend a half hour of easy whittling time with a wooden shake and have fun making yourself one of these high-flying shingles.

CARVE IT OUT: Any kind of wooden shingle will do as long as it's thicker at one end than at the other. You might talk the clerk at your local lumberyard into giving you seconds (new shingles with flaws in them), or when you see an old barn or shed being torn down, you could ask the building's owner to let you pick through the rubble. And if you're ever splitting your own cedar roofing shakes, watch for those that diminish in thickness from one end to the other. Since they're heavier than

the store-bought variety, homemade shingles make the best flyers of all.

Once you have your raw material in hand, use a sharp knife to carve it into an arrow shape, making sure the point is at the thick end of the shake, and the fin is at the thin end. The fin should take up one-third of the total length of the toy and be about 3-1/2″ wide, while the shaft, which ought to be about an inch wide, will use up the remaining two-thirds.

Since shingle wood splits easily, it's best to cut from the back toward the point of the missile. That way, there's less danger of accidentally slicing off the fin.

After the rocket has taken shape, find its center of gravity by balancing the high flyer horizontally on your finger. Then whittle a 3/8″-deep notch at that central point, angling the cut approximately 45° toward the pointed end.

LAUNCHING THE FLYER: You'll need a rocket launcher to blast your creation into the clouds. Use a stick that's about 2 feet long and an inch thick. If the wood is green, say a good springy branch of ash or oak, it'll give the shingle a greater boost. Tie an 18″ length of strong cord (3/16″ nylon clothesline works well) near one end of the wand and loop a tight knot into the line's free end.

Then find a wide open space for your firing range. Until you get the hang of aiming your shots, it's wise to practice away from greenhouses, beehives, and the garden patch with that perfect prize melon you plan to take to the county fair.

Make your final preparations for blast-off by grasping the launcher with one hand in the manner shown in the photographs. With the knot caught in the notch of the rocket's shaft, pull the cord taut by grasping the fin with your other hand. With your arms straight, swing the rocket and launcher back, then whip them forward and up in a smooth arc as if you were tossing water from a pail high into the air, and release the wooden arrow the instant the launcher is directly over your head.

Practicing the shingle rocket launch is half the fun. Toss it high into the air, watch it fly, and then run for cover!

A good throw will sling a shingle rocket two or three hundred feet straight up, where it'll hang for a moment before it comes hurtling back to earth.

A WORD OF WARNING: It is possible, of course, to modify your missiles by creating different shapes, sizes, and weights. But whatever the configuration, be sure you're quick on your feet!

Not knowing where the pointed projectiles are going to land is part of the great adventure. All the dashing to and fro only adds to the general merriment. However, with a group of young rocket launchers, it's prudent to have them send up just one missile at a time.

SHINGLE ROCKET

TUNNEL SLIDE

This tunnel/slide/rocker combination may help keep you from going off *your* rocker on those days when "there's nothing to do blues" overcome your little ones. To make this multiuse plaything, you'll need a 42"-square section of 3/4" plywood, a 32" X 48" piece of 1/4" plywood (be sure the panel's grain runs perpendicular to the 4-foot dimension), ten 16" lengths of 1 X 2 (which can be bought in strips or cut to 3/4" X 1-1/2" from wider boards), and the two sizes of screws called for in the illustration.

Start by upscaling the pattern provided onto a large piece of paper to form a full-size template. Then transfer the twin shapes to the 42"-square sheet of 3/4" plywood and mark the positions of the necessary screw holes. Cut out the two sides, clamp them together, and bore the holes in "two birds with one stone" fashion.

Next, secure the ten ribs—broad sides exposed—between the rocker's sides, using 1-3/4" wood screws and countersinking the heads slightly. Cut the remaining plywood board in half against the grain, and using glue and screws, secure the two resulting pieces to the upper and lower faces of the rib bed. Hold the sheets fast at one end with four countersunk 3/4" screws, then "walk" the panels into position, anchoring them as it becomes necessary. The number of fasteners will depend on the flexibility of the 1/4" plywood.

Finish the project by covering the screw holes with filler, sanding all the surfaces lightly, and painting the rocker the colors of your choice.

I SQUARE = I INCH

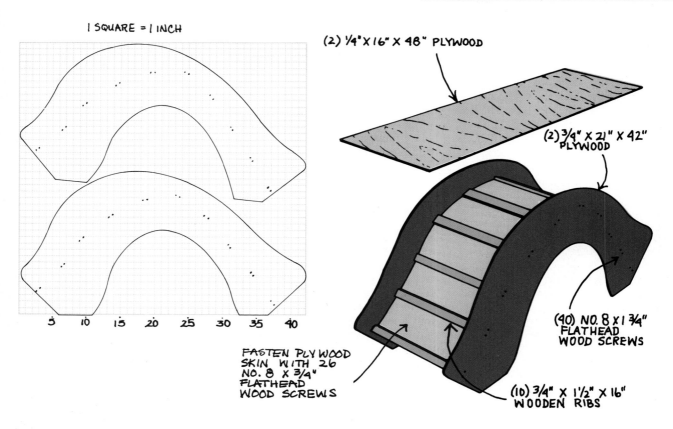

(2) 1/4" X 16" X 48" PLYWOOD

(2) 3/4" X 21" X 42" PLYWOOD

(40) NO. 8 X 1 3/4" FLATHEAD WOOD SCREWS

FASTEN PLYWOOD SKIN WITH 26 NO. 8 X 3/4" FLATHEAD WOOD SCREWS

(10) 3/4" X 1 1/2" X 16" WOODEN RIBS

WOODEN SOLDIER

What's the holiday season or a birthday without a wooden soldier or two to join in the festivities? To make a pint-sized sentry, take a scrap of wood that measures 1-3/4" X 2" X 7-1/2", a second odd piece about 1/2" thick by 3" square, and a 2-1/4"-long section of broomstick or dowel.

Cut or sand the corners from the block, round one end of the billet, and cut a slot, as shown, to simulate a pair of legs. The guardsman's arms are made by cutting the dowel lengthwise down its center, then sanding and beveling the two resulting pieces as indicated. To make the base, trim the 3" square of wood to form a circle, and smooth off its top edge.

Paint all the parts, tack the arms in place, and glue the figure to its stand. To complete the setting, transfer the scaled-down template provided here onto a 10" X 20" piece of stiff cardboard and form and color the sentry's guardhouse.

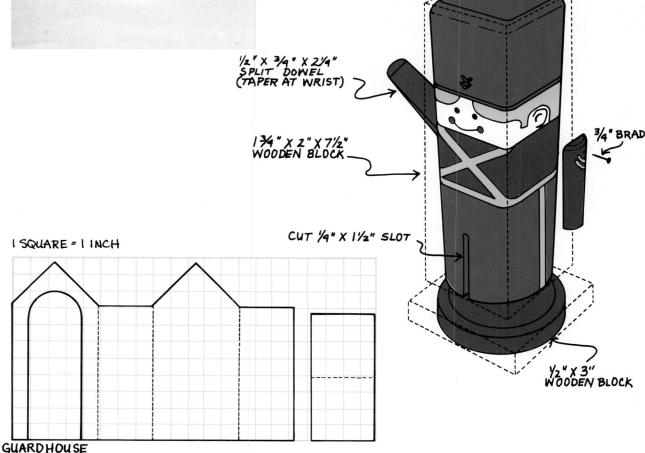

½" X ¾" X 2¼"
SPLIT DOWEL
(TAPER AT WRIST)

1¾" X 2" X 7½"
WOODEN BLOCK

¾" BRAD

CUT ¼" X 1½" SLOT

½" X 3"
WOODEN BLOCK

I SQUARE = I INCH

GUARDHOUSE

BANTAM BACKHOE

The junior "hardhats" on your gift list will really like this down-to-earth gadget, once you've taken the time necessary to size and assemble it. The materials include two 10' lengths of 3/4" electrical metallic tubing (E.M.T.), a 39" piece of the same conduit in 1/2" diameter, an 18" section of 1" E.M.T. bent to a 90° arc (these are available preformed, but they can often be found in an electrical contractor's scrap pile), a section of 18-gauge sheet metal measuring 13" X 16", a 7" X 7" piece of 3/4" plywood, and an assortment of plumbing and fastening hardware.

Cut the tubing to the lengths indicated in the accompanying illustration, drill holes at the spots shown, and paint the metal to suit your youngster's taste. Next—with a pair of tinsnips—trim the galvanized sheet to shape, using the pattern as a guide. Then carefully contour the back of the bucket by bending it around a solid curved object. (The 2-1/4" retaining tang at its end can be folded over a 3/8" bolt or rod.) Finish the scoop by bending up its side, drilling holes at the points designated, and giving it a coat of paint. Now, cut the plywood section into a circle. This round disk serves as the seat.

Finally, just assemble the parts, sand or file them smooth as necessary, bolt the seat onto the stand, and let your young backhoe operator have at it, preferably in soft soil and at a spot that you don't mind seeing excavated!

TOYS FOR ALL AGES

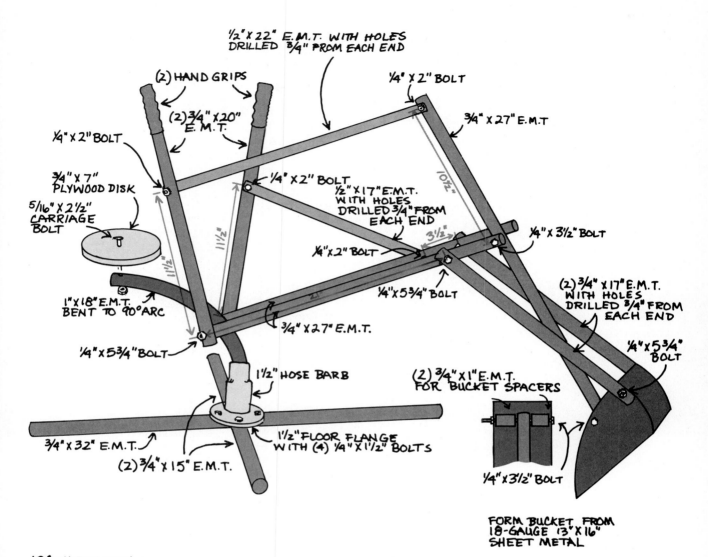

½" X 22" E.M.T. WITH HOLES
DRILLED ¾" FROM EACH END

(2) HAND GRIPS

(2) ¾" X 20"
E.M.T.

¼" X 2" BOLT

¾" X 27" E.M.T

¼" X 2" BOLT

¾" X 7"
PLYWOOD DISK

½" X 17" E.M.T.
WITH HOLES
DRILLED ¾" FROM
EACH END

5/16" X 2½"
CARRIAGE
BOLT

10½"

3½"

¼" X 3½" BOLT

¼" X 2" BOLT

1" X 18" E.M.T.
BENT TO 90° ARC

11½"

11½"

1½"

¼" X 5¾" BOLT

(2) ¾" X 17" E.M.T.
WITH HOLES
DRILLED ¾" FROM
EACH END

¼" X 5¾" BOLT

¼" X 5¾" BOLT

1½" HOSE BARB

(2) ¾" X 1" E.M.T.
FOR BUCKET SPACERS

¾" X 32" E.M.T.

1½" FLOOR FLANGE
WITH (4) ¼" X 1½" BOLTS

(2) ¾" X 15" E.M.T.

¼" X 3½"
BOLT

FORM BUCKET FROM
18-GAUGE 13" X 16"
SHEET METAL

1 SQUARE = 1 INCH

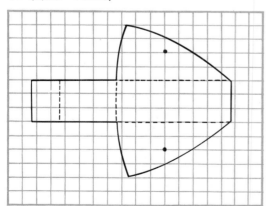

BANTAM BACKHOE

ARTS AND CRAFTS PROJECTS

HARDWOOD COMBS

This is just the project for anyone with a workshop littered with hardwood scraps.

By experimenting with both the design and the shaping of these beautiful bits of wood, you can create hardwood combs for pleasure and possibly for profit. So dig out several fine-grained wood pieces and give it a try.

EQUIPMENT AND RAW MATERIALS: A table saw does a great job of cutting each comb's teeth, but for those blessed with steady hands and careful natures, a miter box and handsaw will do the job. Stay away from a band saw, which tends to make wavy, uneven cuts.

In addition to a saw, round up several grades of sandpaper ranging from coarse to very fine, and a belt sander to speed up the shaping process and to taper and sharpen the comb's teeth. Disk sanders and sanding blocks will work, too, but they take more time.

Be sure to wear a good mask over your nose and mouth when sanding for prolonged periods, since the very fine dust given off by hardwoods can irritate the nasal passages and lungs.

A bit of No. 3 steel wool and one can each of shellac and linseed oil will round out your supplies.

Almost any kind of tight-grained hardwood is suitable for this project: Walnut, zebrawood (which has nice grain patterns), bird's-eye maple, purpleheart, rosewood (it darkens with time), cocobolo, and teak all make up into beautiful combs. Naturally, the exact dimensions of the wood will vary with each scrap and each comb design, but as a general rule, start with pieces that are between 3/8" and 1/2" thick. When selecting wood, bear in mind that the teeth of each comb *must* follow the direction of the grain, or they may snap off while the comb is being made or later when it's being used.

Local lumber dealers are a good source for raw material for those whose workshops do not abound in leftover wood scraps, as well as for those interested in starting a hardwood comb minibusiness. Note that wood costing only about a dollar can produce combs that retail for three times that amount.

MARKING AND CUTTING THE TEETH: Select a hardwood scrap, and pencil in a line to mark the end of the saw cuts for the teeth. This line can be curved, straight, angled, or whatever shape pleases you. In any case, it should be made across the wood's grain and about halfway up the piece of wood.

Now comes the delicate operation of cutting the teeth. With a table saw, use a blade that will give a cut 1/8" wide and set the blade so that it cuts all the way through the wood. Brace the wood against the fence and make the first cut about 1/2" in from one edge of the scrap, sawing right up to the penciled mark. Next, move the block over 1/8" and make another cut. Either "eyeball" the spacing of these cuts or, better yet, use a guide. Continue to cut teeth across the entire block—leaving 1/8" slits between 1/8" teeth—until you come to within 1/2" of the scrap's other edge.

At this point, flip the comb over and carefully let the saw's blade retrace each cut, extending it by 1/4". This will produce the identical saw angle and design on each side of the comb. If a handsaw and miter box are used, this recutting is unnecessary.

SHAPING THE HANDLE: First—on *both* sides of the comb—outline the handle's intended final shape. There's no need for fancy French curves here. Just select any handy object with the approximate radius you want. Be playful. Experiment. Try several designs before you settle on the one that suits you best.

Saw and/or sand the comb, working it down to the finished shape. If you're using a belt sander, remove the corners of the handle quickly with coarse sandpaper, then fine-sand it from there. A band saw or coping saw will speed the roughing-out process for those without access to a power sander.

A FEW POINTERS: Before going any further, sand the comb's teeth until they taper to a point. Otherwise, the comb, viewed from above, will be correctly shaped, but viewed from the side, will have teeth that don't taper to a point but remain

3/8" or 1/2" thick all the way down. And that kind of comb won't do!

Press the piece of work first against the belt of your sander—teeth facing "downstream" in the direction of the belt's rotation—and gradually apply increasing pressure to the teeth to make them taper evenly. Then flip the comb over and sand the other side to the same taper. Continue this until the ends of the teeth are sharp (but not feather-edged) and till the comb's handle is between 1/4" and 1/2" thick.

Now, it's time to actually put points on the ends of the tapered teeth. To do this, loosen the belt on the sander so that it can be slipped over about 1" beyond the edge of the machine. Then [1] turn the sander on, [2] hold the comb so that the extended edge of the belt is positioned between two teeth, [3] angle the comb a bit so as to sand away part of the tip of one tooth, and [4] turn the comb over and sand the other side of

the same tooth to a point. Do this for each tooth, and try to give all of the teeth the same shape and degree of sharpness. This operation can also be done by hand.

Finally, sand the edges of the comb at an angle to put a point on the comb's 1/2"-wide end teeth.

THE FINISHING STEPS: With sandpaper of increasingly finer grit, smooth any rough spots, especially on the insides of the teeth. Don't rush. It takes time to do this job properly.

To bring out the texture and natural beauty of the wood, apply a light sealer. For a quick but effective finish, combine equal amounts of shellac and linseed oil (about three ounces of each) and apply the mixture sparingly, rubbing it in well with a rag so as not to leave any excess oil. (If even a trace of oil remains, you'll gunk up your hair!)

After the oil-shellac mixture has soaked in and dried, buff the entire

surface of the comb with No. 3 steel wool. This will bring out the grain's texture even more and give it a rich gleam.

The comb can also be left as it is, with the hair's natural oil eventually working its way into the wood.

The finishing process doesn't have to stop here, however. Mother-of-pearl or semiprecious stones can be inlaid into a comb's handle, or a design may be carved into it.

PRODUCTION AND MARKETING: Those who master each step of the process will have no difficulty turning out two completely finished basic combs per hour. Naturally, the more sophisticated a person's equipment, the faster the job will go.

Marketing this work is simply a matter of letting people know it's available. Even in these high-tech times, folks still enjoy buying fine handcrafted wooden items for gifts as well as for personal use.

GLASS WIND CHIMES

Here's a way to help clean up the trash that litters roadsides, beaches, and picnic areas and, at the same time, turn out unique works of art: It's the age-old craft of making wind chimes out of discarded materials.

These shiny, translucent, and often colorful chimes produce a clear, melodic ring that will entrance just about anyone within earshot. It's a craft that requires little initial investment and presents a good moneymaking opportunity.

EQUIP YOURSELF: A kiln is essential, so buy, borrow, or barter for one, preferably an electric kiln. A gas, wood, or coal burner can be used, but—with such a device—you'll have to bake in a muffle (an inner chamber which protects the glass from flames and gases) and won't be able to keep an eye on the process. Fortunately, the kiln doesn't have to be an expensive unit, because it only has to reach 1500°F (pottery requires higher temperatures). You'll also need several shelves and some 4" posts, which can be cut from soft firebrick.

And while a kiln may cost you a bit of money, the only other piece of equipment needed is a bottle-cutter kit, which can be located in almost any crafts store and comes in manual and electric models. If you do happen to get hold of an electric glass cutter, the heated wire will eventually burn out. It can be spliced

once by twisting the two broken ends tightly around each other. When it burns out a second time, however, replace the wire. It's wise to take the cutter apart occasionally to clean the electrical connections, but this job can be avoided if all the nuts and bolts are replaced with noncorroding brass parts.

Then, besides the free-for-the-gathering bottles, you'll need a spool of 12-pound-test monofilament fishing line to tie the chimes together, a diamond-tipped tool for scoring glass, and calcium carbonate (also known as whiting) to prevent the

glass rings from fusing to the kiln shelves as they're fired. This powdery substance can be used over and over again indefinitely and is available from stained glass suppliers.

BOTTLE RECYCLING: The first step when making chimes, of course, is to gather bottles. Next, soak them in hot water and scrub away the labels and any glue. Be certain to remove *all* the adhesive, too, or the glass will have a frosted appearance. Then wash away the dirt, though it's easier to finish cleaning the *inside* of the containers after their bottoms have been removed.

Actually, you don't really "cut" the bottles; you just make them break apart, and no matter what kind of kit is used, the principle involved is the same.

Wearing work gloves to avoid burns and cuts, use the diamond-tipped tool to score a line around the bottle wherever you want it to break. Space the scored rings approximately 1″ apart. (On champagne and thick wine bottles they can be spaced as close as 1/2″ apart.)

Next, with a candle flame or other heat source (in the case of the electric glass cutter, a hot electric wire), heat the score line and then apply ice water with an eyedropper. The sudden change in temperature will cause the glass to crack. Just grasp that section and break it off. (Sometimes the cold liquid makes the glass fracture so suddenly that a ring will pop off by itself, so be alert to catch the piece should this happen.)

Once the bottom is off the bottle, wipe the dirt from the inside with a rag or paper towel, but be extremely careful because the sharp edges can give you a nasty gash! Again, gloves can provide protection.

LOAD AND FIRE: With the rings cut, it's time to cover the kiln

floor and all the shelves with a good layer of calcium carbonate. Next, place the glass doughnuts in the kiln, making sure they're about 1-1/2″ apart in all directions and the same distance from any posts and from the shelves' edges. Because hot air rises, the bottom of the kiln will stay a little bit cooler than the top, and—since brown glass will "slump" (or melt

An electric bottle cutter heats and scores the glass so that a drop of two of cold water will cause the lines to crack. Rings of glass can then be removed from the bottle and melted into interesting shapes to be used in making wind chimes.

and collapse into the appealing shapes shown in the photos) at a slightly lower temperature than rings of other colors—it should go on the floor and lower shelves. Clear glass should be placed in the middle, and green up above.

To fuse two or more pieces (as is done when forming the top segment of the wind chime), place one glass ring so that it overlaps the rim of another (of either the same or a different color). Double-ring combinations must always be placed on the very *top* shelf so the two pieces will fuse properly, as should any extra-thick circles.

Unlike pottery, which must be baked slowly with the temperature rising gradually, bottle glass tends to be weakened by slowly increasing the heat. Therefore, turn the kiln up to "high" right away.

It'll take between two and three hours to complete the firing operation, and visual inspection—made through the kiln's peephole—is the only way to tell when the load is "done". (It's best if you can see the rings on the kiln floor, since they'll be the last to flatten.)

Always remember to let the kiln cool completely before you open it. As a general rule, the cooling process takes three times as long as the firing. After opening the kiln, remove the rings and dust off as much of the whiting as possible. (You can unload and reload in one operation to save time.)

Once you've washed the little gems, they're ready to be strung in whatever fashion your imagination conceives. You can, for example, use

two or three fused rings for the top of the wind chimes, or employ lengths of driftwood, branches, bamboo, or other material for this purpose. The glass circles can also be used as Christmas ornaments, and they add a distinctive touch to macramé.

You'll find it's difficult to run out of raw material, even if you use more than 100 bottles a week. There are so many littering the roads that you'll always have a fresh supply. There may even be a bunch of bottles cluttering up your neighborhood, just waiting for some clever recycler like you to turn them into tinkling music-makers, as well as cash!

CHRISTMAS LAMP

Christmas just wouldn't be . . . well, Christmas, without a few old-fashioned artifacts and handcrafts to get us all into the holiday spirit. And this fancy but homemade little oil lamp is just the kind of holiday decoration that can do the job. It isn't hard to put together, either. With a few basic power tools, the project can be completed in one evening.

Start by gathering two 3/4″ X 5-1/2″ X 5-1/2″ pieces of quality hardwood, a 3/4″ X 3/4″ X 24″ piece of the same wood, 8″ or so of 1/4″ dowel, a 1″ stub of 3/8″ dowel, and four pieces of 3-3/8″ X 5-7/8″ single-strength glass. Also round up a glass bulb about 2-1/4″ in diameter (check at drugstores, hobby shops, or novelty shops for one like that shown in the photo and illustration), a 4″ X 8″ piece of fine felt, velour, or velvet, some cotton "stuffing", an ordinary pipe cleaner, and a piece of 3/16″ glass or copper tubing that's about 1/2″ longer than the height of your glass bulb.

Begin your shopwork by routing out a 1/8″-deep, 3/16″-wide groove down the center of two adjacent sides of the 3/4″ X 3/4″ X 24″ piece of wood. Use a router or shaper to cut a decorative border around all four sides of the upper surfaces of both 3/4″ X 5-1/2″ X 5-1/2″ squares of wood. These borders can be any shape, but don't cut more than 3/8″ in from the edges.

Now, drill four 1/4″ holes—each 1/2″ deep—into the corners of the 5-1/2″ squares of wood. These holes are spaced 3-7/8″ apart on center. Drill one set of four holes into the "top" or "finished" side of one block

and drill the other set of four holes into the "bottom" or "unfinished" side of the second block. This is a good time, too, to drill a 13/32″ hole about 1/2″ deep in the exact center of the square which will be the lamp's base (the one with its set of four holes in the top) as well as a 2-1/2″ hole right through the exact center of the square which will form the lamp's cover (the one with its holes in the bottom).

Cut the 24″ length of wood (the piece with the two grooves routed in it) into four 5-7/8″ lengths. Drill a 9/32″ hole 5/8″ deep into the exact center of both ends of all four pieces of wood. Sand these four wooden corners, the base, and the lamp's cover. Finish all six pieces of wood with stain or tung oil.

Next, cut the 1/4″ X 8″ dowel into eight equal lengths and glue one into each of the 1/4″ holes drilled into the corners of the two 5-1/2″ squares of wood. The four 3/4″ X 3/4″ X 5-7/8″ corner supports are then glued—with their grooves facing "in"—to the dowels that were just fitted to the lamp's base. Before this glue dries, it's a good idea to slip all four of the panes of glass down into the corner support grooves and to put the lamp's cover into place, temporarily, just for fit. Do not glue the cover in place.

Glue the 1″ piece of 3/8″ dowel to the bottom of the glass bulb with epoxy, and while it's drying, sew up the cushion that will go under the bulb. This is done by stitching the fabric into a little pillow (with a 3/8″ hole through its center) that will measure 3-1/2″ X 3-1/2″ after it's stuffed about an inch thick with cotton. Sew around three sides of the cushion, stuff it, then stitch up the fourth side and make the hole in the middle of the pillow.

Finally, thread the pipe cleaner through the glass or copper tubing and trim it off so that both ends are just even with (or slightly recessed into) the ends of the tube. Fill the bulb with either charcoal lighter or a pleasantly scented lamp oil, slip the cushion up over the dowel on the bulb's bottom, remove the lamp's cover, and fit the dowel into the 13/32″ hole in the lamp's base. Then very carefully slide the tube/pipe-cleaner wick down into the neck of the glass bulb and position it so that the wick is standing up straight.

You'll be able to light your Christmas lamp and replace its cover just as soon as the fluid soaks up into the wick. To adjust the flame, merely slide the wick up or down within the tube. And don't worry about replacing that pipe cleaner: As long as it doesn't protrude above the tubing's top end, the flame will burn above, not on, the wick.

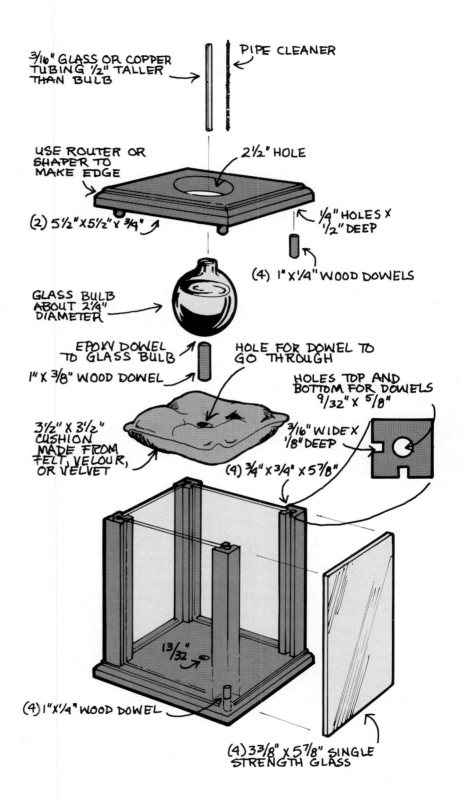

3/16″ GLASS OR COPPER TUBING 1/2″ TALLER THAN BULB

PIPE CLEANER

USE ROUTER OR SHAPER TO MAKE EDGE

2 1/2″ HOLE

(2) 5 1/2″ X 5 1/2″ X 3/4″

1/4″ HOLES X 1/2″ DEEP

(4) 1″ X 1/4″ WOOD DOWELS

GLASS BULB ABOUT 2 1/4″ DIAMETER

EPOXY DOWEL TO GLASS BULB

HOLE FOR DOWEL TO GO THROUGH

1″ X 3/8″ WOOD DOWEL

HOLES TOP AND BOTTOM FOR DOWELS 9/32″ X 5/8″

3/16″ WIDE X 1/8″ DEEP

3 1/2″ X 3 1/2″ CUSHION MADE FROM FELT, VELOUR, OR VELVET

(4) 3/4″ X 3/4″ X 5 7/8″

13/32″

(4) 1″ X 1/4″ WOOD DOWEL

(4) 3 3/8″ X 5 7/8″ SINGLE STRENGTH GLASS

CHRISTMAS LAMP

REED BASKETS

Everybody loves a basket! And whether you're using it to tote vegetables from the garden, display fruit on the kitchen table, or just stash away an unfinished needlework project, your chores will be far more enjoyable if the basket is one you've made yourself.

There are many materials available for crafting these lovely carriers, but one of the best is reed. Strong, pliable, and light, reed comes from the core of the long shoots of the rattan palm, which grows in tropical forests in the South Pacific. These shoots reach lengths of 200 to 600 feet as they trail over the floor of the jungle or hook onto other trees and plants. Once the thorny outer bark has been removed, the smooth, glossy inner bark is stripped off in widths suitable for caning chair seats and such.

Beneath this layer is actual reed—the core of the vine—which is harvested and machine-processed into round and flat strips of varying diameters and widths. The sizes range in diameter from No. 0 at 1/64" (used for making miniatures) to No. 12 at 3/8" (used for sturdy handles). As a rule, the spokes (which are the ribs, or framework) of a basket should be two numbers coarser than the weavers (which are the flexible strands that are woven over and under the spokes).

Reed is sold in one-pound bundles and can be purchased from craft stores or else through mail order suppliers.

ON NATURE AND BRISTLES: Since reed is a natural material, each of the strands will have its own character. Soaking a bunch of them in water (the first step in the basket-weaving process) will reveal some lengths to be very strong and sturdy, while others will turn out as soft as cooked spaghetti. To sort out the No. 5 (1/8") reed generally used for the basket spokes, leave an entire bundle in warm water for five minutes. Because the spokes must be firm and strong, discard any that feel spongy or soft. No. 2 (5/64") reed is often selected for the weavers, and all but the most brittle of these can be used. Save the more pliable ones for starting the base of the container, though, as that's where the coils are tightest.

Be careful not to soak too much reed at a time, because if the material is kept wet for too long, it becomes "hairy", and although some reed is naturally bristly, prolonged soaking will bring out an abundance of these whiskers. It's best to leave the selected strands in water for no more than ten minutes before using them, and after that, keep them under a damp towel as you work. Adding a teaspoon of glycerin to each quart of soaking water will usually help prevent fraying. Any hairs that do show up on a finished basket can be burned off with a propane torch or over a gas stove. Wet the container before moving it rapidly over the flame, or your masterpiece might catch fire! Don't use a match or candle for this purpose. Both give off carbon, which will blacken your basket.

Finally, to keep it from mildewing, let any wet reed dry thoroughly before you put it away.

WEAVING IN THE ROUND: The basic round basket illustrated here is made with what's called *separate base* construction, which simply means that the bottom is woven first and then more spokes are added to make the sides. *Japanese weave* is used for the base, and *triple* and *chasing weaves* for the sides. The border is a *four-row trac*, and the handles have a *rope wrap*.

For this project, gather several sizes of round reed: one-half pound of No. 2 for weavers, one-quarter pound of No. 5 for spokes, and either two 15" lengths of No. 8 (1/4") for side handles, or one 33" length of No. 10 (5/16") to make a single handle. (If No. 10 is unavailable, use two 33" lengths of No. 5.)

Other necessary articles include diagonal cutters, needle-nosed or round-nosed pliers, an awl (bone is best), a knife, a tape measure, twist-ties, a plastic dishpan, an old enamel pan (one that you don't mind staining), a towel, and powdered dye (for the basket shown here, rust and evening blue were used).

PREPARING THE REED: Once all the materials have been assembled, carefully cut all the outer bands of a No. 2 bundle, but do *not* cut the bands that hold the smaller groupings of strands together. Gently pull out one long strand at a time, roll it into a 6" coil, and wrap the end two or three times through the center to hold it.

With a number of coils prepared this way, fill the enamel pan with eight cups of water and the whole package of rust dye. (Leftover mixed dye can be saved for later use.) Bring the water to a simmer, then drop in three of the coiled strands of No. 2 reed. Let them absorb the dye for three or four minutes, turning them frequently. When the color looks dark enough (remember, it'll become lighter again as it dries), remove the strands and rinse them thoroughly in cold water. Check their color, and if they still don't look dark enough, put

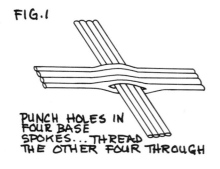

FIG. 1

PUNCH HOLES IN FOUR BASE SPOKES...THREAD THE OTHER FOUR THROUGH

FIG. 2

A

D ——— B

SHORT   LONG

C

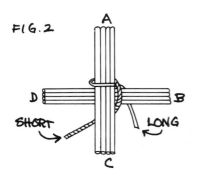

FIG. 3

B

A ——— C

LONG   SHORT

D

TURN CROSS SO THAT YOU ALWAYS WEAVE OVER ARM AT RIGHT

FIG. 4

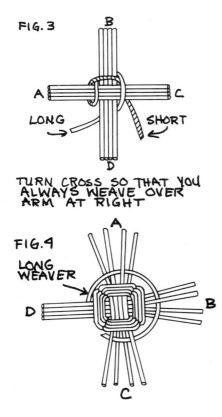

LONG WEAVER

A

D ——— B

C

the strands back in the dye for another few minutes. Be sure the material is rinsed well after it's dyed, or the colored reeds, when soaked again prior to being woven, may stain the rest of the basket. (It's best to soak each shade of dyed reed in a separate container.)

Prepare the package of blue dye in the same manner as the rust. The blue color takes longer to set, so allow eight strands of No. 2 to simmer for five to six minutes this time. Again, rinse the reed thoroughly.

FROM THE BOTTOM UP: To start the base of the basket, cut eight 7-1/2" spokes of No. 5 reed and soak them and a handful of No. 2 reed in warm water for five minutes. Then, with the awl, punch a hole in the center of each of four of the spokes, carefully making the holes large enough to thread the other four spokes through, as shown in Fig. 1.

Take a long, pliable No. 2 weaver and fold it at a point 20" from one end. Hold the spoke cross with arm A at the top (see Fig. 2) and slip the weaver over that arm with both ends to the back and the short end of the weaver on the left. Take the long weaver down behind arm B, holding it snug but out of the way so it isn't crossed over on the next step. Then draw the short weaver end behind arm A, up over the long weaver end and B, and under C.

Next, turn the cross so that B is up. Hold the short weaver tight but out of the way, and bring the long weaver in front of C and behind D (Fig. 3). Turn the cross so C is up, and take the short weaver in front of D and behind A, this time holding the long weaver out of the way. Go on to repeat this maneuver, weaving and turning the cross, until there are four rows on each arm, front and back.

At that point, leave the short end under A, and working with the long end of the weaver, begin to separate the spokes with Japanese weave: over two spokes and under one (Fig. 4). Always keep the same surface facing you and weave only in a clockwise direction.

The first few rows of Japanese

weave will probably look a bit square. This situation is quite common and is the result of not separating the spokes enough. Don't be afraid to pull and tug on both the spokes and the weavers to remedy this. They're very strong and can take a lot of stress. After about half an inch of weaving, the spokes should be splayed out evenly like those on a wheel.

Check your work along the way to be sure the base spokes are lying straight (the weavers should do all the bending). The rows of weaving should also be very close together, so when a strand goes over two spokes, pull it in toward the center of the base from the back before bringing it up to the front again. When a weaver passes under one spoke, leave enough play so that it doesn't bend the spoke and, again, draw the weaver in toward the center button of the base. (At this point in your project the Japanese weave will look rather jumbled, but after seven or eight rows it'll begin to take on a more recognizable pattern.)

Of course, the initial weaver strand will be used up somewhere along the line and must be replaced with a new one. To do this, simply end the first strand behind a spoke and add a fresh length, starting behind the same spoke and crossing over the top of the old weaver in the process (see Photo 2).

Continue using Japanese weave—pushing down gently on the spokes to curve the bottom of the basket slightly—until the base measures 7-1/2" across. The completed piece should look like an upside-down saucer. And with the finished item resting top side up on the table, the center of this saucer shape should be a full half-inch from the table's surface. (The top of the base, of course, is the side on which the spokes are completely covered, and it will become the inside of the basket.)

Finish the 7-1/2" base by trimming the last weaver a half-inch from the last spoke, crimping or folding this end over, and pushing it down along the spoke to hold it.

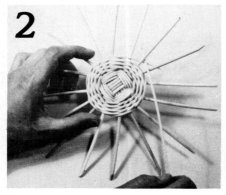

2

3

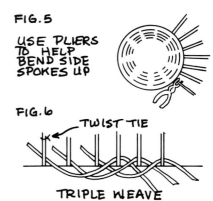

FIG. 5

USE PLIERS TO HELP BEND SIDE SPOKES UP

FIG. 6

← TWIST TIE

TRIPLE WEAVE

SIDE ISSUE: With the base done, it's time to begin the sides. First, cut 32 No. 5 reed spokes, each 20″ long, and soak them and more No. 2 weavers in warm water for about ten minutes.

Then turn the base over, cut one end of each of the side spokes on a slant, run the awl down along the base spoke to open up a space, and slide the side spoke in about 2″. Once it's in place, trim the base spoke as close to the weaving as possible, then run the awl along the other side of the same base spoke and insert a second side spoke. (This whole process is called *bi-spoking*.) Be sure to trim a base spoke *only* after a side spoke has been inserted. If you trim them all at once, there will be nothing to hold the base weavers in place!

When all 32 new spokes are in place, hold the underside of the base toward you and—using your pliers—crimp the side spokes as close to the base as possible. Pinch firmly, then gently push the spoke away from you

(Fig. 5). If a spoke starts to crack, soak it before pinching it once again. If the crack goes more than halfway through, replace the spoke.

To form the container-to-be's sides, begin working from left to right on the outside of the basket, using triple weave. Lay three No. 2 weavers behind three consecutive spokes and mark the first spoke with a twist-tie (Fig. 6). (When instructions say that a weaver goes "behind", "in back of", or "under" a spoke, they mean toward the inside of the basket. "In front of" and "over" mean to the outside.) Take the left weaver in front of the next two spokes to the right and, at the same time, over the top of the other two weavers. Then, run it behind the third spoke and back to the outside (Photo 3).

Be careful to catch each spoke with this weave. It's easy to go in front of three spokes instead of two if you lose track of which spoke the weaver is behind. (If in doubt, pull the weav-

ers out at a right angle to see which spokes they're coming from.) It's also important that the weavers end up on the outside of the basket after each move.

The secret to shaping the container's sides properly lies in pushing the spokes in with your left hand and pulling the weavers taut with your right. Practice and more practice will help you learn the correct balance between these two forces. Shaping is undoubtedly the most difficult aspect of basket weaving.

Do seven rows (or about 1″) in triple weave, ending over the three beginning spokes (count the rows on the long weavers between the spokes), and cut off all three weavers at the end of the seven rows.

Incidentally, while doing the triple weave, you may notice that the loose ends of your weavers are getting all snarled up! The best way to get rid of such tangles is to grasp the three weavers together near the basket and gently free one at a time.

A new weaver is added to the bottom (Photo 2), and a triple weave is used to start the sides (Photo 3). The boarder is finished by weaving spokes first from the inside to the outside (Photo 4) and then back to the inside (Photo 5). A gathering wrap completes a single handle (Photo 7) but is not used on a two-handled basket (Photo 8). Finished examples are in Photos 1 and 6.

4

5

ARTS AND CRAFTS PROJECTS

ROUND AND ROUND: The next section is done in chasing weave. Begin at a spot several spokes to the right of the end of the triple weave, and mark the first spoke with a twist-tie. Weave in front of the next spoke, behind the one after that, and so on until you come around to the second spoke to the left of your starting point. Then add a second weaver behind the spoke directly to the left of the marked one, and go on to weave in front of the marked spoke, behind the next, and so on, so that the second row alternates with the first.

Be sure to keep the two weavers separate as you come around each time: Drop the weaver you're working with and weave a row with the *other* strand. Each weaver thus "chases" the other. When 1-3/8" have been woven, ending over the two beginning spokes, cut off both weavers.

The basket's midsection is triple weave: the first row in rust, the next five in evening blue, and the final row in rust. Be sure to stagger the beginnings of each color so there won't be a jumble of ends all in one place, and use the step-up (described next) at the end of each row.

STEP TO IT: A step-up is used to make each row look complete in itself. To achieve this effect, end the first row of rust with the weavers coming from behind the three spokes to the left of spoke 1 (Fig. 7). Then take the right weaver in front of spokes 1 and 2, behind 3, and out. Then cut off all three weavers.

THE STEP UP: TAKE RIGHT WEAVER FIRST

Make a step-up at the end of each of the five rows of blue, cutting off the weavers at the end of the fifth row, and go on to weave one more row of rust.

Continue the body of the basket with another inch of chasing weave,

ending over the two beginning spokes. Then add a third weaver behind the next spoke to the right, and do seven more rows (1") of triple weave before cutting off all of the weavers.

BORDERING: To make the four-row trac border, soak the spokes for ten minutes, then crimp them close to the weaving so that they bend to the right (Fig. 8).

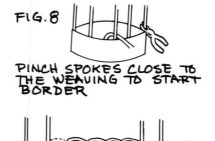

PINCH SPOKES CLOSE TO THE WEAVING TO START BORDER

FIG.9. BORDER: ROW 1

Row 1: Working to the right, bend down the first spoke and take it behind the next one, and out. Repeat this procedure with each spoke, interlacing the last with the first and going from the inside to the outside (Fig. 9 and Photo 4).

Row 2: Bring each spoke, in turn, in front of the two spokes to its right, while holding down those that are sticking out to the front. Run each spoke to the inside, going under the loop formed by the first row (Fig.

10). If you pull the first two spokes out about 2", the last two will be easier to interlace (Photo 5).

BORDER: ROW 2

Row 3: This row doesn't interlace with either of the other two rows, so pull it close to the rest of the border as you weave, because it'll have a tendency to be loose. Looking down into the inside of the basket, hold three spokes straight out. Attach twist-ties at the bend of each of the first two spokes. Then bring the left spoke over the two right ones, and push it down under the third (Fig. 11). Continue taking each spoke on the left over the next two to the right and under the third.

FIG. 11

BORDER: ROW 3

Row 4: This row is woven in the same manner as Row 3 and is directly underneath it. Trim the spokes with a slant cut so that a half-inch is visible under the fourth row.

HANDLE WITH CARE: If you want the basket to have a single handle, cut a 33″ piece of No. 10 reed (or two 33″ lengths of No. 5) and soak it for ten minutes. Each end must be tapered for easy insertion into the basket. Starting about 3″ from each tip, shave the inside of the handle ends to about half their thicknesses (Fig. 12). Also, make a diagonal cut so that point will fit next to the spoke beside which it's inserted.

Run the awl along a spoke to open a space, and push the handle 4″ into the basket. When that's done, count around to the sixteenth spoke and insert the other end of the handle in the same manner.

To make a rope wrapping for the handle, run a long, pliable No. 2 weaver under the border, from the inside to the outside, at point A (Fig. 13). Weave the starting end to the left and in behind spoke B, to hold it. Then take the long, free end and wrap the handle, as shown, following the arrows. Keep the first loop that goes through the basket as far to the left as possible, and add the subsequent wrappings to its right, filling the space between the first loop and the handle (Fig. 14).

Continue wrapping the handle until there are no empty spaces. When a weaver runs out, just leave it on the inside, at either end of the handle, with at least a 4″ tail. Add a new weaver as you did when you began wrapping the handle—that is, from the inside to the outside—right next to the one that's run out. The ends that are inside will be woven to the right and underneath the border after the handle has been completely covered.

FIG. 12

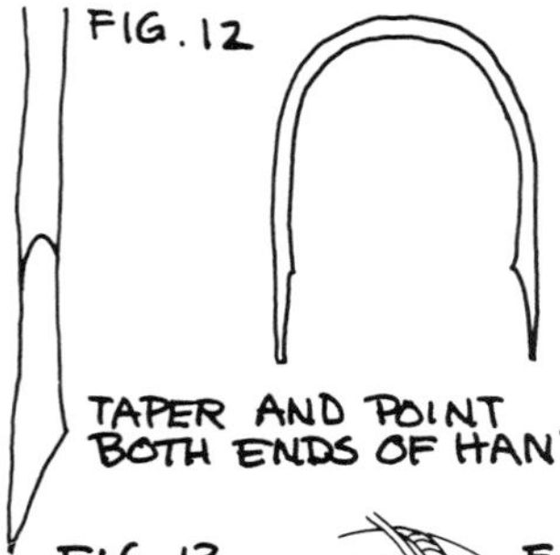

TAPER AND POINT BOTH ENDS OF HANDLE

FIG. 13

FIG. 14

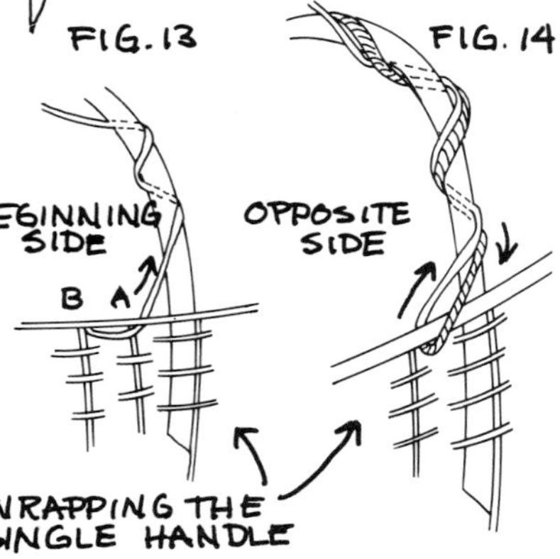

BEGINNING SIDE

OPPOSITE SIDE

B A

WRAPPING THE SINGLE HANDLE

FIG. 15

TAPER AND POINT ENDS OF SIDE HANDLE

FIG. 16

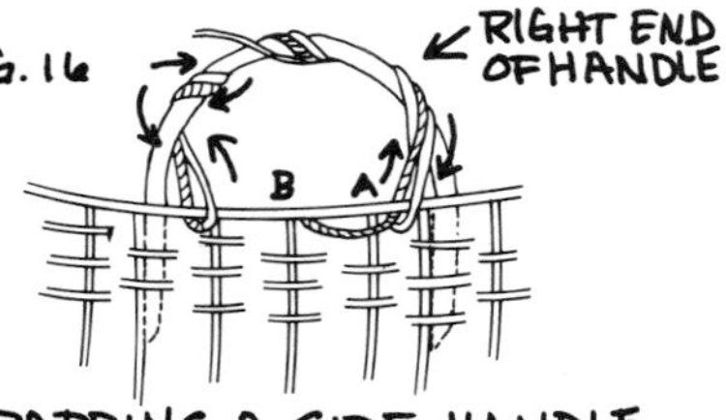

RIGHT END OF HANDLE

B A

WRAPPING A SIDE HANDLE

Finish the wrapping by running a pliable weaver about 2″ down into the basket along the right side of the handle. Bring it behind the handle at a point an inch up from the border and wrap it tightly, from left to right, seven times. Then run the awl carefully through the handle, put the end of the weaver through from right to left (Photo 7), and cut it off flush with the handle. The spring action of the handle reed holds the wrap in place.

A basket with two side handles can be made by cutting a pair of 15″ lengths of No. 8 reed, then tapering and cutting each end on a slant (Fig. 15). Run the awl along a spoke and push one end of a handle in about 3″. Insert the other end beside the fifth spoke to the right. Skip the next 11 spokes and insert the second handle's ends alongside the twelfth and sixteenth spokes.

To wrap each side handle, run a long, pliable No. 2 weaver under the border from the inside to the outside at point A (Fig. 16). Then weave the end to the left and in behind spoke B, and use the free end to wrap the handle (Fig. 16 and Photo 8) following the arrows. Now—easy does it—keep the first loop that goes through the basket at the right end of the handle to the handle's *left*, adding subsequent wrappings to the right of the loop. Be sure the first loop at the left end of the handle is on the handle's *right*, while you add subsequent wrapping to the left. When the handle is completely wrapped, weave the ends away under the border.

FINISHING OFF: Since reed is a porous material, use a polyurethane finish on your basket after it has dried. Regardless of whether you seal the surface of your handiwork, however, the reed can be scrubbed in mild soapy water if it gets a bit dirty. With a little maintenance, a woven reed basket can last for years as a decorative, functional household item.

SOLAR ETCHING

Solar etching is a woodburning technique that uses "double-lensing": One lens acts as an amplifier for the focal point of a smaller lens in order to produce tiny lines. With practice, it's possible to etch lovely, intricate details into lamps, beds, doors, and other wooden objects and to earn extra money as a result.

This overview gives just a hint of the process involved. But if you decide to try this craft, be prepared for an admiring audience, and for sales, every time.

PREPARATION TIME: It can easily take five days to ready a wooden canvas for the sunlight. The first steps are to cut, laminate, and hand-plane the lumber and to make the frame. After the etching is done, the wood is sanded, cleaned with an eraser, and coated with three coats of lacquer or polyurethane varnish.

COOPERATIVE NATURE: Common subjects for sun etchings are boats, plants, trees, and landscapes. These are usually burned into California redwood and pine with an 8″ plano-convex lens. Brooks pine is also a choice material because of the blue (as well as other natural colors) running through it. Redwood is used for making frames, too, and for color accents in some of the laminates. (It's just as easy to burn an image into dense oak, maple, or walnut, but these hardwoods are quite expensive in some parts of the country.)

The plano-convex lens is so powerful that it can strike a flame the instant the sun's rays passing through it are brought into focus, and the light is so bright that a set of No. 5 welder's lenses are necessary for safety's sake.

Most people are quite astonished when they first see the lens turn sunshine into fire, but they also seem to be a bit disappointed to see the artist sketch in his image first with a pencil. They consider it a form of cheating. But feel free to predraw your designs, so that you can erase anything

The solar etcher, using a double lens that focuses the flame, can produce lovely works of art in almost any size.

you don't like *before* burning the wood. (Erasing—or simply lightening the image—can also be accomplished by sanding the surface.)

A WAY OF LIFE: Solar etching is an absorbing craft whose artisans attract much attention and many customers. It is a way to break out of your economic straits (some pieces sell for hundreds of dollars) and to let your imagination soar.

HAND-CARVED SPOONS

There's something special about handmade wooden spoons, something that distinguishes them from the imported utensils lining the shelves of discount supermarkets. They reflect not only quality but also the honored tradition of hand-carving. Unfortunately, such fine hardwood kitchen utensils are hard to come by in this day and age.

WHAT YOU'LL NEED: A supply of hardwood (such as ash or maple) is, of course, the first requirement for spoon carving. It may be possible to obtain all the lumber you'll need at no charge from high school and college shop classes, furniture factories, or local lumberyards. Spoon-sized scraps are often discarded, so you probably can get them for free.

The necessary tools include a wood rasp, a good pocketknife (it must take and hold a keen edge), a small woodcarving gouge, coarse and fine sandpaper, and a handsaw. The saw isn't absolutely necessary, but it comes in very handy once in a while.

STEP BY STEP: Sometimes the idea of putting tools to wood can be more intimidating than the job itself, so it's best just to learn by doing. Begin by drawing a rough pattern on the piece of board, letting the grain and color of the wood do most of the design work for you. And don't expect the sketch to be exactly like the finished product. The shape will change as the spoon evolves.

After sketching the design, saw any excess wood from either side of the handle and cut the corners from the bowl portion to bring that part of the rough spoon bowl closer to its eventual oval shape. Be sure to leave plenty of space to allow for errors or changes of plan. (In fact, if there isn't much extra material around the pattern, skip this "roughing out" step completely.) The resulting shape should resemble a miniature canoe paddle.

Now, pick up the rasp and carefully use it to round the spoon's handle and to shape the outside of the bowl. This is the most tedious part of the entire operation, but resist the temptation to use a blade to remove large areas of wood in a hurry. Instead, stop often to check the shape, and remember that a knife doesn't offer nearly as many second chances as a rasp, which removes wood more slowly.

The really ticklish part of the project is at the transition point between the spoon's bowl and handle. It's perfectly natural to be very nervous when starting to shape this compound curve, to fiddle around, and—finally—to do something that looks like total ruination (such as cutting too sharp a shoulder between handle and bowl, or carving the stem too thin). But out of what appears to be too sharp a shoulder or too thin a stem comes the spoon's final shape. It was in there all along. Once the outline of the bowl is nearly finished, begin to form the cavity. Use the gouge to cut the wood away, but leave plenty of material all the way around to avoid punching a hole through the wood at a thin spot.

As soon as the project is correctly shaped, start to sand it, first with coarse paper and later with a finer grit. This will be a pleasant task, because sandpaper does noticeably improve the appearance of a "roughed-out" carving.

After sanding the utensil's surface until it's "smooth as a baby's bottom", wash the spoon (or put it through a cycle in the dishwasher), and let it dry completely. If that raises the wood's grain enough to make it feel rough again, give the spoon another rubdown with fine-grained sandpaper. Finally, oil the scoop with plain salad oil, and it's ready to use!

WHY MAKE A SPOON? For one thing, a do-it-yourselfer with modest skills (and a jigsaw or band saw) can make good money by turning out a line of hand-carved spoons to sell at art fairs and in craft and gift shops.

Furthermore, wooden spoons make great gifts. Anyone who cooks would be more than pleased to receive them for any occasion.

Of course, you might also want to make a few spoons to keep for yourself, and that's fine, too. Use them for years and years, and then pass the durable utensils along to your grandchildren. So why not carve a spoon or two? You just might start a family tradition!

BARK BASKET

The traditional Appalachian basket, made from the bark of young tulip poplar trees and laced together with smooth strips of hickory, is about as useful and beautiful as any receptacle around. Better yet, once you become an experienced basket-maker, one of these rustic carryalls can be made in less than half an hour and will certainly come in handy the next time you find yourself in one of those once-in-a-lifetime berry patches!

TREES AND TOOLS: Old-timers say that the best time to strip bark from a tree is in the spring and early summer, during the main sap flow that peaks under the new moon in July. Although some skilled artisans use the bark of tulip trees to form baskets and the inner bark of hickories for lacing, basswood may be used for both.

The bark of quaking aspen will also do, but this material is not as durable as the others. Just experiment with whatever species are available to find one that works about as well as the more traditional materials.

Bear in mind that regardless of the type of tree used, the bark that forms

ARTS AND CRAFTS PROJECTS

the basket itself will be most flexible immediately after it's removed from the trunk. So, have all of the other materials ready before starting to "skin" that sapling.

A good knife is essential for basket crafting, and an awl blade will come in handy for punching the holes through which the container is laced. An adjustable leather punch would make the poking job even easier, though, and a small ax or hatchet is needed for felling the trees and stripping the bark.

BARK UP THE RIGHT TREE:
Begin the basket by cutting the lacing from a young hickory or basswood. Just start at the bottom of the trunk and peel an inch-wide strip of bark, pulling the material toward the top of the tree (Fig. 1). The first strip

FIG. 1

may break off after only a foot or two is obtained, but the pieces will come free much more easily, and be longer, with each band of bark removed.

Each strip must be peeled apart and the outer bark portion discarded (Fig. 2). The remaining ribbons of inner bark can then be cut into thin laces.

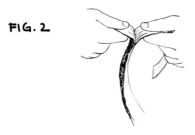

FIG. 2

A tree will die when its bark is stripped, so choose specimens that need to be cleared anyway. Once the sapling is felled and stripped of the protective bark, its trunk will yield a

supply of fast-drying kindling as well as enough lacing for several baskets.

The basswood or hickory "strings" will be ready to use immediately or may be coiled and dried for storage. To better preserve the laces, simply soak them in water for an hour or so before working with them.

A hoop to reinforce the basket's rim can be made from the inner hickory bark, too, but any thin, flexible limb will also do the job.

Once the lacing and hoop have been gathered, prepare the "body" of the basket. Locate a young tree 3" to 5" in diameter, and on a smooth area of the trunk, mark off a section twice the depth of the proposed basket. This piece of bark should be peeled

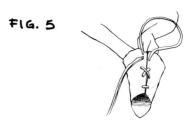

FIG. 3

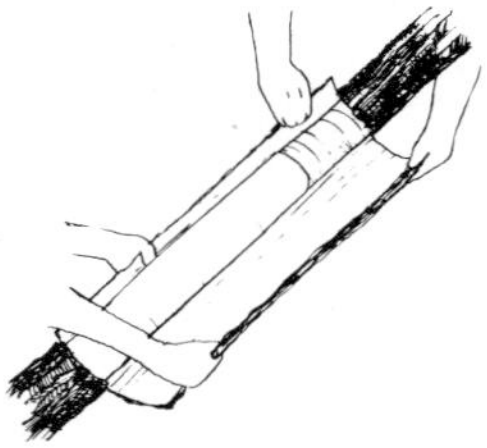

in one sheet from the entire circumference of the tree (Fig. 3). (Again, use a tree that needs to be cleared anyway, cut it down, and gather the material for several containers from its trunk.)

THE "MOUNTAIN" METHOD:
To assemble the basket, take the sheet of tulip tree "hide" and spread it out bark side up. Draw a line across this material dividing the sheet in half lengthwise. Scribe an elongated arc on either side of this line to form a football shape that extends from one side of the sheet to the other. Use a knife to score the

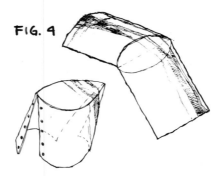

FIG. 4

curved markings through the outer bark only. Carefully fold the material along the cuts and the basket will begin to take its final shape (Fig. 4).

Using a small knife blade, awl, or leather punch, make a series of holes —about 2" apart and 1" in from the bark's edges—along each of the four "borders" that will be pulled together to form the container. Just lace up the basket's sides as you would a pair of shoes (Fig. 5).

FIG. 5

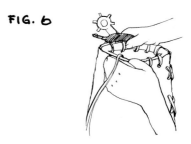

Next, whittle the rim of your container until it's smooth. Then bend the "hoop" stick or bark into shape, set it in place around the mouth of the basket, punch another series of holes, and lace the wooden circle onto the container (Fig. 6). A pair of

FIG. 6

lacing loops left hanging from either side will make it easy to fasten a handle to the carrier.

THAT'S ALL, FOLKS: You'll find that your finished baskets get lighter and more rigid as they dry, and these beauties really last: It's not unusual to find them still in service after 20 years of summer picnics and berry-picking expeditions.

In addition to being sturdy, long-lasting, and useful, bark baskets can provide a ready source of income. They always sell well at area craft fairs, and their homespun charm brings pretty fancy prices, too!

ENERGY-SAVING PROJECTS

In the first place, the walls of such a tank are at least three times as thick as the metal in a 55-gallon drum, which means that a water heater tank will make a tougher, longer lasting stove.

Second, when you build a firebox from a junked water heater tank, it's very easy to make the stove as airtight and efficient as many commercially manufactured woodburners.

Third, proper construction of the heater means it will be easy to load, it will have excellent fire and temperature control, and it will be presentable in any room of the house.

Fourth, you can build a stove from a water heater tank for even less than most people spend fabricating one from a 55-gallon drum. If you can find salvaged materials, the stove may cost you only a day's labor to build. In fact, once you've found your junked, but still intact, water heater tank, about three-quarters of your woodstove is already "custom made".

Finding one of these tanks isn't difficult because they abound in most junkyards around the country. Any discarded, ungalvanized electric water heater (gas ones are unsuitable for this project) with a 30- to 50-gallon capacity will convert nicely into a stove, but many people feel that the 30-gallon tanks (with a diameter of 20″ and a length of 32″) make the most attractive woodburners.

Pick and choose from your friendly local junk depositories—or from the alleyways behind appliance stores—until you find just the tank or tanks you want. If you're doing your

HOMEMADE WOODSTOVE

Most homebuilt woodburning stoves are recycled 55-gallon drums. They more or less serve their purpose, despite the fact that they rapidly burn through and are inefficient, difficult to regulate, and so unsightly that people tolerate them only in the workshop or garage. Low cost is the one redeeming feature of the drum heater. A better way to assemble a homemade woodburner is to use a discarded electric water heater tank, and there are four excellent reasons:

"shopping" in a junkyard, strip off the lightweight sheet metal "wrapper" and the insulation right there in order to make sure that the main tank inside isn't rusted out or filled with corrosion, excessive mineral deposits, or dirt.

Anyone with a cutting torch and welder will find the rest easy, and if you don't own or operate such equipment, scout around for a welding shop where the work can be done competently and at a reasonable price.

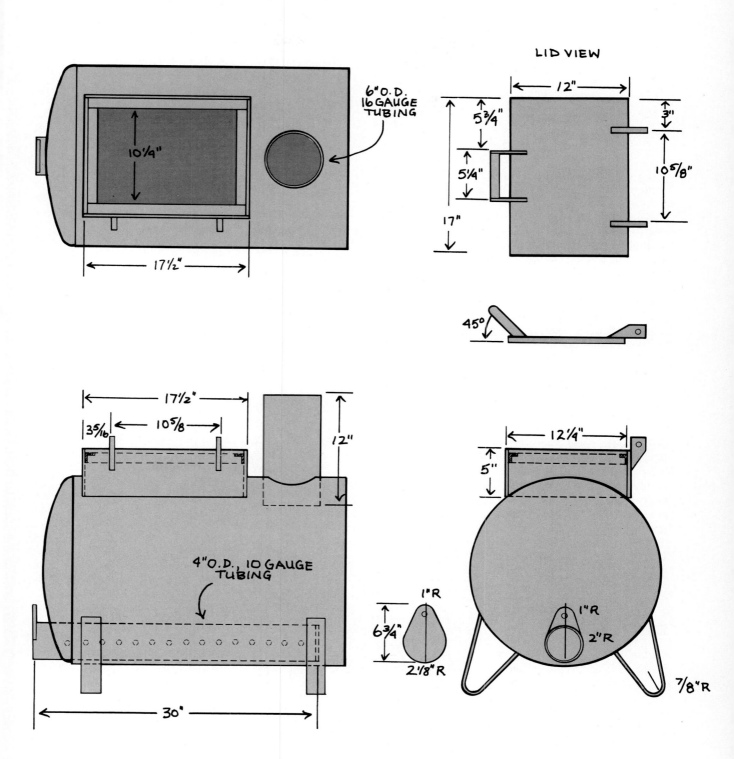

LID VIEW

6" O.D. 16 GAUGE TUBING

10¼"

17½"

12"

5¾"

5¼"

17"

3"

10⅝"

45°

17½"

10⅝"

3⁵⁄₁₆

12"

4" O.D., 10 GAUGE TUBING

30"

12¼"

5"

1"R

6¾"

2⅛"R

1"R

2"R

⅞"R

HOMEMADE WOODSTOVE

Lay the container on its side and add legs and the "loading hopper box with hinged lid" as illustrated in the accompanying drawing. Then weld in the exhaust stack or "smoke boot" as shown. Make sure that all seams are airtight and that the hopper box lid fits snugly and is airtight, too. The draft control is, perhaps, the most critical part of all. If it's well made and doesn't leak, you'll have a good and positive command of your finished stove's blaze and temperature at all times. So, work carefully and do the job well.

Once the stove is completely assembled, paint all its outside surfaces with rust-resistant black paint or "high temperature engine paint". After proper venting and careful positioning on a heat resistant floor pad away from the walls, the waste-not woodburner is ready for use. And even if you bought everything (approximately 65 pounds of steel) except the recycled water heater tank, the project remains cost-effective.

One of these woodburners will warm an entire 1,100-square-foot house while leaving only a small amount of ashes. Also, the heater can hold a fire overnight. In the morning, just jar the stove a couple of times, open the draft a bit, and the log-burner will snap to life.

You can even cook on this stove, but the appliance's 3/8"-thick top requires such a long heating-up period that the air in the room grows unbearably warm except in sub-zero weather. Before resigning yourself, though, to using a conventional range in all but the dead of winter or escaping to a cooler room to eat the food cooked on the woodburner, try a minor modification.

Get a piece of 1/8" sheet steel that's the same size as the stove's loading door. Then fine-trim this extra "lid" to fit just right and add a handle, and your "cooktop" is in business.

With the thicker top turned back, the thinner plate will warm up rapidly and reach "frying temperature" without overheating the house. It's also capable of several very convenient tricks. For example, the plate (which rests at a slight incline on the loading box frame) can slide back toward the stovepipe to open a crack at the front of the loading hole for additional air intake. Admittedly, doing so will reduce the fuel's burn time, but the really fast blaze will speed up the early morning coffee.

Then again, when it's turned sideways, the cooktop allows space to insert a popcorn popper or a grill and still keeps the smoke headed up the chimney where it belongs. In fact, the ventilation is so good that you hardly get a chance to smell those T-bones cooking!

By inserting a small drum oven, you can even bake with this woodburning heater. Just install the unit above a stovepipe damper, and you'll find that it's nearly always ready for some type of cooking. A banked fire will provide low heat for slowly roasting peanuts, while the blaze left from finishing a meal on the cooktop will leave the oven hot and ready to receive a pan of biscuits.

The stove's air intake, the damper, and the choice of two cooktops make baking control fairly easy. However, the oven is small and the temperature inside can change rapidly. Therefore, it's best to stay snuggled up to the stove with mending or reading when any delicate treat, such as a cake or meringue, is in progress.

Installing the little oven will cut down on the draft to a small degree, but that reduction of airflow will cause trouble only on those days when the stove's draw is particularly sluggish anyway.

Overall, the oven actually contributes to the heating as well as the cooking capacity of the stove. And when food isn't baking, you can leave the door open, increasing the effect.

Needless to say, life with this little woodburner can be a real joy. The homey stove will heat your house, dry soggy boots and mittens, and cook rib-sticking meals, filling the air with sounds of cheerful crackling.

CLOTHES-DRYER RACK

One of the worst home-energy gobblers—aside from the heating system and water heater—is an automatic clothes dryer. Not only are such appliances power hungry, but they're also incredibly wasteful: All the nice warm, humid air they produce is usually blown outside!

In the summer, of course, it's easy to avoid the energy waste by using an outdoor clothesline. But what can be done on those all-too-frequent rainy spring and snowy winter days when the weather refuses to cooperate?

The answer may be an indoor clothes-dryer rack similar to the one pictured here. Of course, there's not much new about indoor rack-type dryers, and many families have been using them for years. The trouble with most of the homemade wooden ones, however, is that the heat and humidity—coupled with all those heavy, wet clothes—puts such a strain on them that they usually fall apart in a few years.

This homemade all-aluminum drying rack is sturdier than the old wooden ones, and it's relatively simple to build, hangs over the top of any door in the house, and stores easily. It's a natural energy-saver, too, since no fuel is used other than the warm air already in the house. Also, the wet clothes will help humidify dry indoor air. The sturdy frame can handle anything from diapers to blankets, and it'll usually dry a full load of wash within 24 hours.

CONSTRUCTION: Basically, the portable clothes rack consists of four parallel bars riveted to two endpieces to form a square frame. Three hanger units secure the contraption to the top of a door. Clothespins are then attached—using nuts and bolts—at regular intervals along the crossbars. Each rack takes 22 feet of aluminum flat bar (the best size is 1/8" X 3/4"), 42 inch-long bolts and 84 nuts, 26 rivets, and 42 clothespins (it's best to use wooden pins with large springs, because plastic fasteners and pins with small springs just don't last as long as do the "old-fashioned" kind).

Before putting the drying rack together, divide the aluminum into several different lengths. First, cut four 33-1/2" pieces, and bend the metal—using a vise—to a 90° angle at points 2" from each end of every strap. These will become the crossbars from which the wet clothing will hang.

Next, cut two 29-1/2" lengths (don't bend these sections) to serve as the ends of the frame. To fashion the

hanger bars, cut three 12-1/4" pieces. Then, on one end of *each* of them, form a 90° angle at the 2" mark, and another at 3-1/2". (Naturally, these measurements may be modified to fit any size door.)

Finally, cut two 17"-long pieces to act as braces between the end hangers and the frame (see the diagram). Bend each brace at a point 1" from one end to an angle that will allow the support to be riveted flat against its hanger. In addition, use a vise to twist the metal, as illustrated, into a 90° "turn" so that it'll rest flat against the horizontal crossbar.

Drill holes for the clothespins at regular intervals along the four crossbars and along the outside end bar (the one that will *not* be attached to the hanger units). To allow for clearance near the door, make the first hole in each crossbar 4" from the inside end bar, then make eight more holes spaced 3" apart. At each opening, attach a clothespin by running a bolt through its spring and securing it with a nut and washer. All clothespins should be placed to the insides of the aluminum bars that form the frame.

Next, drill the necessary holes and rivet the frame together. The rivets that secure the hangers to the rack should be flush to avoid scratching the door, but go ahead and drape a towel over the top of the portal before the rack is hung up, just in case. For further protection, simply glue strips of felt to the underside of each hanger unit.

That's really all there is to it: Make one of the racks in a couple of hours and use it for years! Although the dryer *can* serve as a household's only means of drying clothes, for speedier jobs, it's a good idea to combine the capabilities of the over-the-door helper with those of a modern electric or gas dryer. Start by tumbling a load of wet clothes in the dryer on low heat for five to ten minutes. Then before hanging the laundry, switch to only air for another ten minutes to use any heat left in the clothes. This system removes wrinkles (eliminating the need for ironing) and saves energy!

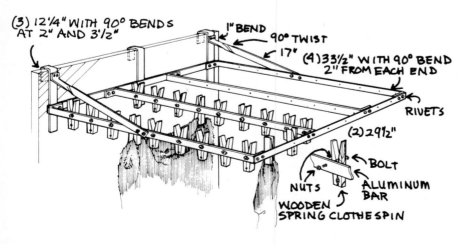

(3) 12¼" WITH 90° BENDS AT 2" AND 3½"

1" BEND

90° TWIST

17"

(4) 33½" WITH 90° BEND 2" FROM EACH END

RIVETS

(2) 29½"

BOLT

NUTS

ALUMINUM BAR

WOODEN SPRING CLOTHESPIN

WOOD CARRIER CRIB

Folks who lay in hearty supplies of timber to keep cozy during the winter months find that although a massive stack of cordwood certainly looks impressive on the front porch, such a pile on the hearth does little to complement a home's interior.

For those who don't enjoy lugging armloads of loose firewood through the living room, here's a "fetching" canvas-and-wood solution to all your timber-totin' problems.

An attractive firewood crib can be put together in a matter of hours, and you shouldn't have to spend more than a few dollars on the project. To make the crib shown, gather an 80" length of 2 X 4, four No. 12 X 2-1/2" flathead screws, eight No. 8 X 1" flathead screws, glue, wood putty, four 1/2"-diameter wooden cap buttons, two 1" X 24" wooden dowels, a 19" X 72" piece of canvas, a 17-foot length of bias edging tape or piping, and some strong thread.

Start by ripping the 2 X 4 lengthwise into two sections: one 1-1/2" X 2" and the other 1-1/4" X 1-1/2". Next, saw each of these boards into four 20" lengths, then take two of the 1-1/4" X 1-1/2" X 20" pieces and cut 3/4" X 2" notches from both ends of each strut.

The four 1-1/2" X 2" X 20" leg posts should be cut in the following manner: Take two measurements—one 3-1/4" and the other 4-1/2"—one end of each leg, and cut 3/4"-deep notches into the broadest side of the board between these pairs of points. With this done, fashion 1" X 1" contoured slots at the opposite ends (which will become the tops) of the legs with a coping saw (see drawing). Finally, use a No. 12 adjustable countersink tool to drill a hole through the center of the wide face of each of the legs and about 6-1/2" from the bottom end. The combination countersink and drill will not only bore the hole to the correct size, but will also sink it to the 3/16" depth that's necessary to accommodate a cap button to be installed later to cover the screw heads.

Now that the wooden components

of the log crib have been shaped, go ahead and sand all the parts, including the dowels, before assembling the frame.

Once the wood is smooth, begin putting the frame together. First, place the notched supports into their respective grooves in the legs, (see drawing). When the fit is just right, use a No. 8 adjustable countersink tool to drill two holes into *both* parts of each joint. With this complete, glue all the joints, screw them securely together using the No. 8 X 1" flathead wood screws, and fill the countersunk openings with wood putty.

Next, fasten the unnotched cross supports to the frame. To do so, butt the ends of these struts against the

previously drilled holes in the legs, making sure the supports are centered. Using a No. 12 adjustable countersink tool, run through the openings once again, only this time let the bit drill a pilot hole into the horizontal supports. Glue the joints between the legs and the crosspieces, and secure them with No. 12 X 2-1/2" flathead wood screws. For a finished appearance, cover the holes with 1/2"-diameter wooden cap buttons, glued in place, and then stain all the wood.

Prepare the canvas hammock by doubling the piece of material—right sides together—to produce a single 19" X 36" rectangle, and making sure the corners are square, stitch a seam to close the open ends. After turning the loop right side out to hide the rough edges of the seam, mark off and cut out a 4"-deep and 5"-wide half oval at each end of the sling for handle holes. Fold the bias binding or piping over all the raw edges, catching a single layer only, and stitch it in place.

Next, slip the two wooden dowel handles through the ends of the loop formed by the sling. Then stitch both layers of canvas together—near the ends—to form two sleeves for each handle. Run a lengthwise stitch down both sides of the sling at the borders and also stitch around the handle holes, following the piping.

Your kindling crib is now complete. When it's time to fetch more fuel for the fireplace or woodstove, just lay the sling open on the ground and pile on the wood. You'll be able to carry quite a load into the house without dropping half the parcel.

ENERGY-SAVING PROJECTS

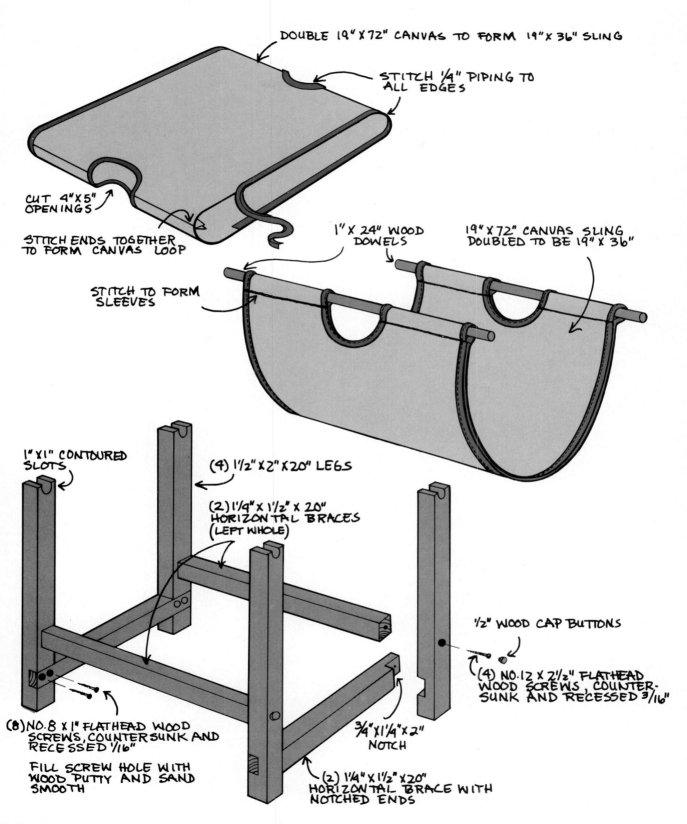

DOUBLE 19"×72" CANVAS TO FORM 19"×36" SLING

STITCH 1/4" PIPING TO ALL EDGES

CUT 4"×5" OPENINGS

STITCH ENDS TOGETHER TO FORM CANVAS LOOP

STITCH TO FORM SLEEVES

1"×24" WOOD DOWELS

19"×72" CANVAS SLING DOUBLED TO BE 19"×36"

1"×1" CONTOURED SLOTS

(4) 1½"×2"×20" LEGS

(2) 1¼"×1½"×20" HORIZONTAL BRACES (LEFT WHOLE)

½" WOOD CAP BUTTONS

(4) NO.12 × 2½" FLATHEAD WOOD SCREWS, COUNTER-SUNK AND RECESSED 3/16"

(8) NO.8 × 1" FLATHEAD WOOD SCREWS, COUNTERSUNK AND RECESSED 1/16"

FILL SCREW HOLE WITH WOOD PUTTY AND SAND SMOOTH

¾"×1¼"×2" NOTCH

(2) 1¼"×1½"×20" HORIZONTAL BRACE WITH NOTCHED ENDS

WOOD CARRIER CRIB

Start this project by finding out what types of plastic film are available. You'll probably find polyester, polyethylene, fiberglass, and vinyl. But polyester is expensive, polyethylene ages and turns brittle in a matter of months, and fiberglass isn't transparent enough (you want to see out as well as let the sunlight in).

A clear vinyl is probably your best bet as it has little or no visual distortion, stays flexible in subzero temperatures, and remains clear for two to three years in direct sunlight.

Glazing of this material should last almost indefinitely in north-facing windows (which get no winter sunlight to speak of) and should hold out up to ten years in south-facing windows, since the plastic will be in place only three or four months of each year. In addition, the cost of vinyl is quite reasonable.

Frames may be built of 1/4″ X 3/4″ molding and may be secured with 1/2″ and 3/4″ wire nails.

Start by measuring the inside of the window casing, and then cut the molding strips for the storm windows so that—when they're assembled—the finished frames will be 1/4″ shorter, both vertically and horizontally than what was measured. This insures that the completed storm window will slide into place next to the existing glass window. If the storm window turns out a little too small, it's possible to fill in around it with weatherstripping, but if the frame is too large, there's no way you can force it into position.

The accompanying drawings show how to make sandwich-style storm windows using two layers of plastic and three of wood. The two layers of the vinyl film will create two separate pockets of air between the inside of the house and the chilly outdoors (plastic film, air, film, air, glass of the regular window). For even greater insulation, consider putting more layers in your sandwiches. And note, too, the way in which the corners of the homemade frames should be overlapped for extra strength.

To construct this type of storm window, lay the first four pieces of mold-

STORM WINDOWS

Storm windows can keep a home significantly warmer in winter, but the cost of manufactured units forces many folks to just put up with chilly drafts.

Why not build your own from inexpensive wood and plastic rather than the currently popular ones made of aluminum and glass? These do-it-yourself units do the job for a fraction of the price of ready-mades.

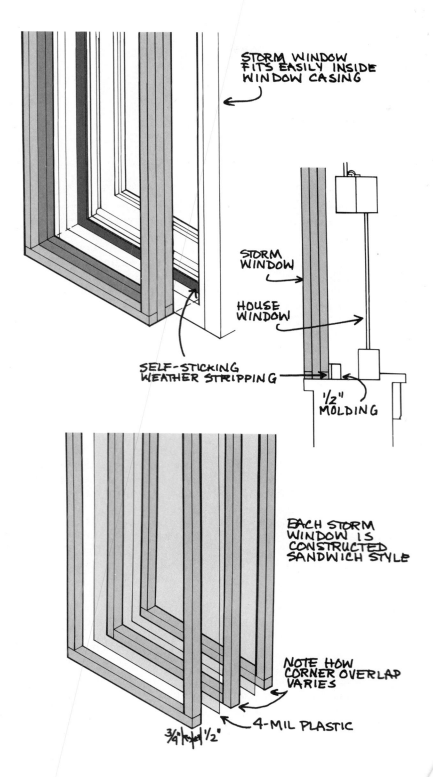

STORM WINDOW
FITS EASILY INSIDE
WINDOW CASING

STORM
WINDOW

HOUSE
WINDOW

SELF-STICKING
WEATHER STRIPPING

1/2"
MOLDING

EACH STORM
WINDOW IS
CONSTRUCTED
SANDWICH STYLE

NOTE HOW
CORNER OVERLAP
VARIES

4-MIL PLASTIC

3/4" × 1/2"

ing down in the shape of a rectangle on any flat surface. Then spread a sheet of vinyl (cut with an inch overhang all around so you'll have something to hold to when you stretch the plastic taut) over the strips. Lay four more strips on the vinyl, positioned so that their ends overlap at the corners in the opposite direction of the overlap of the first strips, and next, tack this first "half" of the storm-window sandwich together with 1/2" nails while someone stretches the plastic tight for you.

Now, roll out another layer of vinyl, top with the third set of molding strips with the corners lapped in the same manner as those on the bottom layer of the frame, and nail through the complete sandwich (wood, plastic, wood, plastic, wood) with the 3/4" nails while your partner stretches the second layer taut. Trim off the excess plastic if desired, but it's not at all necessary.

That's it. The storm window is finished. If you worked carefully, it'll be square. If it's not, however, you can still make it fit the window casing you built it for and make it airtight too. Just nail a strip of 1/2" mold around the inside of the casing the "front" surfaces of this li self-sticking foam weatherstr push the storm window up a stripping enough to comp you'll have a completely

That should take care windows, say 3' X 4'. perhaps 4' X 6', fo general plan, but p molding in betw vinyl. Because it larger pieces of ful to leave a b them. Actua than a 3' X that the frame to ter off ring s

Th real m s

175

STORM WINDOWS

PROJECTS FOR PROFIT

TOOLING UP: The first step is to check the toolshed for a jigsaw, saber saw, or band saw, a brace or drill and some 1/2″ and 5/8″ bits, and a rasp or file (a four-way rasp is helpful). Also locate a hammer, sandpaper, a sturdy pair of scissors, and some contact cement.

Once the necessary implements are gathered, search through scrap wood for boards 3/4″ to 1″ thick and a minimum of 6″ wide and 14″ long. If the planks are worn and weathered, all the better. The best-selling bellows are made from rugged barn ding with an appealing finish.

LOCATING MATERIALS: Be by visiting furniture upholstery s. Introduce yourself to the proors, spend a couple of moments ing about the coming cold is (a perfect lead-in to a descrip your business), then ask them heir scrap piles. It's quite posey've got stacks of leftover quality leather and vinyl too small for upholstery use be discarded anyway.

hop owners will jump at unity to see these scraps eir hands. To those who t, offer to take the whole for one of your finished if that doesn't do it, a ll probably buy enough 0 blowers!

need to buy a quantity pholstery tacks, which e purchased at the obtain your vinyl ps have box after holding 1,000, or

BELLOWS BUSINESS

Anyone who delights in the feel of wood and leather, enjoys building practical tools that also please the eye, and doesn't mind making some extra money while indulging these inclinations is a prime candidate for a bellows business. Start-up costs are minimal, since many of the raw materials may be had for the asking, and most craftspersons probably already own the necessary tools. To create a successful business, you'll need to offer a broad selection of styles and sizes. By mastering the following techniques, it's possible to build a large number of bellows in a lot less time than you'd ever imagine.

enough to decorate over 20 bellows) of the fancy fasteners in every style and color imaginable. Brass-colored tacks in size 1 or 2 are suitable for most bellows and can probably be picked up for a third of what they sell for at a hardware or variety store. In fact, if the upholstery folks take a shine to you, they'll often throw in a handful of standard 1/2″ carpet tacks (another useful item) for almost nothing.

The next stop should be the best "bargain" hardware store you know of. Pick up a quart of contact cement (or a gallon, if you're really counting on a lot of business). Do not buy the little 4-ounce bottles, as their cost per ounce is so high it will eat up your profits in no time!

Now, move on to the largest retail/ wholesale plumbing or air-conditioning supply house in the area and buy a stock of 1/2″ X 1/2″ male-to-male compression pipe couplers and 1/2″ brass flare nuts. These items are used to make decorative nozzles for your

blowers, with almost no manufacturing time required on your part. Get one coupler and one flare nut per bellows. Be sure to insist on the classy-looking "extended" flare nuts with a smooth finish. Male-to-female air nozzles intended for spray equipment will also serve as attractive tips.

Finally, drop by a few secondhand stores and check out their supplies. Discarded nozzles can often be had for pennies, and good leather from wrecked or junked furniture or cars can be found, too. But concentrate on quality materials only; your customers will know—and appreciate—the difference.

PUTTING IT TOGETHER: At last, you've come to the most fulfilling part of the bellows business (next to pocketing the profits, that is): creating your designs. Let your imagination flower, since it's subject only to the limitations of the scrap leather and wood you've gathered. Keep in mind that your customers will want practical sizes—usually 14″ to 20″ long—with plenty of blowing power. There is a market for everything from the hefty models fit for a blacksmith's forge to the svelte trout-shaped units appropriate for the small fire of a fishing camp.

For your first attempt, however, it may be best to stick with a basic pattern. Begin by outlining an attractive-looking bellows design on newspaper or light cardboard, remembering to allow for the length of the nozzle. Fold

the pattern in half lengthwise and cut out both sides at one time to achieve symmetry. Open up the paper again and hold the bellows-to-be in your hand to get a feel for the design.

Once you're satisfied with the pattern, pick out a scrap board that's big enough to accommodate the two identical sides of the bellows. Lay the paper pattern on the wood, trace it twice, and cut out the paddles. Be sure to save successful paper patterns because you might want to transfer them to thin wood stock so they'll stand up to repeated use.

Next, align the two halves and—using a rasp or file—trim off excess wood around the edges until the paddles are identical. If you plan to give the wood a smooth finish, now's the time to sandpaper the surfaces that will be exposed when the bellows is complete.

Choose the most attractive paddle and set it aside for the moment. Take the other half and draw a centerline the length of the piece. Drill two 5/8″ holes along this line: one centered in the handle and the other at a point about midway into the main body of the paddle. The first hole will later be fitted with a thong with which to hang the bellows, and the second will be part of the flapper valve mechanism that makes the tool work.

Then draw a centerline on the paddle you set aside, and pencil another straight line that intersects the first scribe at a right angle about 1-1/2″ to 2″ up from the nozzle end. Saw along the second line, then glue the severed endpiece to the matching portion of the paddle with the holes (Fig. 1).

FIG. 1 CONSTRUCTION DIAGRAM

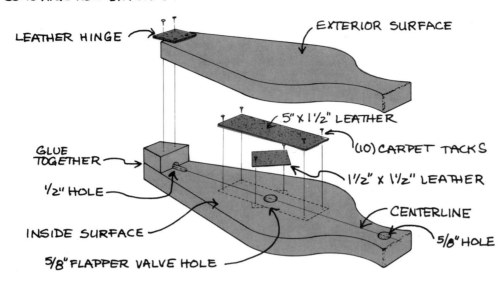

LEATHER HINGE

EXTERIOR SURFACE

5" X 1½" LEATHER

(10) CARPET TACKS

GLUE TOGETHER

½" HOLE

1½" X 1½" LEATHER

INSIDE SURFACE

CENTERLINE

5/8" HOLE

5/8" FLAPPER VALVE HOLE

FIG. 2 PATTERN LAYOUT

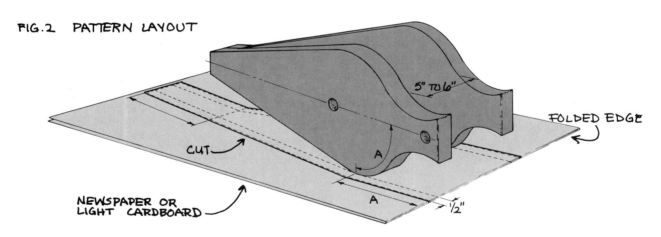

5" TO 6"

FOLDED EDGE

CUT

A

A

NEWSPAPER OR LIGHT CARDBOARD

½"

FIG. 3 BOOT PATTERN

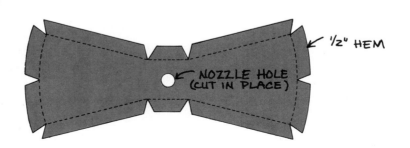

½" HEM

NOZZLE HOLE
(CUT IN PLACE)

When the adhesive is thoroughly dry, bore a 1/2" hole along the centerline clear through the center of the joint where the block and the paddle meet. This forms a tunnel to bring the air from the interior of the bellows to the metal nozzle that will be installed later.

START TO FINISH: Before continuing construction, put a nice finish on the wood. The best treatment for rough, weathered lumber requires the use of a small propane torch and a stiff wire brush. Holding the torch head about an inch from the surface of the wood, draw the flame along the grain, overlapping your strokes as you move the fire back and forth. Keep the flame moving so it merely scorches the surface, making it smoke a bit. Using this technique, blacken the two exterior sides of the paddles and the inside surfaces of the handle grips. Then, working with the grain, scrape away the charred wood with the wire brush. This procedure raises a very attractive rustic pattern and leaves the wood a pleasant deep brown color. To add yet more depth to the finish, wipe it down with some boiled linseed oil and let it dry.

Smoother surfaces and new wood can be sanded and then coated with brown shoe polish (the paste kind) rubbed in well. To produce a black, ebonylike finish, soak some rusty nails in white vinegar for a couple of weeks. Wait till the mixture begins foaming, and when it's ready, brush the liquid into the wood. This produces a great stain and does so at no real expense. There are also commercial wood stains and finishes available. (Either Danish or tung oil works very well.) Bellows-makers with an artistic bent may want to decorate the face of the paddle without holes, drawing landscapes or other designs and painting them in acrylics or oils. This sort of artistic touch can turn a handcrafted implement into a real piece of folk art and increase its selling price significantly.

Furthermore, if the bellows turns out to be particularly striking, why not autograph your work? Just use a black permanent-ink marking pen, the kind with a very fine point, to print the name and phone number of your company across the inner surface of the handle grip that doesn't have a hole.

FLAPS AND HINGES: To complete the leather or vinyl portion of the bellows, you'll need, at most, about four square feet of matching material (the exact amount will depend on the size of your design). Choose a piece that complements the wood finish, and from a small corner of it, fashion the flapper valve according to the following instructions:

After cutting a section about 1-1/2" square and a second piece that measures approximately 1-1/2" X 5", place the square—finished (or grain) side down—across the inside opening of the valve hole with any two of its opposite corners aligned along the center scribe (Fig. 1). Use carpet tacks to secure the other two corners. Place the rectangle of leather along the line so that its center point rests over the middle of the square and tack the strip's four corners down.

To test the valve, cover the corresponding hole in the wood with your mouth and blow. A good valve will let air through when you exhale but will prevent it from returning when you inhale.

For the hinge, cut a small square of leather or vinyl; the heavier it is, the better. Join the two cut-apart sections of the paddle with the hinge piece, first using some contact cement (always be certain to provide plenty of ventilation when working with this adhesive) and then some carpet tacks.

SKIRTS AND BOOTS: The care taken in measuring and installing the leather skirt can make or break a bellows, so the magic word is pattern. Each design will have its own shape, and to avoid wasting good materials, cut out a paper pattern before taking scissors to anything. But whatever the shape, the following method can be used:

Measure along the edge of the bellows, starting at the widest point on one side of the paddle, going up over the shoulders and across the base of the grip, and then down again to the opposite widest point. Now, place the bellows on edge on a folded-in-half sheet of newspaper, positioning the wide points of the paddles at a distance in from the fold that's exactly half of your previous measurement. (See "A" in Fig. 2, which applies to most standard designs. For styles like the fish shown in the photo, you'll have to experiment a bit.)

With that done, open the paddles so there is a 5" to 6" gap between the ends of the handles. Be sure both paddles are positioned the same distance from the fold of the paper and have the same angle toward the tip.

Trace along the outside edges of both paddles and draw another line about 1/2" out from the first. When you reach the widest point on either side, extend the scribe straight back to the fold of the paper. Then at the nozzle end, bring the pencil lines straight out a good 4".

Remove the bellows, cut along the outer line of the pattern, and open up the paper at the fold. To check the fit of the pattern, fold in the edge along the inner pencil line and position the resulting paper skirt on the bellows.

Once you're satisfied, reflatten the fold, trace the pattern onto the leather or vinyl, and cut out the skirt. Then tuck under the skirt's 1/2" border all around and seal it in place with contact cement.

Next, make the boot, which is a decorative cover that fits on the nozzle end. Cut a piece of leather that's long enough to pass down over the hinge, across the nose, and up the same distance on the opposite side. Again, leave a 1/2" margin all around (Fig. 3).

Often when working with leather, you'll find that the raw edges lying across the faces of the paddles are attractive enough to leave unhemmed. If not, fold them under along with the rest of the boot's edges. By cutting small notches as shown, you can easily fold the hem under and secure it with glue.

FINISHING STEPS: Coat the skirt hems and the matching narrow side edges of the paddles with contact cement. Let the glue dry and then carefully press the skirting into place along one paddle and then the other. (The adhesive assures that your bellows will be airtight all around.) With that done, bring the extended ends of the skirt around and across the nose of the tool and cut them off evenly where they meet over the midpoint of the nozzle hole.

The final steps are easy. Nail decorative upholstery tacks along the narrow edges (and across the boot lip, if you like the look), spacing them 1" to 1-1/2" apart. Be certain that they match, in both location and number, from one side to the other. Cut out the piece of leather that blocks the nozzle opening, and—after coating the threaded end of the brass coupling piece with glue—twist that component into the hole, using a wrench if necessary. Then screw a flare nut onto the coupling. Cut a long thong from matching scrap leather, tie it through the hole in the grip, and you're ready to make those coals glow!

BELLOWS AS A BUSINESS: Now that you've made your first bellows, how can you best use your newly acquired skill to make money blow your way?

Begin by creating five or six designs that you enjoy making, looking at, and using. Then, to produce these and future beauties efficiently, plan to make several at once. Cut enough paddles for, say, six finished blowers and assemble them, two at a time, at your leisure. While the glue on one is drying, proceed with the next step on the second bellows. With practice, you should be able to assemble two of them in about an hour.

It's best to give each style a colorful title, such as "Sirocco", "Zephyr", or "Blowhard", so merchants can order them by name. And a memorable moniker for your business will help folks remember and recognize your distinctive products.

The next step is to take color photographs of each style and to place them in a small folder or album. Carry this sales tool—along with two or three samples of your favorite mod-

els—when you head out to market your wares.

As an added touch, make up a single, photocopied page of instructions to give out with each purchase, including simple suggestions on the care of the wood and leather. This sheet will keep the name and address of your business before buyers, retailers, and interested friends of those people who've already discovered the delights of your product.

When setting prices, you might want to check out the competition first. There are *very* few bellowsmakers in this country, and usually the products imported aren't likely to rival your quality creations. Calculate your expense, then time yourself —after you get the knack of construction—and decide just how much to charge per hour. And since fine workmanship is what people really appreciate and *pay* for, it doesn't matter that you may have obtained your materials inexpensively.

TO MARKET: The recent popularity of wood- and coal-burning heaters, cookstoves, and fireplace inserts has triggered a growing interest in bellows. Most folks buy the windmakers as gifts for fellow woodburners, so fall and winter are obviously the prime sales seasons. It's smart to approach retailers by late summer, since that's when they're busy ordering their stock for the winter.

Woodstove dealers will probably be the best retail outlets, but you may have to show the store owners just how efficient—and valuable—your product is. Many have never used a bellows and think that their modern heating devices don't need such old-

fashioned fireside implements. A good way to sell these people on carrying your line is to let them see for themselves what a quality puffer can do. If you don't get an order, offer the free use of a bellows for a couple of weeks, under the stipulation that if the dealer finds the device to be a great help in tending fires and/or fun to use, he or she will stock them for customers. Whether your offer is accepted or not, leave one bellows as a gift for the shop. That gesture will bring you far more than the value of the tool, both in goodwill and future sales.

When dealing with store owners, keep in mind that the retailer has to mark up items 40% to 50%, so set a wholesale price for your bellows that will give the businessperson room to charge a reasonable retail price. It's best to avoid consignment deals whenever possible and always try for a cash sale.

In addition to stove outlets, you can confidently approach chain-saw dealers, hardware stores that sell woodburners and related accessories, and stores that sell local arts and crafts. In tourist areas, gift shops (even those in airports) are also likely marketing targets.

It's not necessary to rely exclusively on retailers. You might, for instance, join a craft guild in order to sell at crafts fairs in your vicinity. (Your local chamber of commerce can usually supply you with the locations, dates, and sponsors of festivals near you.) Many arts and crafts fairs are now juried, and only the finest workmanship is accepted for display. Shows are held almost year round in many areas. Visitors to these affairs tend to spend freely for unusual gifts of quality, and handcrafted wood-and-leather bellows usually win immediate interest and sales.

Finally, use your imagination to make your marketing efforts come to life. How about approaching firewood dealers or chimney sweeps? The growth of your business (and your enjoyment of it) will depend largely on the energy and thought you put into it.

WOODEN SIGNS

Handsome, well-designed, wooden signs can enhance a country landscape or city scene, while plastic and neon advertisements are considered—at best—unattractive necessities. If more folks were making wooden signs, and more businesses were using them instead of the garish kind, how much more beautiful the landscape would be! True, sign making is an uncommon occupation, but it's both satisfying work and a good way to earn a living. It also works as a part-time business, bringing in some handy supplemental income.

APTITUDE: A good sense of design is indispensable to the craft of making wooden signs, and a graphic arts background is very useful. However, having the soul of an artist isn't nearly as important as having the hands of a craftsperson. The work also requires patience to cope with such mundane tasks as endlessly guiding power tools around rigid patterns. A bit of business sense doesn't hurt, either, as this occupation calls for making sales, drawing up contracts, keeping accounts, and collecting payments.

CAPITAL: Starting a sign business requires only a small amount of cash, because when you take on a job, you should collect a 50% deposit to cover all immediate expenses such as wood, glue, paint, hardware, tool rental fees, and extra help you may need. Anyone who's a woodworker may already have most of the required tools, so he or she could make a profit with the very first sign.

SHOP AND EQUIPMENT: A garage or other outbuilding can make a convenient workshop, and since the work is noisy and dusty, doing it in the basement or house can't be recommended. Those who lack a permanent wind- and water-tight shop can erect a partial shelter, but will have

to limit their operation to good weather, since wet power tools can deliver an electrical shock and because the type of glue used will set only at a temperature above 70°F.

A truck in which to visit customers, carry materials, and so forth is useful, though deliveries can also be made in a trailer pulled behind a car.

Standard hand tools used in sign-making include the following: hammer, saw, tape measure, level, steel yardstick and T-square, bar or pipe clamps six feet or longer, mallet and assorted wood-carving tools, and a tall stepladder.

A number of power tools are also necessary: a router with assorted bits (preferably carbide tipped), an electric drill with a full set of bits (including at least one masonry bit), a circular saw, a belt sander, and a power planer. For stability and accuracy, bench versions of these tools would be a good investment, but portable tools fitted with long extension cords are fine for a start.

HOW TO CHOOSE AND BUY WOOD: The first step after entering into a contract for a sign job is a visit to the lumberyard to pick out dry, seasoned, unwarped, and unsplit lumber.

The kind of wood you select depends on the nature of the work to be done. Although pine, fir, and spruce can be used for exterior signs that will be stained or otherwise protected from the weather, redwood, cedar, and cypress are far better. But beware of heavy, wet cypress! After weeks or months of drying in the sun, it will split badly, destroying the sign's appearance.

Pressure-treated lumber is acceptable when used in large chunks (say, for posts), but smaller pieces warp badly. Plywood will split apart after a year outdoors unless the outer layers are marine grade or smooth fiberboard.

Exotic woods such as mahogany, teak, and rosewood are superb in color, grain, and general appearance. They go well with fine furnishings and are excellent for either exterior or interior settings where a luxurious appearance is desired.

The form in which you buy lumber depends on the size of the sign, its design, and the image it's supposed to project. For instance, will thick tongue-and-groove stock adorned with cutout symbols and letters give the desired appearance? This is the fastest and least expensive construction method for dimensional wooden signs (Fig. 1).

If a sign is two-sided, paneled background boards may be nailed horizontally, diagonally, or vertically over a 2 X 4 framework. If a sign is one-sided, simple back reinforcement strips may suffice (see Fig. 4).

FIG. 1

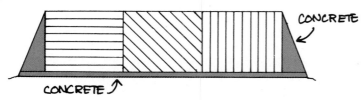

CONCRETE

CONCRETE

For a more interesting surface, you may decide to cut the symbols and letters directly into their background with a router. In that case, tongue-and-groove stock is inappropriate, and if the planned sign is too large to be contained on one board, it will mean gluing several together edge to edge. It will also mean that the surfaces to be joined must be made perfectly straight and flat so that they'll butt against one another without gaps. If you have no jointer-planer, you can arrange to have the planks edge-planed at the lumberyard or a local cabinetmaking shop.

Another consideration in shopping for lumber is how much—if any—extra material will be necessary to reinforce the sign to make it sturdy. A large display made of inch-thick planks, for instance, will require a supporting framework of heavier stock, 2″-thick boards need less strengthening, and 4″-thick timbers remain strong even when deeply carved on both sides.

Once the materials are lined up, it's time to start creating the sign, beginning with the construction of the background.

PANELED BACKGROUNDS OVER FRAMEWORK: A paneled look is easily achieved by building a framework of 2 X 4's (Fig. 2) and covering it—on both sides, for neat appearance—with either tongue-and-groove or plain-edged stock. Boards of any width can be used for this planking, though narrower stock means a larger number of joints and fastenings and thus additional work.

Paneling can be attached to the framework with nails or screws. If the sign is to stand outdoors, brass screws are the best fasteners to use, but they are expensive, so dull-finish galvanized nails may be preferred.

If screws are used, give the job a finished look by concealing the heads as follows: Drill the screw holes with a 1/2″ bit to a depth of 1/4″, insert the fastenings, and fill what's left of each hole with a short length of dowel or a plug of matching wood held in place with glue (Fig. 3). These fillers can be sanded down even with the

FIG.2

USE METAL L-BRACES WHERE NEEDED

CHECK SQUARENESS WITH FRAMING SQUARE

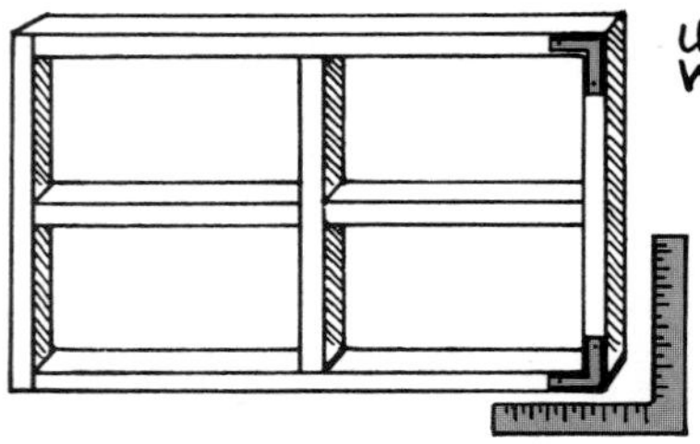

FIG.3 SCREW CONCEALMENT

Drill 1/4″ deep with a 1/2″ bit to make a hole for a 1/2″ plug or dowel. Use dowels where appearance won't matter. Use wood plugs (cut with plug cutter) when wood grain and color must match that of the background.

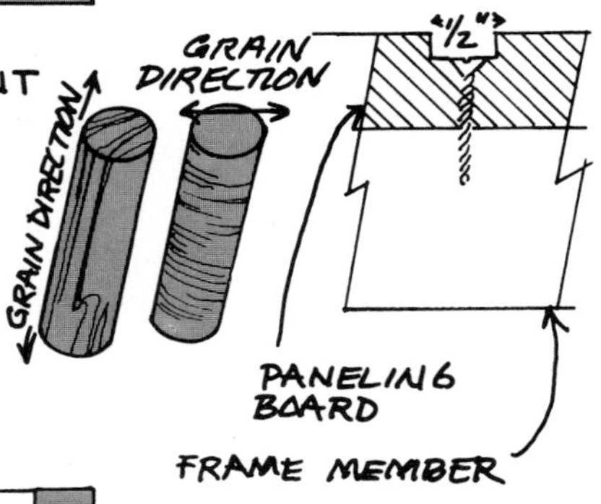

GRAIN DIRECTION

GRAIN DIRECTION

PANELING BOARD

FRAME MEMBER

FIG.4

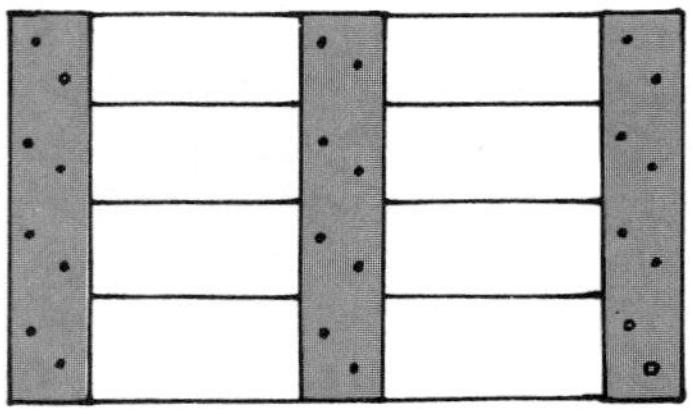

BACK VIEW

REINFORCEMENT STRIPS

FIG.5   GLUE-UP ARRANGEMENT

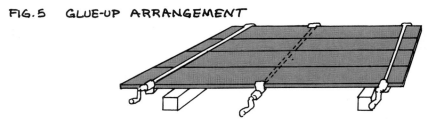

sign's surface after the adhesive has cured. It's possible, incidentally, to create decorative effects with plugs or dowels, but keep in mind that this is a time-consuming process. If screws are used instead of dowels, the heads can be disguised with an enamel varnish that matches the surrounding boards.

When the boxlike framework has been covered on both sides with paneling, it may be necessary to saw off a few protruding ends because some boards are longer than others. An appropriate stain or finish will complete the background. Letters and art can then be cut out with a heavy-duty sabre saw and attached (over 1″

spacers if added depth is desired). Such signs look neat and sophisticated, especially if the paneling matches the exterior architecture of the building to which the billboard or nameplate is affixed.

Of course, it's possible to produce a low-cost, one-sided paneled sign by fastening tongue-and-grove lumber directly to reinforcement strips (2 X 4 or thinner) attached at right angles to the signboard planks (Fig. 4). This method should be used only when appearance is secondary in importance to expense, or in locations where the braces won't be visible, such as against a wall or a background of tall shrubbery.

SMOOTH AND "SEAMLESS" BACKGROUNDS: To construct a sign on which the seams between the boards are not apparent, edge-glue the planks together to form a larger, solid area before attaching the background to a framework of 2 X 4's. This method of construction is appropriate for lumber of any thickness and width, but bear in mind that the narrower the boards are, the greater the number of edges that will have to be evened up and glued.

Remember that the adjoining surfaces of the background planks must be perfectly straight before they're joined so that no cracks will weaken the sign or spoil its appearance. If the boards were not edge-planed at the time of purchase, run them through a jointer-planer until they're smooth enough to lay side by side with no

TOP: Raised letters and art show to advantage on a paneled background. RIGHT: Supporting timbers are an extension of this sign of carved cypress.

gaps showing. Extremely rough stock may need to be recut with a table saw before this edge-finishing.

When the boards are ready, build the framework, then set it aside and proceed to the gluing process.

Choose marine-grade plastic resin, resorcinol, or epoxy, all of which have excellent resistance to weather and may be used in sign construction. Don't attempt to substitute white household glue, which is water-soluble and suitable only for indoor use.

Lay the planks that will form the background across a couple of sets of matching 4 X 4's which will support the work during construction. Flip the boards up, one by one, and brush their edges liberally with the adhesive. While glue manufacturers specify exact thicknesses, even a too-heavy application is permissible, since any excess will run off or be squeezed out when the planks are clamped together.

Align the coated edges closely and press them together with the help of several clamps placed at equal intervals. (Don't tighten the fastenings too firmly on 1″ lumber, or the boards may pop out of position.) If

applying three clamps to one set of planks, alternate their placement: If two are laid across the top of the background, the center holder should be placed underneath (Fig. 5). This tends to prevent the entire sign from warping into a shallow curve.

Complete drying is possible only at temperatures above 70°F and will take 12 hours or more. When the glue is dry, remove the clamps and smooth the newly jointed surface with a plane and a belt sander. Start sanding with a roughly textured belt and follow with a medium one. The result will be a perfectly flat background with almost no visible seams.

Screw or nail the background to the framework and run a circular saw around the irregular edges until they correspond perfectly with the dimensions of the frame. Repeat the whole process on the other side of the supporting structure for a neat two-faced signboard, which can be embellished with either a routed design or raised cutout letters and art. (It's best not to try routing or hand-carving 1″ lumber, as it's a little too thin.)

SMOOTH BACKGROUNDS WITHOUT A FRAMEWORK: Edge-glued signboards can be fab-

ricated without underlying frameworks and be braced by other means, depending on the thickness of the stock used in the panels.

A one-sided sign made of edge-glued 1″ lumber can be reinforced with strips of wood screwed to the backs of the planking in the same manner as a seamed, one-sided paneled sign. If a finished appearance is desired on both sides, simply place

FIG.6 CASEMENT FRAME

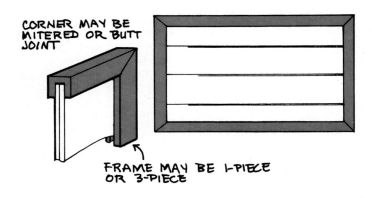

CORNER MAY BE MITERED OR BUTT JOINT

FRAME MAY BE 1-PIECE OR 3-PIECE

FIG.7 END-THREADED DRIFT RODS

NUT AND WASHER

GLUE JOINTS

1" OR LARGER OUTER HOLES FOR SOCKET WRENCH ACCESS

FIG.8 END CAPS AND DOWEL SUPPORTS GLUED AND DOWELED OR LAG-SCREWED

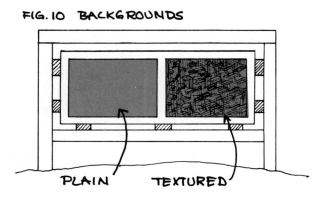

GLUE JOINTS

HIDDEN DOWELS FOR SUPPORT

FIG.9 IRREGULAR BACKGROUND

Jekyll Island

FIG.10 BACKGROUNDS

PLAIN   TEXTURED

FIG.11 ROUTER BITS

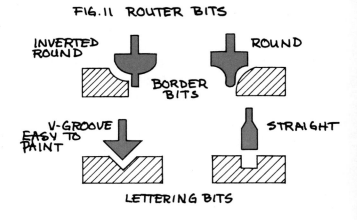

INVERTED ROUND

ROUND

BORDER BITS

V-GROOVE EASY TO PAINT

STRAIGHT

LETTERING BITS

FIG 12 WOODCARVING TOOLS

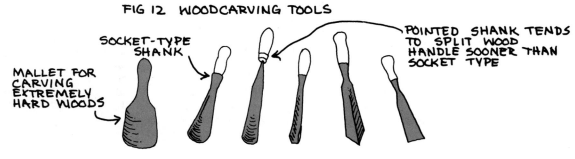

SOCKET-TYPE SHANK

POINTED SHANK TENDS TO SPLIT WOOD HANDLE SOONER THAN SOCKET TYPE

MALLET FOR CARVING EXTREMELY HARD WOODS

PROJECTS FOR PROFIT

two such units back-to-back and enclose the pair in a frame (Fig. 6).

Edge-glued boards that are two or more inches thick can be reinforced with 1/2″ dowels or steel drift rods running right through the planks. These invisible, but extremely effective, braces will insure your sign's permanence.

DRIFT RODS: Run two drift rods through all the boards that make up a laminated background (Fig. 7). The holes—5/8″ in diameter if the rods are of 1/2″-diameter steel—are drilled in two places through every piece of wood, and these holes must be perfectly aligned to receive each reinforcement. You can check the alignment by inserting the fasteners temporarily. Edge-glue the planks as instructed above, and then remove the metal rods before the adhesive starts to dry.

When the glue has hardened, drill an access space at least an inch deep and an inch wide at the ends of the holes through which the rods fit. The lengths of steel (which should be about an inch shorter than the final height of the background panel) are then placed in position. A socket wrench is slipped into the access holes to tighten washered nuts onto the threaded ends of the rods, thus locking the glued boards together even more firmly than the adhesive can hold them. As a finishing touch, the inch-wide openings on the edges of the laminated panel can be filled with plastic wood, which is then stained or painted to match the sign.

DOWELS: This can be tricky, because the fastenings won't fit unless the adjoining holes are aligned perfectly (Fig. 8). A doweling jig is a big help, but with a little skill you can get good results using dowel centers (inexpensive little metal pins of various diameters, used to mark the correct locations of corresponding holes).

To work with dowel centers, drill a 1/2″ hole for the first dowel, at a perfect right angle, exactly in the middle of one board's edge. Then place a dowel center in the hole with its point sticking up. When setting the

next board in position, the metal tip will prick the precise spot of the center of the corresponding hole. Remove the second plank and drill it at the spot indicated.

When all the holes have been drilled into both facing edges, cut thin grooves around the dowels' ends to hold the adhesive, apply glue to the dowels and board edges, fit the pins into their sockets, and push the planks together.

END CAPS: For added strength, dowels or rods may be supplemented with end caps which are themselves doweled in place (Fig. 8). These reinforcements when used alone are of value only on signboards under five-feet long, but end caps are highly recommended on larger signs when used in combination with internal dowels or rods.

IRREGULAR SHAPES AND TEXTURED BACKGROUNDS: If a background of irregular shape is desired, boards can be edge-glued and then the panel cut to any desired form with a band saw or heavy-duty sabre saw (Fig. 9).

Another interesting variation is a textured background, produced with strokes of a gouge, a chisel, an adz, an ax, or some other woodworking tool (Fig. 10). The size of the blade should be appropriate to the size of the area. In other words, a narrow gouge would be the best choice for a small sign.

LETTERS, ART, AND OTHER COPY: Once the background of a sign is complete, it's time to add the letters and artwork. Begin by making a full-sized paper pattern based on the original concept of the sign as approved by the customer.

The pattern is most easily made by transferring the small-scale layout to a background-sized sheet of paper. To do this, mark a grid of 1″ squares on the original drawing. Then decide on a scale. Lay out a full-scale grid on the large sheet and reproduce the design by drawing the contents of each small square in the corresponding large space.

When you have a perfect full-sized copy of the original, transfer the

outlines of the letters and art to the background itself. This is best done with giant carbon paper (sold by art supply stores), because the marks stay put a long time and are dark enough to be seen while routing or carving.

If the sign is to consist of cutout symbols attached to the background, proceed to make and attach the shapes using the transferred outline as a placement guide. Otherwise, go ahead with one of the techniques described in the following sections.

ROUTING: Signs with routed lettering and designs are produced by guiding the whirling bit of a high-speed router around the letters and other shapes of the pattern.

Two kinds of bits—the V groove (its cut is easier to paint) and the straight bit—are normally used in sign work. (Fig. 11.) Border edging bits, available in several contours, are handy to round or otherwise finish the edges of signs and individual cutout components.

The router's cut is clean and fast, especially when carbide bits are used on dry wood. As a rule, however, it's not practical to rout deeper than 1/2″ since the bit's action meets too much resistance beyond that depth. To make a deeper cut, make one pass around the design, then reset your router bit and go over the cuts again.

CARVING: Hand carving, properly done, is by far the most time-consuming way to finish a sign, and yet it's the method that yields the most satisfying results. It's pleasurable to hand-form elegant curves and delicate cuts, but these can be made perfectly only with sharp tools.

Hand-carving equipment is shown in Fig. 12. For roughing out and wood removal, you'll need a set of at least three socket gouges and chisels. A mallet is used to strike the implements with enough impact to remove a fair quantity of wood quickly. Also needed are some lighter duty, pointed-base chisels, semicircular gouges, and V-shaped carving tools.

It's imperative to keep these implements well sharpened and honed, using a stone with both medium- and

fine-grit faces. Instructions generally come with the stone. If not, you can find them in any comprehensive book on wood carving.

If nicks appear in the cutting edges, never grind the blades on a standard, dry, high-speed sharpening wheel, as the heat generated can destroy the temper of the metal. Use either a low-speed sanding belt or a low-speed wheel that passes through water to handle heavy sharpening chores without overheating the cutting steel.

COMBINED ROUTING AND CARVING: In this technique, the V bit of the router is used to make a clean outline around the letters and other shapes, and the background within the resulting line is then removed with hand tools, leaving neat gouge strokes. It's an easy way to get a hand-carved look.

RAISED LETTERS: Raised letters are cut out with a heavy-duty saber saw or a band saw and affixed to the background. To avoid splitting—a real nuisance with cutout

characters, especially small ones—it's vital to have a saber saw that doesn't vibrate and to clamp the material so it can't move while being cut. Any split that occurs in spite of this care can be repaired with a flat mending plate glued across the back of the break, or can be fixed with a corrugated metal fastener such as the type used to repair furniture.

Instead of trying to hand-cut very small raised letters, it is probably best to buy wooden or plastic ones. This is well worth the cost because

PROJECTS FOR PROFIT

This routed cypress sign has been heavily varnished to preserve the wood's natural color.

it's nearly impossible to duplicate their precision in the workshop.

PREPARATION FOR FINISHING: To make the sign colorful and resistant to weather, the completed background, letters, and art must be painted or otherwise finished. In most cases, sanding is a necessary preliminary. The more the wood is rubbed down, the more its natural grain shows through. A belt sander greatly facilitates this job, but a disk sander will leave undesirable circular marks on the surfaces.

Although most signs don't require treatment with wood filler, this may be needed if a really slick finish is desired, or paint or varnish is to be applied over an open-grained wood.

A DISTRESSED FINISH: After an exterior sign with a pronounced grain to the wood has been carved or routed, it may be deeply scorched with a propane torch and then vigorously brushed with a wire brush to eliminate the charred layer and to leave a deeply distressed "driftwood" effect.

To put it plainly, this work is time-consuming and dull. Be sure to wear a protective face mask during the brushing process to avoid inhaling too much floating carbon. A sandblasting unit with an air compressor will give the same effect with less labor, but the cost of this equipment is high.

After the burning and brushing procedure is completed, the surface of the wood will be brown, but it will quickly turn gray with exposure to the weather. The scorching seals the outer layer of the sign and its posts and effectively protects the wood beneath against water. Colorful letters and artwork can be added with paint, as described in the next section.

PAINT: A quick color treatment for signs, paint is applied in at least two layers. The best primer coat is flat white exterior sealer, though there are expensive artists' preparations on the market.

The second coat should be glossy enamel, since it repels the ravages of wind and weather and gives the best outdoor service. (Nevertheless, exterior signs need repainting at least once a year, and more often in rugged climates.) Yacht enamel is also an excellent choice. Be sure to have a paint sample chart handy when making sales, as the color specifications should be included in the contract and on the layout.

Here are two suggestions that will help the painting of signs go more smoothly. First, cutout letters must be painted before they're affixed to a sign, to ease handling and to avoid messing up the background.

The second hint concerns inverted (routed or carved) designs or lettering. Such areas can sometimes be painted with two coats of paint, each of which is allowed to dry thoroughly. The background is then gone over with a belt sander to leave a flawless flat surface surrounding the colorful, recessed symbols. This is a quick

method, since the sanding will remove any slipups and messy applications of finish, and the color will eventually be left only in the recessed areas.

OIL STAINS: Oil stains, which are available in many shades, color a surface evenly and hide natural wood to varying degrees, depending on the product being used and the type of wood. Underlying grain is completely concealed by opaque stain but is partly visible through a semitransparent formulation. (Incidentally, there are very good water-based stains you might want to try, though a varnish must be applied over them to protect the wood.)

Oil stains will hold up for several years and are a good choice when easy maintenance is essential. For a sign that will retain the full vibrancy and warmth of its natural wood, however, varnish is the way to go.

VARNISH: This finish gives a slick, sophisticated look and helps protect and preserve the natural color of the wood. Keep in mind that exterior varnishes contain an ingredient that acts as a sun barrier and tints the protected surface a brownish shade.

Exterior gloss varnish wears longer outdoors than does a low-sheen product, yet both must be reapplied at least annually. Near the sea or under harsh weather conditions, a varnish finish will need attention far more frequently.

GOLD LEAF: Gold leaf, which yields the only lasting gold finish, is applied by an elaborate process (also used in applying silver and copper leaf). Check carefully before quoting on this service! The initial expense of the material—pure gold—is high, and the work takes many hours. There is, however, no satisfactory substitute. Metallic paint invariably tarnishes and is disappointing.

OTHER FINISHES: Some interior signs can be sufficiently protected with an application of linseed oil, lemon oil, or the like every few months. The wood tones will shine through such finishes beautifully. On signs placed indoors, a polished wax finish can be used successfully.

WOODSHOP ANIMALS

Even a "pocket-sized" woodshop always seems to have a box tucked away somewhere filled with scraps of wood that are too small to use for most projects. These discards, however, lend themselves well to making miniature animals you can sell through gift and toy shops or give to your own youngsters.

In addition to their old-fashioned charm, these wooden animals make appealing playthings for several reasons: They mix happily with blocks and other toys, they stack, they encourage creativity, and the little folks who play with them will find them educational, too.

COLLECT YOUR TOOLS AND RAW MATERIALS: Making these toys is so easy that anyone with a drill press, band saw, and sander will find it a snap. Those without such equipment can create the wooden critters with a coping saw, hand drill, and sandpaper. Even pieces of wood that contain minor knots and small cracks can be put to good use in this project. Fill the defects with a mixture of glue and sawdust, and the irregularities will add texture to the natural look of the finished toys.

The designs should be cut from pieces of wood measuring no more than 1-1/2" thick by 3-1/8" by 4-3/4". (This keeps the completed animals small enough—yet thick enough—for tiny hands to stack easily.) Short ends of almost any hard or semihard wood will do. Red alder is perfect, as is Alaska yellow cedar (which isn't a true hardwood but works well since it is tough enough for these toys, looks good, and doesn't splinter too readily). Redwood, being soft and splintery, isn't usually recommended for children's playthings.

DESIGNING YOUR TOYS: Start with one of the rough-cut blocks and draw a compact, chunky animal to fit the dimensions of the piece of wood. When you have something that looks good, cut it out and sand it. There's your original. Get your ideas from life, from books (children's books—especially—have nice, clear illustrations that you'll find inspiring), and from your imagination.

Keep your outlines simple and try to key them to your equipment. The curves on a hippopotamus, for example, can be sized to match the drum on the top of your sander (which, obviously, makes it very easy to sand down a hippo). Avoid fragile beaks or feet that can break off during rough-and-tumble play.

Many of these little creations can be designed so that the space between their front and back legs is a half circle. You can remove the semicircles from two animals at one time by clamping two figures together—base to base—and then drilling with a 1-1/8" bit right through the resulting "crack" where the two blocks abut.

MAKE A PATTERN FOR EACH FIGURE: After perfecting a design, trace it onto a piece of tempered fiberboard or scrap paneling and cut out a master template. Mark the spot for the eye by drilling a hole with a 1/8" bit, and you're all set to duplicate a rabbit, rhinoceros,

or some other animal as many times as you like.

All the basic figures can be modified to make bookends, coat pegs, birthday-candle holders, and other children's items. Pencil holders, for example, are nothing more than stock animals with a few holes drilled into their backs (after a bit of practice, you'll find it easiest to drill these holes before the figures are even band-sawed out).

Another simple way to get more mileage from an especially good design: Just scale it up or down. Some customers will be looking for a "papa", a "mama", and a "baby" elephant. You can easily furnish all three, and except for size, they are all the same animal!

PRODUCTION IS EASY: You can fashion a number of these wooden animals in a short time. Place a template on a block, pencil around it, and mark the eye. Repeat for a second figure. Then clamp the two blocks together (base-to-base as already described) and run the 1-1/8″ drill bit between them to form the animals' legs. Switch to the 1/4″ bit and drill out the eyes. (Auger bits—the ones with little guide screws in their centers—are the best kind to use.)

Next, unclamp the two blocks, and —one at a time, with each held down flat on the band saw's table—cut out the animals with a 3/8″ or 1/4″ skip-tooth blade. Then sand them to shape on your bench sander fitted with a medium-grit belt. Finally, hand-sand each figure to take off all sharp corners and edges (remember, you're creating something special for little children).

Each of the tiny pets is finished by dipping it in a nontoxic sealer. A good choice is thinned linseed oil. It's still one of the best finishes around, and it enhances the natural beauty of wood's grain and color. For efficiency, dip the animals in batches. Then dry them on racks for several days. If you dry them outdoors, keep them out of the sun.

When the oil is dry, rub the wooden figures gently with No. 3 steel wool. Make all the strokes *with* the grain to obtain an extra smooth "feel" that's delightful.

COST AND MARKETING: It's possible, as experience is gained, to make four or five little animals an hour, and by utilizing scrap lumber, the cost is quite low.

The toys always sell well when attractively displayed at craft fairs. No one can walk by without sneaking a glance when you pose your little creatures in totem pole stacks, in games of "hide and seek", or in a zoo or barnyard setting.

It seems that both institutions and individuals welcome the opportunity to buy quality wooden toys. And not just for children: Adults also fall for these natural little charmers, and many will purchase a "pet" pencil holder for themselves.

If craft fairs are scarce in your area, try writing to day care centers and nursery schools and letting the people there know what you have to offer. Or put some of your creations out on consignment in craft and gift shops, advertise them on supermarket bulletin boards, or sell the figures directly from your home or woodworking shop. These little animals really pay off, both in cash and in enjoyment.

APPLEHEAD DOLLS

Years ago, when life was less complicated and most homesteaders lived miles from their nearest neighbors, family entertainment was more often homespun than manufactured. Children had to invent their own games, and—since cash was scarce—parents made toys for their youngsters from a variety of natural materials.

Today, that tradition can be continued by fashioning applehead dolls. This easy at-home craft requires a minimum of low-cost supplies. And best of all, the wizened faces of the small figures will entrance any child. No two of the faces turn out exactly alike, so applehead dolls make delightful conversation pieces and gifts. They also sell well at gift shops, craft fairs, and country produce stands.

The Seneca Indians are thought to be the first people to make dolls out of apples, and the craft was later adopted by mountaineers in Appalachia where such handmade toys are still produced as part of the area's cottage industry. The miniature figures command a surprisingly high price, too.

APPLE WHITTLING: Few supplies are needed to make an "applehead", and you'll probably have most of the necessary materials already on hand. Gather some apples (the larger, the better, because the fruit shrinks quite a bit as it dries), a sharp paring knife, several shallow bowls, a bottle of pure lemon juice, a box of noniodized salt, a few light-gauge coat hangers, a pair of pliers, clean strips of old bed sheets (or other rags), a supply of small cotton balls, and some scraps of cloth.

To start an apple "noggin", carefully peel the fruit and carve out the eyes, nose, mouth, and ears. Try not to whittle too deeply or too shallowly, since an evenly balanced carving will dry into a more lifelike face than will an excessively jagged form. (At this point, try cutting tiny smile lines around the doll's mouth or crow's feet beside its eyes by making small creases with the point of a knife.)

Don't worry if the applehead's face still looks like a bland man in the moon, because it will acquire character during the drying process. Also, be sure to carve more apples than you think you may need (or want),

since some of the faces shrink into unrecognizable, useless, shapes as they dry.

After sculpting the facial features, dip the fruit in a bowl filled with lemon juice. This bath should last about a minute and should be followed by a generous sprinkling of salt, which with the citric acid in the lemon juice helps cure the apple and prevent its rotting. Finally, make the doll's eyes by pressing two whole apple seeds into the carved sockets.

SPEEDY AGING PROCESS: Now the doll's head is ready to be "strung up" for a drying period of two to four weeks. Unbend a large paper clip (or use a length of wire) and push it straight through the apple's core, bending the wire at the bottom—so the fruit won't slide off—and fashioning a hook at the top. Then simply hang the newcomer in a northfacing window away from direct sunlight.

It's fun to watch the dolls' faces slowly change and develop personalities as their soft, babylike roundness "ages" into the craggy countenances of backwoods oldsters. It's really impossible to predict just what kind of

To begin an applehead doll, peel a large apple and carve out miniature facial features. Let the head soak in lemon juice for about a minute. After sprinkling the little face with noniodized salt, string up the "appleheads" on wire to dry for two to four weeks.

PROJECTS FOR PROFIT
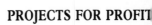

expression will emerge from each apple. Sometimes the most intricately cut features shrivel into oblivion, while a lackluster carving will often blossom into a fascinating face etched with crotchety character lines.

In about three weeks, the appleheads will be totally free of moisture and withered to half their original size. Give each one a thin coat of clear shellac or varnish to protect the fruit from further deterioration.

THE FINISHING TOUCHES: Now it's time to make each of those wrinkled old faces into a complete "person". Pull apart a cotton ball and glue it around the face to form a snowy halo of hair. For a "granny" doll, arrange the fuzz into a tiny bun on top of her head.

To form the figure's body, use pliers to twist a thin coat hanger into a simple stick figure. It's a good idea to shape the limbs with a double thickness of wire, so that the little fellow—or lady—will be sturdy. Next, wrap strips of old sheets around the arms, legs, and trunk of the figure to put a little "meat" on the doll's bones. Secure the rags on the wire form with either rubber bands or adhesive tape.

Simple down-home clothes for the miniature figures can be made from blue denim or other fabric scraps or the usable portions of worn-out garments.

Once you've dressed your "pippin people", attach a head to each body by skewering it firmly on the protruding "neck" of the wire figure. Hands and boots for the dolls can be carved out of wood or made from chunks of dried apple. Finally—to give those applehead oldsters a healthy, outdoor glow—"rosy up" their cheeks with a small brush dipped in red acrylic paint.

That's really all there is to it. It's as easy as apple pie—and fun—to make one-of-a-kind dolls that require no more of an investment than a few common household supplies, a bit of spare time, and some imagination. Give one of your creations to a child, and you'll probably be giving that youngster a delightful first home-made natural toy.

APPLEHEAD DOLLS

STAINED GLASS

Making and selling stained glass items is one of the most rewarding crafts imaginable. And anyone with a little patience and determination can learn the basic techniques very quickly.

GETTING STARTED: Find a roomy work area such as a table or bench in an unused part of the garage, den, porch, or extra bedroom. A sheet of 3/4″ plywood placed across two sawhorses will serve as an ideal workbench and provide plenty of space. It can also be rapidly disassembled if necessary.

If there are small children in the family, make a special effort to keep your work area off-limits to curious fingers, because broken glass pieces and strips of lead are extremely hazardous. So be sure the space set aside for your sun-catching art is quite separate from your home's regular traffic patterns.

MAKING DESIGNS: The easiest way to begin a stained glass project is with a black and white line drawing of the pattern, and though there are several books containing such designs on the market, the plans they present are often too complex for a first effort. So design your first piece yourself,

WRONG **FIG. 1** RIGHT

sticking to simple shapes, straight lines, and gentle curves. Limit the size of the project by keeping both length and width between 10″ and 18″, and restrict the number of glass pieces to between 15 and 25.

Begin by drawing the design on graph paper to keep it square and in proportion. As a rule of thumb, the shape in the pattern should comply with the following guidelines: [1] Never draw a "lead line" (one that indicates the position of the lead that will hold your shards together) that stops in space. All such lines *must* be connected to other lead lines (Fig. 1). [2] Never design a right or acute angle without adding at least one lead line from the apex of the angle (Fig. 2). [3] Always divide any large pieces of

background glass into small shapes, and avoid having tight curves that jut into such shapes (Fig. 3).

Upon completing the design and sketching it full size on a sturdy piece of paper, go over the lead lines with a fine-point permanent marking pen. This pen should draw a line about 1/16″ wide, just the right size for your "lead allowance" (the space which will be taken up by the leading). It's very important to incorporate this allowance into the pattern: If you don't do so, the glass panel may distort as you place the lead strips between its pieces.

CUTTING THE GLASS: Glass cutting is really a simple skill which, for some reason, most folks believe is cloaked in mystery. In fact, the technique is easy to master with a little practice.

When purchasing a glass cutter, follow the recommendation of a stained glass supplier, who may let you experiment with a few different types

 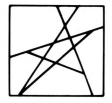

WRONG **FIG. 2** RIGHT

before buying one. A visit to a local commercial glass store or framing shop will usually yield a box of free scrap glass, which will be perfect for practice cutting. Just lay a pad of newspapers on your work surface before you start.

Hold the cutter comfortably in the palm of your hand (Fig. 4), and dip its tip in some light oil or turpentine. Then set the scoring wheel close to the edge of the glass, press down firmly, and push it away from you across the glass surface. Always run the cutter off the opposing edge of the glass, lessening the pressure as you do so, and never go over a score line twice.

After cutting a fine groove in the pane, break the sections apart carefully. If the score line is straight or gently

curving, grasp the glass on either side of the score and snap it in two with a downward twist. However, if the cut is more radically curved, tap the *underside* of the line with the handle of the cutter and then separate the pieces.

Now some folks may tell you that this method of scoring glass is "wrong", because it requires holding and pushing the tool in a manner that's just about completely opposite to the traditional method practiced by most glass cutters. However, by using the procedure described, you're running the cutter ahead of your hand (pushing it as you would a tiny wheelbarrow). This enables you to see exactly where the cutting wheel is going, helping you to follow curved lines around small patterns with accuracy.

After practicing on scrap glass, begin shaping your *stained* glass. Cutting the colored panes will require applying a little more pressure than when working on the "softer" window material. Set the stained glass piece on top of the full-sized pattern (called a cartoon), check the lead allowance, and cut to the *inside* edge of the marker line. Then as each individual shape is cut out, reposition it on the pattern and check to see whether the black marker line shows all the way around the perimeter of the glass.

Of course, some stained glass is so nearly opaque that the pattern can't be seen through it. In that case, draw the shape on white adhesive-backed paper, cut it out, and apply the gummed side directly to the glass. The paper can be peeled off after the piece is cut.

A pair of grozing pliers—tools with little teeth on their rounded jaws, available from a stained glass supplier—will do any glass "nibbling" that might be necessary, and a special glass file will smooth the edges to make the pieces fit the pattern perfectly. Number the shapes with a china marker as they are cut, place a corresponding numeral on the pattern, and set the glass aside.

LEAD AND SOLDER: Before fitting the pieces together, make a frame by nailing two quarter-round wooden

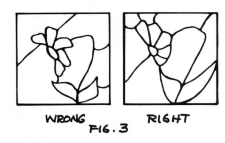

WRONG FIG. 3 RIGHT

molding strips together at a right angle to form a corner on your workbench. Or, if you prefer, prepare a separate piece of 1/4″ or 3/8″ plywood—about two feet square—with molding strips along two adjacent sides. Either way, brace the glass against this molding corner while you're making the window.

The lead used to hold the stained glass pieces together comes in different sizes and shapes. Ask for six-foot lengths—called cames—of 3/16″ or 1/4″ channeled lead in two shapes: The "H" shape, which has a channel on each side, serves as a common border when two pieces of glass meet, while the "U" shape can be used around the *outer* edges of the entire piece (Fig. 5).

The metal will be curved—and perhaps twisted—when purchased, so it's important to stretch the strips before they're sliced into measured pieces. The easiest way to accomplish this is with a friend's help. Each of you should grab an end of the lead came with a pair of pliers, and pull (brace yourself and exert a strong, steady tug) until the came straightens out and actually stretches an inch or so.

Strips of lead can easily be cut with an inexpensive pair of diagonal cutting pliers (wire cutters) that have been ground or filed to a sharp edge. Always sever the lead *across* the open channels to obtain a clean cut. If you close down on the top of the lead, the edges will mash together, crushing the channels, and the joint will then be unusable.

Now, put your design pattern in the corner of your workboard, place two cut lead strips against the square molding corner, and fit your first piece of glass into the channels of the lead. To hold this (and subsequent pieces of glass) against the corner, use flat-sided farrier's (horseshoe) nails, which can be purchased from a stained glass supplier or local equestrian shop. Tap them into your workbench board with their flat sides against the edge of the glass until you've prepared the next length of lead. Continue to fit the glass pieces into the metal channels, cutting and bending appropriate strips of lead as you progress, pulling and resetting the nails to hold everything tight, and always building out from the corner in a logical order. Remember, of course, to keep matching the glass shapes to the pattern underneath.

After all the lead strips are in place, your artwork is ready to be soldered. You'll need a one-pound roll of 50/50 (50% tin and 50% lead) solid-wire solder and a small can of paste flux (both of which are available from a local plumbing supply wholesaler).

Clean all the lead joints with a small, stiff wire brush until they're shiny. Then apply some flux (with a paint or paste brush) and begin soldering. Use a 50- to 120-watt soldering

FIG. 4

← PUSH

FIG. 5

LEAD

GLASS

iron or soldering gun with a chisel tip to mold the soft metal. If you plan to do a *lot* of glasswork, a quality iron would be a good investment. Again, a stained glass supplier will be able to recommend the best one for your needs.

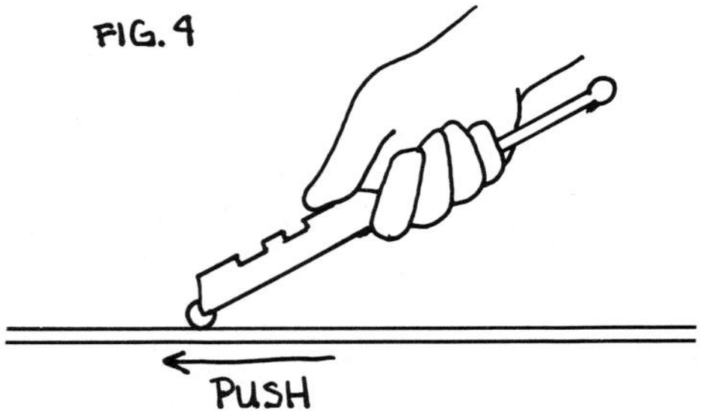

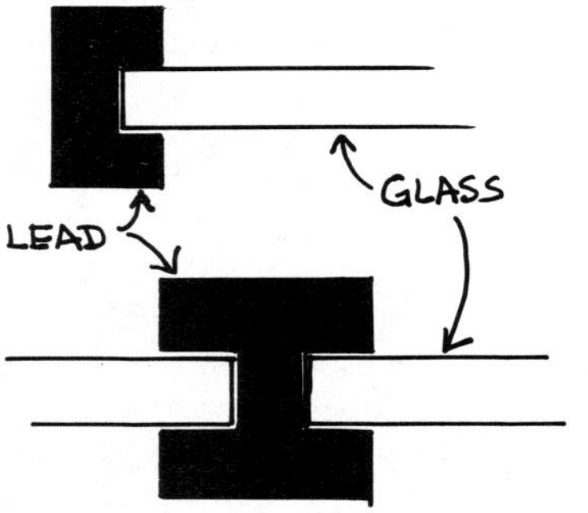

Place about a 1/4″ of the end of the wire solder over the cleaned and fluxed lead joint, and melt it with the heated iron. Then working quickly and gently, move the tip of the iron in a small circular motion, out from the center of the joint and back, finally lifting the tip straight up. With a little practice, you'll soon be able to shape smooth solder joints!

One word of caution: It isn't uncommon for a soldering iron to overheat and begin to melt the lead in a piece being worked upon. To keep the temperature of the iron constant, be sure to unplug the unit when it gets too hot (or install an in-line rheostat to monitor the temperature of the tool). And if the iron has been sitting for a time while plugged in, always test it on a piece of scrap lead before putting it to use!

After completing all the joints on both sides of the window, solder small copper loops to the upper back corners of the panel for easier hanging.

GLAZING AND CLEANING: If your piece of artwork is to be used as an actual window, it'll need to be puttied. Work some glazing compound (available at most hardware stores) under the lead flanges around every glass piece, front and back. This material will make your panel relatively air- and watertight and a great deal stronger, as well. In order to preserve the effect of the clean, crisp lead lines, trim off any excess compound with a sharp knife or an ice pick.

The final step is cleaning. A handful of whiting (use powdered calcium carbonate or plaster of paris) will do the trick. Just brush this material onto the panel with an old scrub brush. Whiting will clean the glass and darken the lead. Then a quick wash with soap and water will leave your panel sparkling and ready to transform every sunbeam into a ray of colored light!

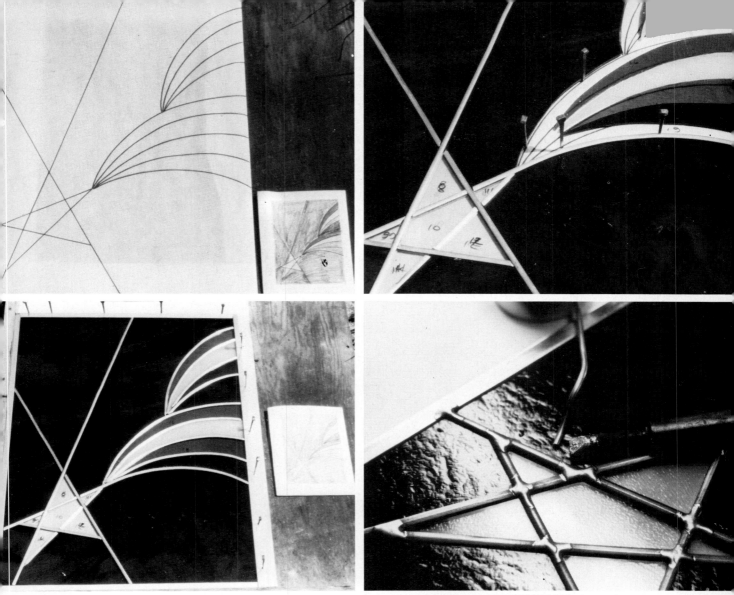

The stained glass pattern is laid out full-scale on paper. The glass and the lead strips are then laid down over the pattern and held in place as the work progresses with flat nails. When all the glass pieces are in place within the rough frame that holds the work, the joints are completed with solid-core solder and a soldering iron.

WORKING WITH LEAD

Working with lead *can* be dangerous if you're unaware of basic safety procedures. The following guidelines should help insure a safe experience.

[1] Never allow children to handle lead or—even worse—to place it in their mouths.

[2] When working with lead, always cover any small cuts on your fingers with adhesive bandages, and—once you're done—wash your hands thoroughly, especially before eating.

[3] If you're pregnant, it's best to play safe and not do any lead work until after your child is born. Studies have shown that high lead levels in a mother's body can adversely affect her unborn child.

[4] Never wash your completed panel with a sponge or dishcloth that could possibly be used later for food preparation or dishwashing. Lead deposits can be transferred to dishes and edibles. Likewise, always position your workspace away from food preparation areas.

CORNHUSK DOLLS

The cornhusk doll is a good example of how much can be accomplished with materials that are generally discarded. It's hard to believe that the demure little lady in full-skirted costume was entirely hand-shaped with string, wire, and the crackly shucks left behind to rustle in the autumn wind after the harvest.

Producing this age-old folk art is an absorbing pastime right from the start. The raw materials are fun to gather and a pleasure to work with (wet cornhusks drape just like fabric). And since most of the makings cost nothing, you can experiment and be as creative as you wish.

This is also a good craft for children, who can make their own versions and still be assured of pleasing results.

Not only do cornhusk people make attractive decorations and interesting playthings, but they can also provide a source of extra cash, for a ready market exists for these quaint dolls.

MATERIALS: The ideal time to gather husks is on a bright, blue and gold autumn day soon after the dogwoods have turned red. Folks who don't raise their own corn can usually find a farmer who'll be happy to part with a bagful or two of shucks.

The husks should be dry, not green, and will last for years if kept free of moisture. If spotted with mildew, they can be soaked in a solution of bleach and water, though this may make them a bit more brittle than unbleached wrappings.

Discard the coarsest parts of the outer husk (which are likely to be discolored and wind-shredded) and gently take apart the many-layered wrapper that remains. Carefully tease away the ample outer pieces of husk from the stalk (some will tear, but can still be used) and save the fullest, heaviest, and cleanest for the doll's skirt. Also select the lighter-weight, silkier, but still-flared portions from the inner layers of the husk. These will come in handy as sleeves. Especially clean and pliable—yet opaque—pieces of shuck make good faces for cornhusk people, and corn silk does well as hair.

Removing all the husk from about five ears of corn will provide more

than enough material to make a doll. Some of the figure's parts don't require any special kind of husk and can therefore be put together from the leftover pieces.

To fashion a doll, you'll need a few other supplies:

[1] Lightweight string, crochet cotton, or similar cord. Color isn't important.

[2] Tan, ivory, or other cornhusk-colored sewing thread to tie the parts of the doll that will show when finished.

[3] Wire or pipe cleaners.

[4] A base for the doll's head. Possibilities include acorns, hickory nuts, black walnuts, beads from old jewelry, or polystyrene foam balls an inch or a shade larger in diameter.

[5] Straight pins.

[6] White casein glue.

To begin working on your first little person, pour lukewarm water into the sink, a pan, or a shallow basin and soak the shucks for a few minutes to soften them. The husks that aren't used immediately can be left to air-dry and then be put away for another dollmaking session.

Next, choose a comfortable, well-lit location, and place a folded bath towel on your work surface to absorb moisture from the husks during handling and to prevent dripping water from making puddles.

HEAD: The head of a cornhusk doll is the first part to be made. Select a long, thin piece of husk—about 1-1/2″ X 6″—and form it tightly around whatever base has been chosen. (Don't worry about the uncovered sides of the head as they'll be concealed by a bonnet.) Pinch the ends together at the neck and tie them firmly with lightweight string. The excess shuck should be left trailing below the tie to help attach the head to the body.

BODY: The doll's body is made from 12 to 15 pieces of husk, each of which is 3″ wide at one end and tapers to a point at the other, a shape that lends itself well to body building. Since additional covering will be added later, don't be concerned about small imperfections in the material.

Pick up the dozen or so chosen pieces by their narrow ends and arrange the tips around the excess that dangles below the head. Placing the tapered ends at the neck helps to avoid bunchiness there. Tie the bundle of pointed husks together with string, as far up and as close to the head as is compatible with a secure knot. Wrap the string around twice and give a good tight pull.

ARMS: Cut a 6″ piece of wire or pipe cleaner. This one continuous length will form both arms, with a hand on each. Place the wire on a piece of husk which measures about 1-1/2″ X 6-1/2″ and roll the shuck around the metal core. When this step is almost finished, fold the outer ends of the wrapper in over the tips of the wire and then complete the roll. Tie the covering with tan thread (doubled) at the wrists and in the center.

SLEEVES: To form the sleeves, take advantage of the cornhusk's natural shape at the point where it was attached to the stalk. Choose a flared piece that's not too stiff and is about 1-1/2″ wide at the narrow "gathered" end, 3-1/2″ wide at the opposite end, and 2-1/2″ long. Fasten this covering around the arm at the wrist by tying it on in the reverse of its final direction, and turn it back for a puffed effect. (For a "rolled-up-sleeves" look, attach the piece at the elbow rather than at the wrist.) Once it's been folded back, tie the open

end of the sleeve to the arm near the center of the length of wire.

The other sleeve is made in the same way, and there's no need to worry if the two don't look exactly alike. When the arms are attached to the body, their coverings will tend to even out.

Take the sleeved armpiece and thrust it firmly as far up under the head as it will go so that half the body husks fall in back and half in front. Then tie a length of string firmly around the torso just under the arms to form a high waist.

BODICE: The next step is to smooth out the bodice. Choose several long strips of husk that are each about 1″ wide. Hold one with your thumb at the left front of the doll's waistline, cross the band over her right shoulder, and hold its end down at the back. Wrap the next strip from the right front, up over the left shoulder, and down to the right side of the back. Continue wrapping strips on alternate sides until the bodice is well built up. Although stained husks can be used for the lower layers, the two final pieces of shuck should be unblemished. Tie a string around the waist to keep the wrappings in place.

At this point there are a lot of long —usually too long—pieces of husk flapping about below the waist. Whack them off with strong scissors so that the finished doll will stand 6″ or 7″ tall.

SKIRT: The doll's skirt is treated in much the same way as the sleeves: Tie it on in the reverse of its final direction and pull it down to produce a bouffant effect with the rough edge hidden under the gathers.

To do this, choose two of the widest, cleanest pieces of flared husk to form the front and back of the skirt. (If you're short of wide material, add an extra section to cover the gap at each side.) Tie on the front first, with the narrow end at the waist and the wider part extending up over the doll's face. Then fasten the back panel in the same way so that it overlaps the first one slightly. With practice, it's possible to attach both sections in one operation, but in the beginning it's easier to proceed as suggested. And don't worry about all that string bunched around the waist; it helps to keep the doll together.

Your doll now appears to be standing on a hot-air register with her skirt flipped up over her head. Gently turn back the two parts of the garment, one at a time, so that they fall as they should. Then find a long, thin strip of scrap husk and pin it loosely around the bottom of the skirt—without actually piercing the "fabric"—to hold the pieces in position while they dry.

HAIR: Remember that corn silk you saved? Select a small hank (about as much would come from one ear of corn), tie a piece of thread around the center of the bundle, dunk the silk in water, and lift it out at once. Then drape the wet wig over the doll's head and use a straight pin to anchor it to the husk covering until the silk dries. Let the hair hang down the doll's back or form it into a bun. You can also make a separate braid and tie it on, tucking up the rest of the hair into the cap.

CAP: A becoming bonnet will cover the sides of the cornhusk lady's head and will help keep her hair in place. Choose a good clean piece of husk about 2" X 3" and wrap it from shoulder to shoulder over the head, holding it together at the neck. At this point, of course, the cap material will be sticking straight out behind the doll, so hold her in one hand—with the headgear still pinched together under her chin—and with the other hand crease the "fabric" (as if wrapping a package) to fit the back of the doll's head. Put a pin in each side of the bonnet, if desired, to hold it in place while you form and tie it. A bow for the front or back can be made and attached from a wisp of husk measuring about 1/8" X 4".

ACCESSORIES: Surrounding these traditional cornhusk dolls with items typical of the colonial or frontier period can lend to the characters' costumes an air of authenticity, and the following items can help enhance that image.

APRON: A protector for the tidy housewife's dress can be fashioned from a piece of flared husk about 2" X 2" or 2" X 3". Such a garment is affixed just as the skirt was: positioned with the gathered edge at the waistline and the wider part extending up over the bodice, and then tied and flipped down. Try making the apron of dark red husk from Indian corn or use fancy calico.

BROOM: Pampas grass seed heads make good brooms. Or try tying pine needles or thin dried grass to a small twig. A somewhat heavier sweeping tool can be made from a dried corn tassel. Look around the yard, hedgerow, or woods for other possibilities.

CHURN: Start with the dasher—a thin stick—and roll a 2"-wide piece of husk around it to a thickness of about 5/8". Tie the wrapping near both ends. Then cut a husk ribbon 1-1/4" wide and wrap the lower end of the stick—or the barrel—until it reaches a thickness of about 1". Again, fasten the roll near both its

top and bottom. Tie or glue the dasher to the doll's hand, or leave the churn free-standing.

BREAD: It's fun to pose the doll with her hands offering a loaf of homemade bread. The next time you bake, set aside a small lump of dough about the size of a golf ball. Divide this into nine parts, roll each into a thin rope, braid three tiny loaves of three strands each, and bake the dough into miniature loaves.

BUCKET: Find a 1"-high tapered cork to serve as a form, wrap a small piece of wet husk around it, and tie the corn shuck in two places with thread. Let the husk dry on the cork. When you remove the form, touch the edges of the bucket with glue and also dab adhesive on the thread binding to hold it in place.

To give the bucket a bottom, cut a circle of husk (or paper) slightly larger than the diameter of the pail at its smaller end and notch the disk's edges with scissors. Spread white glue around the inner edge of the container's wall where the bottom is to fit, and push the paper disk down into position with the eraser tip of a pencil.

For the handle, braid three thin strands of husk, tie the ends of the plait with thread, and glue them to the bucket. Hang the pail over the doll's hand.

KNITTING: Using two round toothpicks as needles, cast on about 12 stitches of lightweight string or wool. Knit an inch or so, then wrap the end of the "yarn" into a small ball and glue the last few strands around the bundle to prevent unraveling. Tie the work to the doll's hands and let the ball of wool fall to her feet or dangle partway down.

A great deal of the fun to be had with this craft comes from modeling sticks, twigs, weeds, and other natural materials into tools for your little people. You should let your imagination run free!

SALES: After a bit of practice and family fun with dollmaking, try selling some of your better efforts, both as a source of extra cash and as a marvelous excuse to turn out still more cornhusk people. The dolls can be sold through a wide range of outlets: farm market stands, fruit growers' sheds, country stores, gift shops, craft fairs, natural foods stores, antique dealers, and interior decorators.

Some shop owners are glad to take articles on consignment (an arrangement by which the dealer pays you when the piece is sold and retains a commission). Others will buy items outright.

While thinking of outlets, don't overlook the possibility of selling from your own house. Word-of-mouth advertising is often the best kind, and selling one or two dolls to friends can lead to a steady stream of customers.

PRESENTATION: You'll offer only your best work for sale, of course, but keep in mind that the way in which the dolls are presented may have a lot to do with how quickly they find a home. They will look more appealing if they're attractively arranged, neatly placed in a box or basket or set on a display shelf that protects them from dust and crushing yet leaves them clearly visible. Try hanging your creations on a sturdy branch that is mounted securely in a base. You might even offer to do a window arrangement for any shop owner who handles your line.

One final point: When selling dolls yourself (say, at a craft fair), display one of each kind on the table and keep your duplicates in a carton beside you.

PRICES: Setting a fair price for your dolls—one that gives the customer a good buy and gives you a reasonable return for your work—depends on several factors. The first of these is the cost of making each item. Although the expense for materials will be very little, it's important to know the exact figure.

A second consideration is your time. The first few tries will be slow going, but the pace will quicken in short order until it's possible to produce about one doll every half hour.

The price these handmade figures can command in an urban area, far from cornfields and other sources of natural materials, will undoubtedly be somewhat higher than what will be considered a reasonable price in rural locations, where cornhusks are plentiful and competition abounds.

RECORDS: An elaborate record system is unnecessary for a small sideline business like this one, but do keep track of what is spent for supplies, when and where to pick husks, what kind of dolls are made, when and where they are sold, and the prices they bring. You'll discover a pattern that will help you plan how to concentrate future efforts more effectively. At some point your business may become successful enough to necessitate keeping very accurate accounts for tax purposes.

LESSONS: There's one fact to face from the start: People will copy your dolls. "Customers" will examine your wares at length and then discuss right in front of you how they're going to go home and make their own dolls!

Don't worry about how this will affect your profits. Enjoy your role as a transmitter of folk art and be aware that there'll always be plenty of shoppers who lack the time, materials, and motivation to make their own heirlooms.

And since your work will be imitated anyway, why not make it official? When you've developed some expertise, arrange through a local craft or gift shop to give lessons in the art of cornhusk dollmaking.

These classes can be run very simply: Seat your students around a big table or on the floor by the fireplace, serve refreshments, and demonstrate how to make a doll while the pupils follow through each step with the raw materials you provide. Charge a few dollars per lesson and take up to ten novices at a time. That way, individual help and encouragement can be given to beginners.

Because of their handcrafted appearance, the many ways in which they can be posed, and the ease of making these low-cost novelties, you should have no trouble selling the cornhusk dolls or finding people anxious to learn how to make them.

GETTING STARTED IN WELDING

WELDING BASICS

It's the busiest time of the year and the tines on your garden tiller just snapped. The welding shop is booked solid for the next week, and it's going to take a month for the local dealer to get parts from the factory.

Sound familiar? Probably, but by setting yourself up with the proper equipment and learning to weld, you can eliminate this frustration and make some money taking the overflow from the booked-up local welder.

OUTFITTING YOURSELF: The heart of your setup is the welder itself. Get a good 230-volt electric arc welder with an amperage range that's adjustable between at least 70 and 200 amps, and ideally between 40 and 224. Both AC and DC units are available, but the first-time user should opt for a DC model which will be fine for medium-duty use.

There are several other pieces of equipment needed for protection, and it's important that you get quality items. A face shield is a must to protect the face and neck from sparks and hot metal fragments and the eyes from the intense light of the welding arc. Good leather gloves that can be flipped off with the flick of a wrist are also necessary. You should wear natural-fiber clothes when welding and don a hat (also of natural fiber) to protect your head and hair. A leather apron will protect your clothes.

For the actual welding, you'll need a supply of E6011 and E6013 rods in 1/8", 5/32", and 3/16" diameters. Be certain to store these in a dry place.

GETTING STARTED: With the necessary equipment lined up and

some scrap steel about 1/4" thick, you're ready to begin welding. Making certain there is plenty of ventilation in your work area, plug your welder into a 230-volt, 50-amp outlet. Place a 1/8" rod in the grooves of the machine's electrode holder and set the amperage to about 95 amps. Connect the ground cable to the piece far enough away from the spot you intend to weld so as not to interfere with your work, or if the steel piece is on a conductive surface, simply clamp the wire close to the scrap of metal on which you are practicing. Then keeping the rod well away from any metal, turn on the welder.

Put on your face shield and warn anyone around not to stare at the bright light of the arc. Strike the arc by holding the rod about 20° from vertical, scratching the tip across

about an inch of the area to be welded, drawing the rod toward you, and then quickly raising the tip about 1/4" above the metal.

When the protective flux is scratched from the tip of the rod, current flows through the rod, leaps across the gap to the workplace, and forms an extremely hot (6500°F) electric arc that melts both the end of the rod and the metal being welded. Molten metal from the rod travels across the arc onto the piece being welded, fusing with that material to form a weld.

However, it sometimes doesn't go that smoothly. Failing to lift the rod from the metal quickly enough can cause it to "freeze", or stick, welding itself to the metal. A strong twist should free the rod, but if it doesn't, more drastic action is needed. First, turn off the welder and release the rod from the holder. After the rod has cooled, wiggle and twist it free or knock it loose with a hammer. With practice, you should develop the

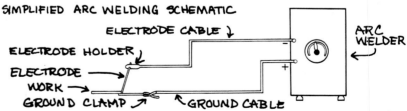

SIMPLIFIED ARC WELDING SCHEMATIC

quick wrist action needed to strike an arc without the rod fusing with your workpiece.

EXERCISE NO. 1: LAYING A BEAD: Once you've struck an arc and are consistently able to hold the stick close enough to the metal's surface to maintain the circuit, the intense heat and flow of molten material will continue until the rod is used up. But before you can expect to put this action to work to join two pieces of metal, you must learn to control the flow/fusion process to the point where you can produce a symmetrical, deeply penetrating weld.

Developing this bit of eye-hand coordination can be somewhat difficult, though, because the quality of the bead you produce will depend on how well you balance three important factors: [1] the amperage setting, [2] the length of arc, and [3] the speed at which you move the electrode, known as "rate of travel".

The amperage setting required will depend mainly on the thickness and type of metal you want to weld and on the size of the electrode used to do the job. (The owner's manual with your machine will probably include a table of recommended rod sizes for given metal thicknesses.) While learning, however, stick with the approximately 1/4″ steel and a 1/8″ rod. An amperage setting of between 85 and 115 will be appropriate. (Start at a setting of 90 amps and then adjust up or down as you observe the

results you get on each bead.)

With your face shield down, hold the electrode so that it leans toward you at an angle of 70 to 80° to the work. Starting at the edge of the piece farthest from you, draw the electrode back toward your body. Don't try any side-to-side movement for now. Just pull the rod back in a straight line, evenly and steadily: not too fast (speed will cause you to produce a weld that's shallow and too narrow) and not too slow (the material will pile up and ripple excessively). By looking closely, you'll be able to see a crater forming in the metal at the end of the arc. Try to keep the flow of material into the back of that cavity smooth and consistent.

While you're doing your best to control the rate of travel, another complication is taking place: Your welding rod is melting, and—as a result—the length of your arc is getting longer. So as you pull the electrode toward you, you must also continually push the tip gradually forward to compensate for the rod's ever-decreasing length. As a general rule, try to keep arc distance equal to the diameter of the electrode being used. When the gap is correct, you'll hear a

"crackling" sound, but when the arc is too long, you'll hear a hollow, blowing noise.

Once you've completed a pass, let the fresh weld cool from red-hot to black, then use a chipping hammer to knock off the thin slag crust. Underneath will be anything from a disappointing mass of pits and bubbles to an attractive, evenly distributed, deep, strong weld. The ideal bead is about 1-1/2 to 2 times as wide as the diameter of the electrode and as long as the amount of rod used.

You can't expect to get a perfect specimen until you've had quite a bit of practice, so keep at it. Experiment with amp settings and arc distances and travel speed—try your hand at moving the electrode from side to side in a close zigzag or circular motion, too—and analyze each bead's appearance. If you make an honest effort to be your most severe critic, you'll be able to detect what you're doing wrong and correct it. The photo showing beads formed on amperage settings ranging from too low (cold) on the left to too high (hot) on the right should help, but there are some other things to look for.

Slag pockets: black, nonmetallic de-

The far left photo of the beads shows, from left to right, the results of too-cold through too-hot fusion. The fourth bead is the best one. Clamp the work tightly to your workbench before striking an arc.

ARC ACTION
GASEOUS SHIELD
CORE WIRE
SLAG
ELECTRODE COATING
WELD
70° TO 80°
DEPTH OF PENETRATION
MOLTEN FLOW
WORK
CRATER
ARC LENGTH

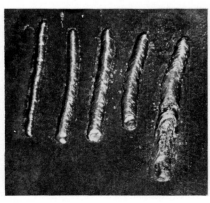

posits in the weld. Try keeping the electrode movement steady and holding the rod closer to perpendicular.

Undercutting: a shallow groove along one side or grooves along both sides of a weld. This usually results from moving the electrode too fast. Slow down a little.

Spatter: droplets of metal around the weld. It isn't a serious problem, but—if adjusting amperage doesn't cure it—you may be holding the electrode too high.

A BUTT WELD: Now that you're running beautiful beads consistently, you're ready to start actually joining two pieces of metal. Again, use 1/4" steel (be sure the edges to be fused are square) and 1/8" rod. If you happen to have two pieces that are *more* than 1/4", you should probably bevel the top edges to about 45° to assure a deep bond.

Position the two sides so that they almost, but don't quite, touch (to allow for expansion) and clamp them down securely. Because of the tremendous heat applied during welding and the stresses created by the variations in temperature along the seam as the work progresses and later cools, the fresh weld and any adjacent metal are especially subject to distortion. Therefore, if the plates are allowed to move, the steel will often twist away from the joint, and/or the electrode material will crack. Clamping the pieces is the easiest way to minimize the effects of these forces, but a "tack weld", a good, penetrating 1/4" dot of metal placed at each end of the joint and used in addition to the clamps, will insure

that you will obtain a positive bond.

Now, set your machine to about 115 amps and strike an arc. Start the weld at the top of the plates and draw it toward you. This time, hold the rod nearly perpendicular and move the stick side to side in a tight "Z" pattern. If you're using an E6011 electrode—which penetrates a bit more deeply than does an E6013 —you may also want to keep the arc length somewhat higher than the rule-of-thumb 1/8". At the end of the run, raise the wand about 1/4" and hold it there briefly to allow the cavity in the final half-inch or so of the weld to fill with metal.

Let the work cool for a minute, then knock off the slag. Ideally, you should have a weld that penetrates into the seam, both horizontally and vertically, about 1/8". The surface of the fresh metal should be only slightly convex.

If you're satisfied with the results, smooth the work with a hand grinder to give it the appearance you'd want for, say, a box stove. On the other hand, if the weld is poor, you may want to break it open by twisting the pieces in a vise or hammering them apart to get a closer look at the results of your efforts. Is fusion complete all along the seam? Are there slag pockets? Keep a critical eye out for weaknesses in the work, and be prepared to practice correcting them.

On subsequent runs, you may want to try welding both sides of the plates . . . or attempt to apply a second layer over the first (completely clean off the initial seam's slag, then use a wide but close zigzag—or crescent *or*

figure-eight—motion to cover the first weld).

A TEE WELD: Now, you're ready to try to join a horizontal 1/4" steel plate to a vertical one. You can use clamps and a length of angle iron to keep the pieces positioned, or, better yet, lay a small tack weld on both sides of each end of the vertical plate, to hold the members in place.

For practicing tee-weld technique, 1/8" rod should be sufficient, but because more filler material is required here than for a simple butt joint, a 5/32" electrode (again, either E6011 or E6013) would be better. When using the smaller wand, you'll need to slow your rate of travel in order to build up sufficient metal in the joint. However, the decreased speed will cause increased heat and—therefore—a higher possibility of metal distortion, so if you have the larger-size electrode available, or if you're working on a "for real" project, 5/32" is the way to go.

Set your machine for about 130 amps and strike an arc. Now, hold the rod so that it bisects the 90° angle formed by the two pieces (in other words, so that it's 45° from vertical) but leans at an angle of about 80° out from the corner where you intend to

The surface of a finished butt weld is only slightly convex and should be ground smooth for a perfect joint. Grinding is complete when the joint is scarcely discernible to the touch.

GETTING STARTED IN WELDING

start the weld. Point the tip of the electrode in the direction of travel, aim the arc directly at the juncture of the two plates, and use a forward, oscillating, circular motion to bring the weld metal up and into either side of the seam. Keep your work as even as possible, and be sure to build sufficient material all along both the vertical and horizontal planes.

When the weld has cooled, examine the seam. Chances are you'll be looking at real messes after your first few attempts. (Undercutting is a common problem with tee welds. To correct it, try increasing or decreasing arc length or reducing travel speed or amperage.) Be sure to break the weld with a hammer to get a closer look at the degree of penetration. If it isn't deep enough, try, try again.

IS THAT ALL THERE IS TO IT? Well, the answer to that question is yes *and* no. You'll be able to handle most simple projects once you've perfected the fundamentals outlined here, but there is certainly much more to learn about welding and welding equipment. There are dozens of types of welds, hundreds of kinds of electrodes for various purposes, and scores of special procedures. And your arc machine can do more than just weld: It can cut (not as smoothly as an oxyacetylene outfit, but you can grind the edges after cutting to get an acceptable surface), it can be used to thaw frozen pipes, and with the proper attachments, it can even braze and solder.

Learning to weld is like learning to do almost anything: The best way is just to do it. Concentrate on the basics until you really have them perfected. And if you know someone who welds or if you have access to an adult education or technical school course of some kind, you're sure to benefit from face-to-face instruction.

The key is practice, and as soon as you've perfected your skills sufficiently, you can even get paid while you learn . . . by making simple—but salable—items such as flowerpot stands and the like.

Before long, you'll be saving—and making—money as a welder!

WELDING TABLE

Any serious welder knows that one of the most useful—and versatile—tools in the shop is the *table* on which the work is accomplished. That surface is often far more than just a waist-level workbench for metal fabrication. Ideally, it's a welding station "headquarters", set up to accommodate a head shield, clamps, chippers, and electrodes (along with the handle that fits them). It should also serve as an accurate measuring device both for gauging lengths and for squaring corners, a solid foundation to which components can be clamped when the job must be "just right", and a base upon which other useful tools such as bending brakes and jigs can be mounted.

LIST OF MATERIALS

(6)	1-1/4″ X 20′ tubular steel, 11-gauge, cut as follows:		
	(2) 78-1/4″	(2)	27-3/4″
	(12) 6″	(8)	12″
	(2) 30-1/4″	(2)	13-1/4″
	(6) 75-3/4″	(5)	10″
	(2) 29-3/4″	(2)	33″

(2) 1-1/2″ X 12″ tubular steel, 16-gauge
(2) 1-1/2″ X 1-1/2″ flat stock, 16-gauge
(2) 3/4″ X 1-1/2″ pipe, Schedule 40
(2) 3/16″ X 2-1/2″ X 8-1/2″ flat stock
(4) 3/8″ X 1-1/4″ X 2″ flat stock
(4) 3/8″ X 1-1/4″ X 5″ flat stock
(1) 3/8″ X 2″ X 8″ flat stock
(1) 3/8″ X 2″ X 5″ flat stock
(4) 1/4″ X 1″ X 14-3/4″ flat stock
(2) 1/2″ X 35″ threaded rod
(2) 1/2″ nuts
(2) 1/4″ X 2″ angle iron, 1-3/4″ long
(2) 2″ swivel casters and mounting bolts
(2) 4″ solid wheels and mounting bolts
(2) 5/8″ nuts
(2) 5/8″ X 2-1/2″ leveling feet
(1) 3/4″ expanded-metal sheet, 16-gauge, 29-1/4″ X 77-3/4″
(1) pint of paint

The table shown here incorporates features found on a number of commercial models and is specifically designed to provide convenience while handling a wide variety of welding tasks. For example, its open construction lets grinding dust and slag fall through, rather than collect upon, the work surface. And its dimensions (30-1/4′ X 78-1/4″) allow the bench to be rolled through most doorways—either wheelbarrow-style or tipped up vertically—by means of the casters mounted on the legs and the upper corners of one end.

Other practical touches include the use of leveling feet on the non-wheeled supports and a bare metal upper surface to promote conductivity, not to mention "holsters" that keep a supply of rods and the electrode handle within easy reach.

Maybe the project's best feature, though, is its cost, which is one-quarter that of equivalent commercial models. And even that comparison doesn't tell the whole story, because none of the industrial versions has the flexibility of this design.

GATHER THE MATERIALS: Although advanced welding techniques are not required to complete this project, steadfast attention most definitely is. Since the finished table will become the "standard" by which everything made upon it is gauged and squared, it's important that the parts be measured accurately and assembled correctly!

Ideally, do the work on a bench that's level and that allows the table's parts to be set and clamped while they are joined. You'll need a tape measure, a carpenter's square, a hacksaw, a power drill (with an assortment of bits), a hand grinder, and welding equipment.

Begin by collecting the components given in the list of materials, including 120 feet of 1-1/4", 11-gauge tubular steel, which generally comes in 20-foot sections, for the frame. Then carefully cut all this square tubing to the lengths indicated in the materials list, and prepare to fasten it together section by section.

Because it's important that the bench be constructed in a step-by-step fashion, the accompanying illustration has been color coded to indicate the proper order of assembly. Once the parts shown in the first color have been welded together, go to work on the next group, and so on until the basic chassis is completed. Then supply the finishing touches such as wheels, leveling feet, and holders.

START BUILDING: When you're ready to begin, tackle the construction in the following sequence:

[1] The two sides are put together—with the horizontals placed 10" from what will become the upper ends of the legs—to form two broad "H" shapes.

[2] The components that make up the center section are added, starting with the cross braces at the ends, moving on to the longitudinal central

"spine", and finishing with the two short lengths that join the middle horizontal bar to the two at the sides. At this point, the project should look like a bed frame. Note that an extra piece of straight tubular steel or angle iron clamped to the frame can provide a good guide—and a temporary mount—for the to-be-welded components.

[3] The eight 12" corner braces are installed. Make sure their ends are cut at 45° angles so they'll fit flush against the frame.

[4] Four of the five 10" uprights

are placed on the frame's perimeter, each midway between two of the corner stanchions. The fifth is welded at the cross in the middle of the assembly, as illustrated.

[5] The adjustable belly truss—which is used to square up the entire table—is added at this stage. It's nothing more than an inverted "T" (formed by a 5" length of 3/8" X 2" flat stock joined to an 8" section of the same material) fastened to the *bottom* of the central cross and connected to 1-3/4" lengths of 1/4" X 2" X 2" angle iron. These, in turn, are centered at the underface of each end cross brace with pieces of 1/2" threaded rod. Four sections of 1/4" X

1" X 14-3/4" bar stock form two "V's" which support the "T" from the sides. Once the truss is completed, it's important that the bench be trued by tightening the end nuts and checking the assembly with a square—making adjustments as necessary—before progressing to the next step.

[6] The expanded-metal sheet is trimmed to size, cut out to accommodate the uprights, and then tacked in place to make a platform.

[7] The top section is added. Start by laying down its perimeter (the corners should be mitered to 45°), then fasten the three long horizontals between the upper end-rails so that they're equally spaced. Finish up by welding the dozen 6" spacers between the center rails at 18" intervals. (Again, a length of straight angle or square tube can be used as a guide when making the welds.)

[8] The table's 4" solid wheels ride on 3/8" X 3" bolts that are themselves supported in forks made from 3/8" X 1-1/4" X 5" bars welded to 2" strips of the same material. These struts are fastened to the sides of the legs at one end of the table, and their upper edges are chamfered (using a grinder) to form angled shoulders. The caster rollers are bolted to 45°-ended 3/16" X 2-1/2" X 8-1/2" straps that are welded across the inside faces of the upper corners on the wheeled end of the bench.

To fasten the levelers, simply weld a 5/8" nut into the tubular legs at the table's opposite end and thread the feet in. Finally, seal the ends of two 12" lengths of 1-1/2" tubular steel or pipe with some scrap metal, and tack one of these assemblies obliquely to the uprights at each side of the frame. Then weld a 3/4" X 1-1/2" pipe section to at least one corner post to provide a rest for the electrode holder. Finish up by painting the entire table—except for the work surface and the one spot that'll accommodate the ground clamp—with your favorite color of enamel.

Fabricate this table with care, treat it with respect, and be rewarded with years of useful service.

GETTING STARTED IN WELDING

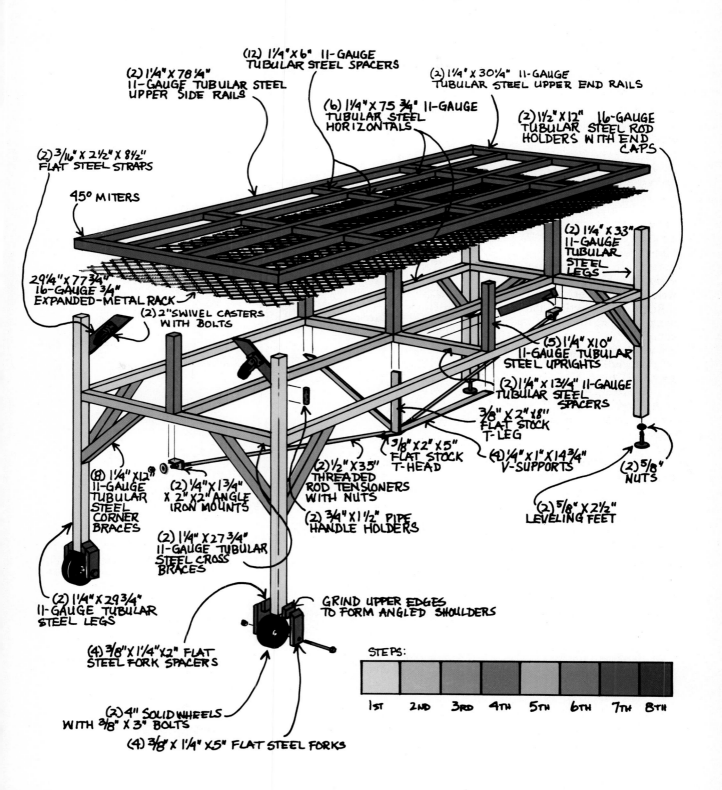

(12) 1¼"x6" 11-GAUGE
TUBULAR STEEL SPACERS

(2) 1¼" X 78¼"
11-GAUGE TUBULAR STEEL
UPPER SIDE RAILS

(2) 1¼" X 30¼" 11-GAUGE
TUBULAR STEEL UPPER END RAILS

(6) 1¼" X 75 ¾" 11-GAUGE
TUBULAR STEEL
HORIZONTALS

(2) 1½" X 12" 16-GAUGE
TUBULAR STEEL ROD
HOLDERS WITH END
CAPS

(2) 3/16" X 2½" X 8½"
FLAT STEEL STRAPS

45° MITERS

(2) 1¼" X 33"
11-GAUGE
TUBULAR
STEEL
LEGS

29¼" X 77¾"
16-GAUGE ¾"
EXPANDED-METAL RACK

(2) 2" SWIVEL CASTERS
WITH BOLTS

(5) 1¼" X 10"
11-GAUGE TUBULAR
STEEL UPRIGHTS

(2) 1¼" X 13¾" 11-GAUGE
TUBULAR STEEL
SPACERS

3/8" X 2" X 8"
FLAT STOCK
T-LEG

3/8" X 2" X 5"
FLAT STOCK
T-HEAD

(4) ¼" X 1" X 14¾"
V-SUPPORTS

(2) 5/8"
NUTS

(8) 1¼" X 12"
11-GAUGE
TUBULAR
STEEL
CORNER
BRACES

(2) ¼" X 13¾"
X 2" X 2" ANGLE
IRON MOUNTS

(2) ½" X 35"
THREADED
ROD TENSIONERS
WITH NUTS

(2) ¾" X 1½" PIPE
HANDLE HOLDERS

(2) 5/8" X 2½"
LEVELING FEET

(2) 1¼" X 27¾"
11-GAUGE TUBULAR
STEEL CROSS
BRACES

(2) 1¼" X 29¾"
11-GAUGE TUBULAR
STEEL LEGS

GRIND UPPER EDGES
TO FORM ANGLED SHOULDERS

(4) 3/8" X 1¼" X 2" FLAT
STEEL FORK SPACERS

(2) 4" SOLID WHEELS
WITH 3/8" X 3" BOLTS

(4) 3/8" X 1¼" X 5" FLAT STEEL FORKS

STEPS:

1ST	2ND	3RD	4TH	5TH	6TH	7TH	8TH

WELDING TABLE